# THE JOURNALISTS/THE WEDDING FEAST/
# THE MERCHANT

Arnold Wesker was born in Stepney in 1932 and educated at Upton
House School in Hackney. From 1948 to 1958 he pursued many trades
from furniture maker to pastry cook. His career as a playwright began
when Lindsay Anderson, who had read *The Kitchen* and *Chicken Soup
with Barley*, brought Wesker to the attention of George Devine at the
Royal Court Theatre; Devine sent *Chicken Soup with Barley* to the Belgrade
Theatre in Coventry, where it was first produced in 1958, under the
direction of John Dexter. A year later, having been turned down by the
Royal Court, *Roots* was directed by Dexter, again at the Belgrade,
Coventry, and in the following months he directed *The Kitchen* at the
Court for two Sunday Night experimental performances 'without
decor'. *The Wesker Trilogy* created an enormous impact when produced
in its entirety at the Royal Court in 1960.

His other plays include *Chips With Everything* (1962), *Their Very Own and
Golden City* (1965; winner of the Italian Premio Matzotto Drama award
in 1964), *The Four Seasons* (1965), *The Friends* (1970) and *The Old Ones*
(1972). In addition to plays, Arnold Wesker has written poems, short
stories and numerous articles. Among these are *Fears of Fragmentation*
(1970; articles and lectures); *Six Sundays in January* (1971), including two
stories, a diary, the libretto for a documentary, *The Nottingham Captain*,
and a TV play, *Menace*; *Love Letters on Blue Paper* (1974), a collection of
stories; and *Say Goodbye! You May Never See Them Again*, a text for a
book of primitive paintings by John Allin. His most recent publications
include *Words – as Definitions of Experience*, an essay on education;
*Journey Into Journalism*, a personal account of a brief stay in the *Sunday
Times*; *Said the Old Man to the Young Man*, a collection of stories; and
*Fatlips* (1978), a book for children.

In addition to this volume, Penguin has published *The Wesker Trilogy*
(Volume 1); *The Kitchen*, *The Four Seasons* and *Their Very Own and
Golden City* (Volume 2); *Chips With Everything*, *The Friends*, *The Old
Ones* and *Love Letters on Blue Paper* (Volume 3); and a collection of
short stories, *Love Letters on Blue Paper and Other Stories*.

Arnold Wesker was artistic director of Centre 42, a cultural movement
for popularizing the arts, primarily through trade union support and
participation, from 1961 to 1970. He lives with his wife and three children
in North London.

# ARNOLD WESKER

# The Journalists/The Wedding Feast/ The Merchant

## Volume 4

PENGUIN BOOKS

Penguin Books Ltd, Harmondsworth, Middlesex, England
Penguin Books, 625 Madison Avenue, New York, New York 10022, U.S.A.
Penguin Books Australia Ltd, Ringwood, Victoria, Australia
Penguin Books Canada Ltd, 2801 John Street, Markham, Ontario, Canada
L3R 1B4
Penguin Books (N.Z.) Ltd, 182–190 Wairau Road, Auckland 10,
New Zealand

—

*The Journalists* first published in Poland by *Dialog* 1974
First published in Great Britain by Writers and Readers Publishing Cooperative
1975
Published in Penguin Books 1980
Copyright © Arnold Wesker, 1975

*The Wedding Feast* first published by *Plays and Players* 1977
Published in Penguin Books 1980
Copyright © Arnold Wesker, 1977

*The Merchant* first published in East Germany by Henschel Verlag 1977
Published in Penguin Books 1980
Copyright © Arnold Wesker, 1977

All performing rights of *The Journalists*, *The Wedding Feast* and *The Merchant* are
fully protected, and permission to perform any of the plays, whether by amateurs
or professionals, must be obtained in advance from Robin Dalton, Associates,
91 Regent Street, London W1R 8RU, who can furnish all particulars.
All rights reserved

—

Made and printed in Great Britain by
Richard Clay (The Chaucer Press) Ltd,
Bungay, Suffolk
Set in Monotype Bembo

*The Journalists*

For VERA ELYASHIV –

journalist and dear friend whose stubbornness
helped shape this play.

# QUOTATIONS

A journalist is stimulated by a deadline. He writes worse when he has time  ..

It is the mission of the press to disseminate intellect and at the same time destroy the receptivity to it ...

The making of a journalist: no ideas and the ability to express them ...

Truth is a clumsy servant that breaks the dishes while cleaning them ...

KARL KRAUS, *German satirist* (1874–1936)

# PUBLISHER'S NOTE

To obtain background material for this play, Arnold Wesker got permission to study at first-hand all the departments of *The Sunday Times*. An unforeseen offshoot of this two-month period of research was a long essay called *Journey into Journalism*, written in December 1971. But repeated attempts by the author to gain permission from *The Sunday Times* to publish the essay led to confrontation. Certain journalists on *The Sunday Times* objected strongly to its appearance, and after an embattled, sometimes acrimonious correspondence which added some 10,000 words to the original slim document, Wesker felt honour-bound to withdraw his essay from publication.

About this misadventure, Wesker has stated, 'My journey into journalism was an unhappy one – an affectionate excursion which went sour . . . It's sad since I'd been very impressed with what I'd encountered in my eight weeks with them and thought I'd written a fair, serious and, though critical, yet affectionate piece. They didn't agree and so, since I'd obtained their cooperation for a play, I couldn't abuse it by publishing something they felt unfairly represented them.'

*The Journalists* is a fictional, dramatic account of the workings of a present-day Sunday newspaper. It is of course based on personal observation; but it is not a *pièce-à-clef* or simple documentary of *The Sunday Times* – nor is it the author's purpose that the play be misread as such.

*The Journalists* is indeed real, not in any narrow sense, but on the scale of social and work relations – the elements of stage rhythm in the best Wesker tradition already familiar to playgoers who applauded *The Kitchen* and the epic *Their Very Own and Golden City*.

# INTRODUCTION

All drama is open to many interpretations. And they are made!

It *is* true that the writer doesn't perceive all the implications of his work, but equally true that the experience he's assembled in the order he's assembled it is intended to be evidence of one or a set of specific statements.

They may not be the only statements his work makes – it's in the nature of any assembled evidence that it will suggest the proof of different things to different men, but of all the possible statements a work makes – whether poetically or with a greater degree of prose – one will sound the loudest simply because the author has directed all the selection of his material into making it. One pattern will emerge the strongest because the author has delineated its shape with greater emphasis. What he has taken out in his various drafts he has taken out because he's said: that detracts from my theme, blurs my meaning.

When directors and actors interpret a play they are engaged in the act of discovering that one sound which is louder than the others, that one pattern which is stronger than the others.

Whatever sounds or patterns my audience will find in this work there is only one main one which I intended; may not have achieved but had hoped to.

*The Kitchen* is not about cooking, it's about man and his relationship to work. *The Journalists* is not about journalism, it is about the poisonous human need to cut better men down to our size, from which need we all suffer in varying degrees. To identify and isolate this need is important because it corrupts such necessary or serious human activities as government, love, revolution or journalism.

Swift wrote a novel which gave this cancerous need a name – Lilliputianism. The lilliputian lover competes with his (or her) loved one instead of complementing her. The lilliputian journalist resents the interviewee's fame, influence or achievement rather than wishing to honour it or caution it or seriously question it. The lilliputian bureaucrat (involved in the same process, but in reverse) seeks to maintain his own size by not acknowledging the possibility of growth in those over whom he officiates; he doesn't *cut* down to size, he *keeps* down to size. The lilliputian revolutionary is more concerned to indulge resentments or pay off private scores than to arrive at real justice.

Thus government, love, revolution or journalism are time and time again betrayed. It is this with which my play is concerned.

ARNOLD WESKER

London, 24 January 1975

# NOTES

## THE SET

An impressionistic layout of the main offices of *The Sunday Paper*. There is a 'cut away' called The Centre Space where the action outside the offices is played.

In order that action and dialogue are evenly distributed over stage area, the designer must pay careful attention as to which office is near which.

But however the rest is laid out, The News Room must occupy a large space, for most of the final activity goes on there.

To the rear is a screen upon which are projected the huge printing presses. At a point near the end of the play the projection is taken over by a film of the presses beginning to roll.

## PRODUCTION

Activity must be continuous in all sections throughout the play while the plot weaves its way stopping here and there – sometimes for a lengthy exchange, sometimes for a few lines. Occasionally conversations will take place on the telephone between individuals from different offices.

While the audience focuses on one 'frame' (section) at a time, the orchestration of what happens *at the same time* in each remaining office is a director's problem. The following may help:

The rhythm of a Sunday newspaper office is one of a slow beginning at the start of the week (Tuesday) working up to an agitated flurry, which culminates at about six in the evening on the Saturday when the button is pushed to start the printing presses rolling for the first editions.

It is important, however, to remember this: it is a Sunday paper, not a daily one; therefore a lot of the pages will be laid out early on in the week. Many articles, indeed, have been set up weeks in advance. This means that not every department is hectic on the Saturday. For example the Arts pages are well advanced, but Sport – which is waiting for stories of the Saturday matches – is frantic

The two real centres of Saturday's activity are The Stone – where the printers and journalists lay out the pages and make the last minute changes (this area is not shown); and The News Room – where the editor and his closest advisers shape up, on blank sheets, the final product (this area is shown).

I have not indicated every action, but certain routine movements are continuous throughout – growing in intensity towards the end of the play, and the following actions can be drawn from to help the director in his orchestration:

Messengers taking copy from 'the stone' or from one department to another.

Reporters writing or subs correcting copy at their desks.

Journalists reading newspapers – endlessly! or official documents.

Journalists in conversation in each other's departments.

Journalists shaving themselves with electric razors, women making up (could toilets be shown? they are constantly washing print off their hands).

A woman pushing a tea trolley is ever present; reporters flow to and from it for tea and sandwiches.

Reporters, secretaries at typewriters.

The constant making or receiving of telephone calls.

Individuals with special information being interviewed.

Clatter is continuous but, of course, volume of noise must be regulated or projection of dialogue will be a constant fight for the actors. Could it all be on tape? then actions could be mimed. I'm thinking particularly of typewriting.

Journalists are alert, fast-thinking and fast-talking individuals. The clue to achieving the right rhythm is to maintain a quick delivery of lines – but in the beginning to have long pauses *between departments* which become shorter as the play continues thus giving the impression of increasing activity.

When action takes place in The Centre Space the rest of the action and noise freezes.

## TIME

This may be a problem since there are many assignments which are concertina-ed. It must be imagined that we are covering a week of five days *but* this week is also five weeks. That is to say we've taken our Tuesday from the first week, our Wednesday from the second week and so on. Time is therefore taking place on two planes, and some stories belong to the week, others to the five weeks.

The first professional presentation of *The Journalists* took place on 15 June 1978 on French radio under the auspices of Lucien Attoun's France-Culture. Jugoslav TV presented a television version of the play, setting it in a TV house instead of a Sunday newspaper. The first production in the UK was an amateur one given by the Criterion Theatre, Coventry, on 27 March 1977.

The only other performance, to date, has been a reading by professional actors to raise funds for the Jacksons Lane Community Centre in Highgate which took place in the Centre's theatre once in the afternoon and again in the evening of 13 July 1975. The following was the cast:

| | |
|---|---|
| MARY MORTIMER | Sheila Allen |
| HARVEY WINTERS | Ian McKellen |
| CHRIS MACKINTOSH | Sebastian Graham Jones |
| JULIAN GALLAGHER | William Hoyland |
| PAUL MANNERING | Michael Mellinger |
| HARRY LAURISTON | Dave Hill |
| MARTIN CRUIKSHANK | David Bradley |
| ANTHONY SHARPLES | Gawn Grainger |
| MORTY COHEN | Oliver Cotton |
| DOMINIC FLETCHER | John Hug |
| JANE MERRYWEATHER | Katherine Fahy |
| ANGELA GOURNEY | Janet Key |
| SEBASTIAN HERBERT | Bernard Gallagher |
| JOHN PROSSER | Hugh Thomas |
| ERNST GUEST | Brian Badcoe |
| RONNIE SHAPIRO | Harry Landis |
| MARVIN McKEVIN | Jim Norton |
| GORDON FAIRCHILD | John Bennet |
| TAMARA DRAZIN | Lisa Harrow |
| NORMAN HARDCASTLE | Brian Cox |
| CYNTHIA TREVELYAN | Gillian Barge |
| SECRETARY | Liz Hughes |
| PAT STERLING | Jennie Stoller |
| SIR ROLAND SHAWCROSS | Robert Eddison |
| RT HON GEORGE CARRON | Mark Dignam |

| | |
|---|---|
| SIR REGINALD MACINTYRE | Peter Jeffrey |
| OLIVER MASSINGHAM | John Gill |
| A FINK | Jonathan Pryce |
| AGNES | Cheryl Campbell |
| JONATHAN | David Yelland |
| DESMOND | Andrew Byatt |
| MAC SMITH | Fulton Mackay |
| MESSENGERS, SUBS, ETC. | Lindsay Joe Wesker |
| | Arnold Wesker |

Directed by Michael Kustow
Designed by Hayden Griffin
Lighting by Rory Dempster

# CHARACTERS

MARY MORTIMER, *a 'columnist'*

HARVEY WINTERS, *the editor*

CHRIS MACKINTOSH ⎱ *journalists on In Depth*
JULIAN GALLAGHER ⎰

PAUL MANNERING, *News editor*

HARRY LAURISTON ⎱ *News reporters*
MARTIN CRUIKSHANK ⎰

ANTHONY SHARPLES, *Business News editor*

MORTY COHEN ⎱ *Business News journalists*
DOMINIC FLETCHER ⎰

JANE MERRYWEATHER ⎱ *Women's Pages journalists*
ANGELA GOURNEY ⎰

SEBASTIAN HERBERT, *Arts Pages editor*

JOHN PROSSER, *Assistant Arts Pages editor*

ERNST GUEST, *a novelist, reviewer*

RONNIE SHAPIRO, *Sports editor*

MARVIN MCKEVIN, *Assistant sports editor*

GORDON FAIRCHILD, *Foreign editor*

TAMARA DRAZIN, *a foreign correspondent*

NORMAN HARDCASTLE ⎱ *journalists working in*
CYNTHIA TREVELYAN ⎰ *Political and Features*

SECRETARY, *to the Editor*

SECRETARY, *in The News Room*

PAT STERLING, *a freelance journalist*

SIR ROLAND SHAWCROSS, *Minister for Social Services*

RT HON. GEORGE CARRON, *Minister for Science and Technology*

SIR REGINALD MACINTYRE, *Chancellor of the Exchequer*

OLIVER MASSINGHAM, *Under Secretary of State – Foreign Affairs*

A FINK, *a man with 'secret' information*

AGNES ⎱ *sons and daughter of*
JONATHAN ⎰ *Mary Mortimer*
DESMOND

MAC SMITH, *a trade union official – Municipal and General*

MESSENGERS, SUBS, REPORTERS

# ACT ONE

## PART ONE

### THE CENTRE SPACE

[MARY MORTIMER *is interviewing* SIR ROLAND SHAWCROSS, *Minister for Social Services, in his office. There's a tape recorder on the desk.*]

SHAWCROSS: And that, Miss Mortimer, is precisely what democracy is: a risky balancing act. The delicate arrangement of laws in a way that enables the state to conduct its affairs freely without impinging upon the reasonable freedom of the individual. Tilt it too much one way or the other and either side, state or individual, seizes up, unable to act to its fullest capacity.

MARY: But surely, Minister, with respect, and I know you've written standard text books on the subject, you must agree that the *quality* of democracy doesn't *only* depend on the balance of freedom which our laws create between the individual and society, does it?

SHAWCROSS: By which you mean?

MARY: By which I mean that ordinary men are forced, daily, to confront the depressing petty officials who interpret those laws.

SHAWCROSS: Therefore?

MARY: Therefore *you* may give the letter to the law but the spirit of the law filters through to the ordinary citizen in the waiting rooms of hospitals, the offices of the employment exchange, the desks of housing officials, visits of social security officers and –

SHAWCROSS: Go on.

MARY: I could go on endlessly, Sir Roland.

SHAWCROSS: Go on endlessly. I don't see your question yet.

MARY: Well, I'm rather intimidated about going on, you've said these things much better than ever I could.

SHAWCROSS: Be brave.

MARY: All right. Great wisdom and learning may be required to *conceive* statutes but who expects great wisdom and learning in officials? And the ordinary man meets *them* not *you*. He faces the policeman, the factory superintendent, the tax-collector, the traffic warden – in fact the whole gamut of middle men whose officious behaviour affects the temper and pleasure of everyday life.

SHAWCROSS: And your question is?

MARY: What concern do you have for that?

SHAWCROSS: For the gap between the law maker and the law receiver?

MARY: No, with respect, I'd put it another way. For the change in the *quality* of the law which takes place when mediocre men are left to interpret it.

SHAWCROSS: That sounds like a very arrogant view of your fellow creatures, Miss Mortimer.

MARY: Sir Roland, forgive me, I must say it, but that's evasive.

[*Intercom buzzer rings.*]

VOICE: Your car in fifteen minutes, Minister.

SHAWCROSS: Thank you. [*Pause.*] Miss Mortimer, our first hour is nearly up. Tomorrow you're dining with us at home – it is tomorrow, I think? We can continue then. But for the moment I'd like to speak off the record. You've created a very unique reputation in journalism. Rightly and properly you're investigating the minds and personalities of men who shape policy. And you're doing it in depth, in our offices, our homes and on social occasions. I'm surprised so many of us have agreed and perhaps it will prove a mistake. We'll see. But there are aspects of government which it's obviously foolish of us to discuss in public no matter how eager we are to be seen being open and frank. You want me to say what concern I have for the actual quality of everyman's daily life. I could answer simply, and honestly, *every* concern. But where does that get us? I could project myself as an all round humanitarian but – I know I'd not be called upon to demonstrate that humanity. I could offer you phrases which my own, canny experience tells me will look good in print. But you're after something different and I, for one, would like to help you find something different. I'm not evasive but, to be blunt, some of my harshest thoughts could be demoralizing. Ah! you will say, that is the part of the man I'm after. But consider this: how true is the truth? You're right, the ordinary man must face the numb and bureaucratic mind. Our best intentions are distorted by such minds. But that can't really be my area of concern, can it? Suppose it were, I might then be forced to observe that the petty mind is a product of a petty education. Should I then go to complain to the Minister of Education? He might then say education is only *part* of the influence on a growing person — there's family environment to be considered. Should he then interfere in everyman's home? No, no, no! Only God knows where wisdom comes from, you can't legislate for it. Government can only legislate for the *common* good; the *individual* good is, I'm afraid, what men must iron out among themselves. Now, that's the 'truth' about my thinking. But where do I go from there? I don't act on it. My attempts at legislation are not less excellent because I doubt the excellence of men to interpret them. So, which truth will you tell? You have three: that I aspire to perfection of the law? That I mistrust the middle men who must exercise that law? or will you combine the two? The first is pompous, the second abusive, the third confusing.

MARY: And you don't think people would respond to such honesty?

SHAWCROSS: No! Frankly. Most people can't cope with honesty.

MARY: With respect, Minister, but that sounds like a very arrogant view of your fellow creatures.

SHAWCROSS: Ha! [*Pause.*] We'll continue, we'll continue. I must leave.

[*Both go to door which he holds open.*]

And it's not necessary to keep saying 'with respect', Miss Mortimer. Do you enjoy saying it? Funny thing, but people enjoy saying things like 'your honour' 'your Majesty' 'with respect' 'your highness' . . .

**Now the offices of *The Sunday Paper* burst into activity.**

## EDITOR'S OFFICE

[HARVEY WINTERS, *the editor, dictating to secretary*.]

HARVEY: '. . . And so, you ask, "where do the best minds go? Not
into politics or the civil service", you say "there's no role for this
country to perform – instead they go into journalism and the mass
media". Well, I don't agree with your parenthetical observation
but it's a good question and a flattering answer. The best minds
don't want to legislate or exercise power so, they comment!
Journalism as an act of creating self-awareness in society! Good!
And for that very reason I believe it matters intensely the way
newspapers, radio and television report race relations. Spectacularly
in India, the Ahmedabad, A-H-M-E-D-A-B-A-D, the Ahmedabad
riot was touched off by rumours given the apparent veracity of
print: stealthily in Britain, the malformed seeds of prejudice have
been watered by a rain of false statistics and stories. Television
News has been an offender – no, a *gross* offender; the interviewer
asks people in the street what they think and the weirdest notions
of reality are listened to with the respect accorded to truth, as if the
electronic marvel of it all sanctified the instant communication of
ignorance'. [*Phone rings*.] Bloody hell! I'll never finish those letters.
No calls after this. Hello, Winters.

[*It's* ANTHONY SHARPLES, *editor of Business News Section*.]

ANTHONY: You rang?

HARVEY: Tony, yes. I want you to do something on women being
allowed into the stock exchange.

ANTHONY: Love to. Can't claim the privileges of a private club,
now, can they?

HARVEY: I was thinking of a light hearted leader, not an occasion for
solemnity.

ANTHONY: Indeed not, no, indeed. They've made fools enough of
themselves. Now let's see if they're still worried about telling dirty
jokes on the floor. How many words?

HARVEY: About 450?

ANTHONY: Done.

# IN DEPTH

[*Two journalists:* CHRIS MACKINTOSH, JULIAN GALLAGHER.]

CHRIS [*tearing sheet from pad*]: Falling bloody bridges! This subject must have priority over something though God knows what.

JULIAN [*banging on phone receiver*]: Hello? Hello? Blast! Going through to someone else. [*To* CHRIS] Here's that couple of quid I owe you.

# BUSINESS NEWS

*This is a large section, only part of which we see, the rest tails off stage.* [*Three journalists:* ANTHONY SHARPLES, MORTY COHEN, DOMINIC FLETCHER.]

DOMINIC [*who's been listening on a phone, shouts, off-stage*]: There's a stringer here says that the Transport and General Worker's Union in the north have an eccentric official who's bored with head office contracts. He insists that every new contract *he* draws up has to have an original clause in it and this time he's insisted that everyman get a day off on his birthday. Anybody interested?

VOICE [*off stage*]: Try features.

DOMINIC [*into phone*]: An incredibly stupid suggestion from one of my colleagues to try features.

# IN DEPTH

CHRIS: *I* don't know why the bloody bridges fall down. I don't even know why they keep up.

JULIAN [*pointing to pile of documents while hanging on to a phone*]: By the time we read through this lot we'll be able to build them ourselves. Hello hello HELLO!

CHRIS: Have you got hold of anyone yet?

JULIAN: Going through to someone else now. Hello? Press office? At last. It took five people to get to you. Julian Gallagher *The Sunday Paper* here. These bridges that keep falling down. Is your ministry making a statement yet?

## EDITOR'S OFFICE

[MARY *knocks and enters.*]

SECRETARY: Good God! How triumphant she looks.

MARY: They're going to work.

HARVEY: What was he like?

MARY: Shrewd, evasive and charmingly civilized.

SECRETARY: She's obviously enjoying herself.

MARY: Loving it.

SECRETARY: Why Mary Mortimer, you're even radiant.

MARY: Don't I deserve to be? I worked bloody hard to set up those interviews and they're all going to happen.

HARVEY: We all worked hard –

SECRETARY: – had to pull strings you know.

HARVEY: The notorious side of your brilliance isn't the most helpful key for opening the doors of power.

MARY: You've got the best journalist on Fleet Street working for you, stop complaining.

HARVEY: You'll not expect me to do that.

MARY: Quite right, Harvey.

SECRETARY: So you'd better lose that smug radiance before it tempts . . .

MARY: . . . my sardonic colleagues to demolish me with their courteous male chauvinism.

HARVEY: You getting your ministers to talk on the science versus politics issue?

MARY: I'm free ranging over everything.

HARVEY: Because I want us to build up a body of comment on that issue and your profiles will be central. I'm planning TV trailers on them the second you finish the last interview.

MARY: It's not easy. Not everyone sees the future as you do in terms of science versus politics.

HARVEY: We'll help them then.

MARY: And I trust you're planning to plaster the Saturday screen with the maximum spots?

HARVEY: Don't teach your granny to suck eggs.

MARY: Even granny's male pride is a little punctured isn't it?

HARVEY: And don't draw me into one of your sex wars, love.

MARY: Confess. Liberated though you may be, Harvey Winters, women do not a paper make. Confess.

HARVEY: I'm not biting. Now be a good girl and go. Look! Letters!

MARY: I'm going. Got me laundry spinning round the corner.


## WOMEN'S PAGES

[*Two journalists:* JANE MERRYWEATHER, ANGELA GOURNEY.]

JANE [*just entering with mocked-up sheets*]: Not a very inspiring week's work is it? An article about women's bums, one about two awful designers who make men's suits for £150 each and another about wild tea-drinking parties.

ANGELA: We're only supposed to be able to write about boys and knickers. Stop complaining.


## IN DEPTH

CHRIS: Do I want a cigarette? Yes I do want a cigarette. [*Reaching for packet.*] No I don't want a cigarette. Bridges! Christ! What a come down for In Depth.

## POLITICAL AND FEATURES

[*Two journalists:* NORMAN HARDCASTLE, CYNTHIA TREVELYAN.]

CYNTHIA: Look at these photographs. We've created a monster.
NORMAN: Aargh! The maimed, the dead, the diseased –
CYNTHIA: – and the starving. Look at them.
NORMAN: Someone must do them but I don't want to look at them.
CYNTHIA: And I can't get him to snap anything else now. 'Where the violence is, send me there' he says. And he's right. He can't photograph peace. And it's our fault. We've encouraged a morbid squint in his eye. My fault in fact. Bloody hell! they make me feel so wretched.

## EDITOR'S OFFICE

HARVEY: What's on today?
SECRETARY: You mustn't forget to speak to Chris Mackintosh about the collapse of Atlantis Insurance.
HARVEY: After the eleven o'clock.
SECRETARY: After the eleven o'clock. Then lunch with Morgan King MP.
HARVEY: The new fiery socialist super star.
SECRETARY: The very same. Then the boss wants you at five.
HARVEY: Can't see myself in a fit state for him after three hours of wine and fiery socialism.

## POLITICAL AND FEATURES

CYNTHIA: When he first came here he could hardly talk. Just threw his photographs on the desk and asked could we use them. In those days I pretended ugliness had poetry. Blocks of new flats with graffiti on the lift doors, smouldering kids hanging around the stairs, fighting on the roundabouts. Even then he had an eye for violence and desolation and waste. His own background. Look at them. Not even pity is there? Just acceptance. 'This is how it is!' And every time he comes in with a new batch of evidence about cruelty it shows in his own features.

## NEWS ROOM

[*A* SECRETARY, *who spends most of her time answering the phone, taking down messages and handing them to the news editor,* PAUL MANNERING. *Two reporters:* HARRY LAURISTON, MARTIN CRUIKSHANK.]

MARTIN [*waving newspaper*]: Another cutting to give to the honourable Miss Mary Mortimer for her Morgan King MP file.

HARRY: Where's he been speaking this time?

MARTIN: Humbermouth. Quote: 'Opening the town hall in the latest new town of Humbermouth, Mr Morgan King, the socialist MP for New Lanark, upset councillors by attacking what he called "the dead spirit of the place". In a speech which can't have endeared him to the town's architects he said: "But where is your town's spirit? This town hall? A building where functionaries meet to organize your tax and drainage problems? Surely," the fiery MP for New Lanark continued, "a town's heart is its gardens, its concert hall, its swimming pool, libraries, meeting places – where are they?"'

PAUL: Splendid. I've no doubt the bitch'll go to town on that one.

## POLITICAL AND FEATURES

NORMAN: Jesus! I've got a lump in my throat.

CYNTHIA: Give up smoking.

NORMAN: It's all right for you to be flippant.

CYNTHIA: Who's flippant? You got a lump in your throat so stop smoking.

NORMAN: You also think it might be cancer?

CYNTHIA: Norman, for God's sake.

## BUSINESS NEWS

DOMINIC: So I charms into me lap the lovely tennis player, who's also rich, privileged and American, and says to her, 'Ho hum, you think that now you're in my arms I'll not put out that story?' 'But,' she says, 'I thought you were a business journalist not a sports reporter.' 'I am I am,' says I, 'but' I pretend to her, 'the lesbian love affair of a famous Wimbledon player is too good for any kind of journalist to let slip.' With which she jumps out from the comfort of my ample thighs and cries, 'It's a terrible profession, terrible! Have you no standards?' 'Standards?' I say. 'Profession?' I say. 'I don't believe journalists have a profession – I don't know what that profession is anyway. And certainly they don't have any standards. It's the law of the jungle!' I cry, 'and not a very colourful one at that!' But, soft Irish nit that I am, I relent and in the end swop my silence for a night in the net – in a manner of speaking.

## EDITOR'S OFFICE

[NORMAN *visiting*.]

NORMAN: How about letting me take a look at the guerrillas in East Pakistan?
HARVEY: Climate's rotten. You know you catch whatever disease is in the air.
NORMAN: I'm serious, Harvey.
HARVEY: So am I.
NORMAN: You haven't got a better person in this paper to do it.
HARVEY: Bloody hell! The egos in this building.

## WOMEN'S PAGES

ANGELA: We're not used enough. We ought to be more provocative instead of practical. 'Down with children' not 'Cheap canvas chairs from Chelsea'. 'Down with children'. 'Must mothers of handicapped children be martyrs?' That sort of thing. Dammit! We're paid well enough. I want to be stretched. [*With its double entendre*] I luuuuve being stretched.

## EDITOR'S OFFICE

HARVEY [*on the phone to* CYNTHIA]: Cynthia, is Norman nearby?
CYNTHIA: No.
HARVEY: He having problems with his wife?
CYNTHIA: Afraid so. Why?
HARVEY: He's pressing me about going abroad again.
CYNTHIA: Guerrillas in East Pakistan?
HARVEY: The same. What's his illness this week?
CYNTHIA: Cancer of the throat.
HARVEY: Bloody hell! I'll talk to Gordon.

## ARTS PAGES

[SEBASTIAN HERBERT, *arts editor:* JOHN PROSSER, *assistant;* ERNST GUEST, *a novelist and reviewer.*]

JOHN: It's 9000. I've finished counting. Last year we received 9000 books to review of which we succeeded in covering roughly one fifth – nearly two thousand in fact.
ERNST: Is that good or bad?
SEBASTIAN: Very good, my boy. What, 1900 books in 52 weeks? Work it out.
ERNST: You work it out.
SEBASTIAN: I will, I will. That's let's see, 52 into 340, six – that's roughly 36 books a week which, although many are reviews in brief, is pretty good going. *And* you must take into account that with declining advertising the paper's not as big as it can be most of the time. Yes, very good I'd say.

## EDITOR'S OFFICE

GORDON FAIRCHILD *of Foreign Dept. visiting.*]

HARVEY: I'd like the research to begin now, Gordon. Go right back to the Aryan invasions of India, who was Hinduized, which minorities remained, the role of Imperial England in protecting minorities, why did the Muslims survive, right up to partition of Pakistan from India.

GORDON: What about the power of the priests?

HARVEY: Right! You can give a break-down on the sects as well.

GORDON: I'm thinking of something more on the lines of linking the massacres to the religious rabble-rousers.

HARVEY: Too big. It's a separate piece.

GORDON: But central, don't you think?

HARVEY: I know that priests everywhere have a lot to answer for and one day we'll write it – something for Tamara perhaps – but not now. This massacre's enough. O.K.?

GORDON: As you say.


## SPORTS PAGES

[RONNIE SHAPIRO, *sports editor.* MARVIN MCKEVIN, *his assistant.*]

RONNIE: Fascist! That's what it is. All sport is fascist activity. I've just realized.

MARVIN: Only just?

RONNIE: Governed by rules against which there's no appeal.

MARVIN: You've been talking to too many referees.

RONNIE: I mean apply them to a democratic society and they wouldn't hold up for ten seconds.

MARVIN: How about taking over the arts pages for six months?

RONNIE: And what's more fascist than all that crap about healthy body healthy mind?

MARVIN: And character being built on the playing fields of Eton?

RONNIE: All balls. *What* character, that's the point. The arts pages? I'd love to.

## FOREIGN DEPT.

[TAMARA DRAZIN, *foreign correspondent.* GORDON, *just entering.*]

GORDON: Harvey wants us to keep going at Pakistan.

TAMARA [*with irony*]: He's not afraid of 'boring' our readers?

GORDON: Even if it does.

TAMARA: Small blessings.

GORDON: And I agree with him.

TAMARA: And I'm sick. Look at it. [*Indicating telex reports.*] For what? What in this world is worth such savage slaughter?

GORDON: Keep cuts to a minimum then.

TAMARA: Cut it? I want to weep on it.

## ARTS PAGES

ERNST: I can't understand why you don't raise the price of newspapers.

JOHN: Cut down our dependence on advertising? No point really. Newspapers are a dying institution.

SEBASTIAN: Needless to say I don't share that view.

JOHN: Get in all the reviews you can, Ernst my boy. The day of the newspaper mogul is over. We're the honoured custodians of his agonizing death cries. He's screwed everyone, made off with his millions and now the workers are screwing back and between them they'll soon end an era. What you're witnessing is the decline of an industry.

## FOREIGN DEPT.

[TAMARA *is cutting out her clippings and pasting them in her book.*]

TAMARA: Look how full my book's getting.

GORDON: I've an idea which I put to Harvey and he likes.

TAMARA: Do you know why we all keep scrap books of our little bits and pieces?

GORDON: It's a serious long term project for you, listen to me.

TAMARA: So that in twenty years time we can say 'Look! *I* was right. When everyone else was making the wrong analysis of a situation I was making the right one. Here it is. In print!'

GORDON: An in-depth probe into the power of the priests.

TAMARA: Even Harvey.

GORDON: The priests have a lot to answer for, you know.

TAMARA: Even Harvey will point to a passage in a new bill and say 'Look! my wording! Exactly what I wrote in an editorial a hundred years ago.'

GORDON: Something on the lines of linking massacres to the religious rabble-rousers.

TAMARA: 'They've listened to me' we all cry.

GORDON: And for God's sake listen to *me*.

TAMARA: What priests? There are priests and priests.

GORDON: All dogma begins with the priesthood. And where there's dogma there's massacre.

TAMARA: I'm not fit, Gordon, believe me, I'm not fit.


## NEWS ROOM

[PAT STERLING, *a freelance, talking to* PAUL.]

PAUL: I don't think it's our story, Pat, not really. Aren't girls of twelve having abortions all the time?

PAT: But this one had been refused by a National Health Service gynaecologist. Some shrivelled-up hag.

PAUL: We can't help being shrivelled up old hags, you know, and isn't it all over anyhow?

PAT: That's why you can print the story.

PAUL: And the poor child's had her abortion privately?

PAT: 'If you play adult games' says this gynaecologist, 'you must expect adult consequences.'

PAUL: Awful, yes, I know, terrible story. Have you tried the *News of the World*?

PAT: Don't you just *know* what they'd do with it?

SECRETARY: The eleven o'clock in five minutes, Paul.

PAUL [*assembling papers*]: I'm sorry.

## FOREIGN DEPT.

GORDON: Perhaps you should see a psychiatrist.

TAMARA: Uch! They're so immodest.

GORDON: I know a good one.

TAMARA: They imagine every distress is a curable aberration.

GORDON: Did you know I was under one for three years?

TAMARA: Think they can explain everything 'The fault of the past! A sad tangle of human relationships!' Such awful presumptions. I despise them.

GORDON: Why don't you ever listen to me?

TAMARA: And you know why I despise them? Because there's such a thing as *endemic* despair only they're too arrogant to acknowledge it; you can't *pay* to have *that* cut out.

GORDON: Friends can help.

TAMARA: Maybe. But not help to get rid of it, only to live with it. Endemic despair is something you're born with.

GORDON: Or something you have if you can afford it.

TAMARA: That's a vulgar observation.

GORDON: You mean it's vulgar to be so poor that you've no time to reflect upon endemic despairs?

TAMARA: No, but it's crude to observe it.

GORDON: *Crude* to observe it? You've changed your mind? No longer 'vulgar'?

TAMARA: Don't split hairs.

GORDON: Well now, let's take a look at that, then. Crude to observe that the starving child has no time to reflect on life's hopelessness?

TAMARA: Ah ha! The starving child. He had to be brought in.

GORDON: Don't sneer at the starving child, my dear. Without him you'd have no endemic despair to enjoy.

TAMARA: You think I enjoy despair? You're a demagogue, Gordon.

GORDON: Scorn not the man who doth attempt alleviation of man's ills.

TAMARA: Scorn such a man I do not. But man's relentless and ugly stupidities are mine to despair of. You want to do good deeds? Do them. I will give you my cheque and God bless you. But do them silently and not heartily and give me leave to lament what I will.

GORDON: I'm even more convinced you need help.

TAMARA: And don't insult me.

[*She leaves.* MARTIN *passes her, extending a greeting she ignores.*]

MARTIN: She's getting worse.

GORDON: She worries me. She's speaking louder, faster and, with her deep-throated Slavic accent, she's becoming like a Nöel Coward caricature.

MARTIN: A man just rang in, American, freelance. Says he's got a trunk load of documents that reveals the 'truth about Biafra'!

GORDON: That'll make the fourth trunk load of documents I'll have read revealing 'the truth about Biafra'.

MARTIN [*imitating*]: 'Oh boy, man, is this big. Wait till you get a load of this. *This* is really big.'

GORDON: They're all big.


SPORTS PAGES

[MARVIN *entering.*]

MARVIN: Bloody hell!

RONNIE: I'm not interested.

MARVIN: Those phoney sports stories in the *Daily Sun* I've been blasting?

RONNIE: What of them?

MARVIN: Harvey stopped me this morning and said lay off.

RONNIE: *That* he should've said to me.

MARVIN: 'Lay off,' he said, 'my opposite number is squealing.'

RONNIE: Are we trying to change sports reporting or are we not trying to change sports reporting!?

[*Phone rings. It's* HARVEY *from the editor's office.*]

HARVEY: Ronnie?

RONNIE: Yes, Harvey.

HARVEY: Yesterday's *Financial Times.* Page 12. Second column, three up from the bottom. Got it?

RONNIE [*who's been turning pages of the F.T.*]: Got it.

HARVEY: Aston Vale football club is offering you, me and others shareholdings in the club. Might make a good story for 'Bullseye'. Who's selling them, how many, why, and who's buying. O.K.?

RONNIE: O.K. Thanks. [*Phone down.*]


# EDITOR'S OFFICE

[*It has been slowly filling up with people for the 'eleven o'clock' editorial meeting.*
*Present are* ANTHONY SHARPLES, CHRIS MACKINTOSH, GORDON FAIRCHILD.*]

HARVEY [*to* ANTHONY *and having just put down the phone.*]: You going to stop reading that paper and listen to us?

ANTHONY: When *you've* stopped phoning.

HARVEY: Right, gentlemen. And what are we going to do about our beloved leader and his government this week?

GORDON: I think it's about time we tried a touch of irony in our political commentaries. 'Today poverty is your own fault, today you can stand on your own two feet. Anyone can become Prime Minister.'

CHRIS: 'Our beloved leader has proved it.'

GORDON: 'And our nasty chancellor has proved it. All of them self-made and nasty men saying you too can also be self-made and nasty men . . .'

CHRIS: Think they'll get the point? [*To* GORDON] Here's that couple of quid I owe you.


# POLITICAL AND FEATURES

[TAMARA *visiting*.]

CYNTHIA: 'Why so pale and wan fond lover?'

TAMARA: I think what I'd like is a good, old-fashioned nervous breakdown.

CYNTHIA: That's a shocking thing to say, Tamara.

TAMARA: There's such honesty about going to pieces.

CYNTHIA: You mustn't be frivolous about such things.

TAMARA: I feel so guilty to find myself being able to cope with it all.

NORMAN: Guilts! Guilts! Those sombre, Jewish guilts.

TAMARA: Mornings. Wake up. A disc-jockey's forced jocularity.

CYNTHIA: Well thank God for a little jocularity, I say.

TAMARA: These offices. Sour jealousies. Battles for space. Defeated journalists.

NORMAN: *Not* first day of the week, pleeease.

TAMARA [*picking up newspaper and turning pages*]: Then all this. The smug weariness of experienced politicians. The intimidations of bigoted minorities. The tortuous self-defence of money makers. The pomposity of knowledge-glutted academics. Genocide in Pakistan. And us, pretending to stand up to them with I-don't-know-what; our five hundred words here, our six-hundred-word-thoughts there.

NORMAN: The price we pay for the pleasure of your company is the depressing effects of your conversation.


# ARTS PAGES

ERNST [*who is checking his proofs*]: Sebastian, is it your idea of a joke, a correction, or an improvement to change the words of my review from 'to put it mildly' to 'to put it wildly'?

SEBASTIAN: Oh, here's a much better printer's error. [*Reading from a proof.*] 'They become incredibly wound up; yet these is method in their madness for the unwinding is ceremonies and without a bitch.'


## POLITICAL AND FEATURES

CYNTHIA: As a matter of fact I'm about to embark on a long eulogy of disc-jockeys.

TAMARA: Really.

CYNTHIA: All about the joy they bring to drab lives.

TAMARA: And how their constant stream of gaiety denies the existence of unhappiness?

CYNTHIA: Not denies, just by-passes.

TAMARA: There's nothing more gloomy than laughter at all costs.

CYNTHIA: It's not laughter at all costs, it's music at all costs.

TAMARA: *Music?*

CYNTHIA: Yes! Yes! Music!

TAMARA: No! No! *Not* music. Energy, perhaps, of a spurious urgency. And a relentless loudness to cover up for poverty of talent.

CYNTHIA: You're growing old and square.

TAMARA: What an easy vocabulary of insults we have these days. 'Square' presumably is the state you need to think others are in so that you can feel young? [*She leaves.*]

CYNTHIA: How complicated these mid-European ladies are.


## EDITOR'S OFFICE

[*Editorial continuing.*
PAUL *from news desk entering.*]


HARVEY: Hello, Paul. Our problem is that we're all in agreement that government's wrong and we're right.

ANTHONY: Oh, I don't know. I'm more inflationary than you.

HARVEY: Are you? Well you're wrong then. I think we're entitled to be absolutely critical of *all* aspects by now and it would be absolutely consistent with our policy to criticize the government's economic strategy.

ANTHONY: There *is* no economic strategy.

GORDON: But there *is* a philosophy. I mean 'let lame ducks go to the wall and stand on your own two feet' *is* a philosophy.

ANTHONY: Yes, but it's not a strategy.

HARVEY: Anyway, they're changing doctrines. State subsidy, for industries suffering from 'non-culpable decline'.

ANTHONY: From what?

HARVEY: 'Intervention in industry' says the minister in today's *Times*, 'is respectable in areas of non-culpable decline'. What do we say to that?

GORDON: Sounds like a very sad and touching excuse for death. 'Please, everyone, forgive my non-culpable decline.'


# BUSINESS NEWS

MORTY: The great thing about Arnold Weinstock is – the man's so sane.

DOMINIC: What is there about shop keepers, d'you think, that mesmerizes the intelligent journalists of Business News?

MORTY: If he has to sack 5000 men because of waste he'll do it. And he'll justify it by saying it's better for the sacked ones because men get depressed hanging around doing nothing, lose self-respect.

DOMINIC: Compassionate man, Weinstock.

MORTY: And those that stay know that they're good because Weinstock has kept them and so they're men of confidence.

DOMINIC: A Solomon, no less!

MORTY: His prime task? To weed out a waste.

DOMINIC: A gardener, to boot!

MORTY: He appeals to men's greed but, paradoxically –

DOMINIC: – paradoxically –

MORTY: – paradoxically he must elicit from them a high degree of *cooperation* in order to satisfy that greed.

DOMINIC: Paradoxically.

MORTY: His approach is precisely that of a good business journalist – determined to cut through half truths and vague generalizations.

DOMINIC: Really?

MORTY: 'Never believe anything,' he says, 'all information is suspect.'

DOMINIC: Arnold Weinstock's attitude is rather like that of the baron of whom it was asked: 'Why do you build your walls so high and strong?' To which the baron replied: 'In order to give the peasants' hovels something to lean upon.'


## EDITOR'S OFFICE

[*Editorial continuing.*]

HARVEY: Where are we on the Soviet spaceship deaths?

PAUL: No further than any other newspaper.

GORDON: Anyone know why the monkey died last time?

ANTHONY: Boredom, I think.


## POLITICAL AND FEATURES

[MARY *rushes in with her bag of laundry.*]

MARY: I'm late for the 'eleven o'clock'.

NORMAN: We've got another Morgan King quote for you. Cynthia?

CYNTHIA [*reading from a cutting*]: 'Addressing the annual Durham Miners' gala over the weekend, Mr Morgan King, the new fiery socialist super-star member for New Lanark, said: "I believe that before any legislation can be passed in parliament there must exist the machinery to communicate an understanding of that legislation otherwise we will be forced to *drag* a community behind us."'

MARY: What the bloody hell does he think newspapers and television are for?

CYNTHIA: '"Nor is it enough to print, however vast the quantity, our complex blue bills and white papers which few can read or understand, nor to leave their interpretation to the not-always-adequately-briefed and random intelligence of busy, information-drunk journalists who interpret according to bias or the quality of their mind."'

MARY: The impertinence! The incredible impertinence of the man. How dare he? 'The quality of their mind'. Who the bloody hell does he think he is. A jumped up miner's son with exaggerated notions about the value of self-education!

NORMAN: Uh-uh-uh-uh!

MARY: Well *I'm* not intimated by working-class haloes – the pain of poverty has never blinded me to its product of ignorance, and underprivilege was never a guarantee against charlatanism and *that's* the function of journalism – to protect society from shabby little charlatans like him.

NORMAN: And who will protect society from shabby little journalists? We traffic in human blemishes, Mary. Don't you find it washing over your own life?

MARY: I'll take you on some other time. [*Rushes out.*]


## WOMEN'S PAGES

JANE: Do you know what Mary said to me when I first came to work here? 'If you're young and in charge,' she said, 'and you want to deflate an old journalist, my advice to you is this: when she – or he – brings his piece to you, you flip through it and then throw it on the desk and say – well, honestly, I didn't expect you to show me something like this.'

ANGELA: That sounds like our Mary. What made you think of that?

JANE: Don't know. Remember the time we invited the politicos to our ideas luncheon and we ended up giving *them* ideas? Well I gave the idea for those in-depth interviews of cabinet ministers to Norman and – well – oh, I don't know. Credit grabbing is one of the sicknesses of this profession. Takes it out of you.

## IN DEPTH

[NORMAN *visiting.*]

NORMAN: Where's your master?

JULIAN: Don't have masters or deputies in our department. Some of us just get paid more than others, that's all.

NORMAN: Worthy, worthy.

JULIAN: Being someone's deputy is an invitation to assassination. He knows it, I know it, so we drop titles. Lovely life. Easy, civilized, just what I was born to. Scurrying across Europe to investigate this and that, pause for a love affair, a ballet, a bit of skiing. You ever go skiing, Norman?

NORMAN: Are you mad? Skiing? You can break legs and die of exposure and things.

JULIAN: Glad to see you making jokes about your dying and disease. Good to laugh at one's fears, I think.

NORMAN: I'm not laughing. That's the mistake everyone makes. *I* ceased laughing after Molière. Humour for me is an internal haemorrhage, otherwise it's contrived giggles.

## EDITOR'S OFFICE

[*Editorial continuing.*
MARY *entering.*]

HARVEY: Hello, Mary. I think we ought to have someone in India in case war breaks out.

ANTHONY: In *case* war breaks out? With six million East Pakistani refugees on her soil and every major power full of pious platitudes? War? *And* revolution, *and* famine, *and* cholera.

HARVEY: Any volunteers to go?

GORDON: Me please.

HARVEY: You'll bloody stay here and coordinate.

ANTHONY: No free trips this time, my lad.

HARVEY: I'm thinking of sending Norman to take a look at the Mukti Bahani.

GORDON: You thinking or is he asking?

## SPORTS PAGES

[MAC SMITH, *a trade union official, visiting.*]

RONNIE: So it's settled then?

MAC: I can't be sure, Ronnie.

RONNIE: There's very little any of us can be sure of in this life, we know, but, Mac, we met six times last week. Management say they're not yet closing down the garage. Your men are safe, for the moment.

MAC: Ah, but are they? And has management said they're *not* closing down the garage? They've changed the *date* for closure, but *we* asked them to withdraw it.

RONNIE: And haven't they agreed on that?

MAC: The position's very ambiguous.

RONNIE: Industrial disputes usually are, old son.

MAC: Don't be frivolous, brother, the strike threat's not passed yet.

## EDITOR'S OFFICE

[*Editorial continuing.*]

HARVEY: Right, now, science and politics, how's that coming along?

ANTHONY: Morty's getting a good picture of investments in technology. Should have it by the end of the month.

CHRIS: Norman's pursuing the backbone: 'Has technology re-arranged the genes of political issues?' or some such thing to do with futurology.

GORDON: That'll bring them in.

HARVEY: You remain sceptical?

GORDON: I remain sceptical.

MARY: We doing something more about this new book on race by the way?

CHRIS: What do you suggest? Arts reviewed it last week.

MARY: Well have you read it? I mean just look at this paragraph. It's just such unscientific thinking makes me so suspicious of the man.

HARVEY: Send someone to interview him I'd say.

MARY: Ask him if he's erring according to Hudson's law of selective attention to data?

PAUL: That might be a boomerang question, since the journalist's profession is entirely given to just that: the selective attention to data.

## BUSINESS NEWS

DOMINIC: They want to take over the shipyards? Workers' control? Right, here's what I'll want to discover:

One: Can it work inherently? i.e. can they produce workers who can manage and administer, men who can overcome demarcation issues and work in a way to double production?

Two: If they can, will it be allowed to work?

Three: If it's not allowed to work will this produce a chain reaction of protest from workers in other industries?

Four: If it *is* allowed to work will it set up a precedent and example to be followed in other industries?

Five: Most important – *how* will it work? That is to say: will it work in such a way that it would simply produce another hierarchy producing its own set of disenchantments.

As a good barrister by training my questions are already succinctly formulated.

MORTY: And as a good reporter the answers already written, I trust.

## EDITOR'S OFFICE

[*Editorial continuing.*]

ANTHONY: And how's Mary's profiles? Coming along are they?

MARY: Four down three to go.

ANTHONY: Committing themselves on science versus politics?

MARY: Here and there. George Carron will of course.

PAUL: I should hope so, being the minister for science and technology.

GORDON: Do they actually let you come into their houses, fondle their dogs, tickle their grandchildren, pour wine for you and all that?

MARY: All that and more.

ANTHONY: More. Ah ha!

MARY: You're a dirty old man, Anthony.

ANTHONY: It's hardly an issue how dirty this old man is. Question is, how dirty are they?

MARY: Harvey, I'd like, while we're talking about profiles, to pursue someone else I think we should all be keeping an eye on.

PAUL: Morgan King M.P. no doubt.

HARVEY: Oh, the super-star. I'm lunching with him today.

GORDON: You planning to rubbish him? Poor man. He's only just started his political career. I'd've thought small fry for you, Mary.

PAUL: She's actually been having a go at him for some time.

ANTHONY: Under cover of that 'witty, cool and deathly column' of hers.

HARVEY: They're heathens, Mary, ignore them. Tell us.

MARY: I don't know. He smells phoney.

HARVEY: I'll let you know.

GORDON: Don't his crude honesties appeal to you? You're always complaining about political smoothies.

MARY: I'm just saying he needs to be kept an eye on and I'd like to know you'd be interested if I came up with anything.

HARVEY: Providing we don't get snarled up in any more litigations. Our libel insurance is running low.

GORDON: I actually get prickles on my skin every time I see Mary prepare to lunge for a kill. Thrilling. That's my word for it — thrilling.

MARY: Harvey, would you excuse me. I don't think you need me. [*She leaves.*]

HARVEY: You must stop getting at her or I'll begin to think it's professional jealousy, and you wouldn't want me to think that.

PAUL: I think she's lethal.

CHRIS: But a brilliant journalist.

PAUL: *You* all think so, I know.

## POLITICAL AND FEATURES

CYNTHIA: Don't you ever feel uneasy, sometimes, as a journalist? We inundate people with depressing information and they become concerned. Then we offer more information and they become confused. And then we pile on more and more until they feel impotent but we offer them no help. No way out of their feelings of impotence. Don't you ever feel guilty?

NORMAN: Constantly.

## PART TWO

## THE CENTRE SPACE

[*Part of the lounge in the home of the Rt Hon.* GEORGE CARRON, *Minister for Science and Technology.*
*He's playing chess with* MARY.]

CARRON: I'm a bachelor, Miss Mortimer. If I'd been married — nice cultured woman and all that — I might be more interested in literature, films, plays, all that. But I'm not.

MARY: You don't mind me asking, Mr Carron?

CARRON: After three gruelling sessions with the old man? Ask away. I'll tell you what I mind and don't mind. But art? Can't help you there. You'll have to put me down as illiterate. Science and politics, those are my passions.

MARY: And chess.

CARRON: Ah, chess. My only addiction.

MARY: So, it doesn't worry you that all those upstart writers are required reading in the schools?

CARRON: Worry me?

MARY: After all, *their* values point to one kind of society while you're legislating to shape another kind of society.

CARRON: Worry me? Strange question. Check. Look, I'm an old man and, I'll confess, not a very happy one, I began my career as a labour politician from a farm labourer's background and half way changed my politics to Tory – a man's driven by the profit motive, plain and simple, I soon found that out. But, it makes for a lonely life. To be despised. Not nice. You live with it but you never get used to it. Still, that's not the point. What I'm saying is that experience shaped me, not art. I didn't change roads because of what I read in books but because of what I read in man. I don't think I'm a philistine – you mustn't think anything simple like that – but it's – my experience. I'm tone deaf, colour blind and get very impatient with the convenient concoctions literary men make into novels. I saw a play once and I thought to myself, yes, well, them people can behave like that 'cos they got good scripts written for them. I prefer men who write their own scripts. They do it in 'The House' and they do it in the cabinet and they do it at international conferences and that's real. Art shaping society? I doubt it. Science, yes, not books. Still, I've got to believe that haven't I? Minister for Science and Technology and all that.

MARY: Can we talk about science then?

CARRON: You haven't moved out of check yet.

MARY: Sorry. [*She moves.*]

CARRON: Ah! You know what you're about don't you?

MARY: I've got three children who kept calling me bourgeois for playing bridge so I pacified them by learning chess.

CARRON: My one regret – no children. Watch out for your queen.

MARY: The editor wants to focus on the science versus politics debate.

CARRON: Facile divisions. Journalese. Look, the argument goes like this, I know it: there develops, it is said, unnoticed by most of us, a whole range of scientific and technological discovery and invention which creeps up behind societies and suddenly – is there! And each time it happens, the argument goes, then all the moral, religious and political deliberations of decades are rendered useless and we have to begin to formulate our opinions all over again. Right? That's the thesis. And it's one that presents this image of a silent, modest, effective activity – science – alongside a vociferous, self-important and ineffectual babelizing – politics! It's an attractive picture. I can see why people fall for it and I can see why newspapers choose it as a popular controversy ripe for oversimplification. But how accurate is it? How helpful is it? Look at the period between 1900 and 1913, 'La Belle Epoque' we call it. World-wide economic growth, prosperity, scientific and technological advances. The lot!

MARY: And all based on the political and philosophical assumptions of the enlightenment.

CARRON: Right! You've got it!

MARY: Science made possible by politics, not in conflict with it.

CARRON: Exactly! but look what happened after 1913 – something no scientific progress nor philosophical enlightenment can account for nor, I may add, need account for – an idiotic, soul-destroying world war!

MARY: Then who should account for it?

CARRON: Ah! Now you're asking a question which needs the kind of complex answers newspapers can't give and presumably didn't give in those early 1900s. Instead they oversimplified, as you're trying to do. And *they* led to World War One and you and your editor – well, I won't be so presumptuous. Books! History! The interaction of ideas – that's where you'll find your answers and where I think you ought to guide your readers for their answers.

MARY: But, Minister, that's a contradiction. You said *experience* changed men, not ideas from books. Now you're saying certain *ideas* formed the basis for 'la Belle Epoque'.

CARRON: Contradictions? Well, you've got to live with them also. A Jewish M.P. once told me a story about an old rabbi who was asked to settle a dispute between two men. The first man tells his version and the rabbi listens, thinks, and says: 'You know, you're right.' Then the second man presents his side of the argument and the rabbi listens, thinks and says: 'You know, you're right.' At which the rabbi's pupil who was standing by waiting for wisdom says: 'But, Rabbi, first you said this man was right, then you said that man was right. How can that be?' And the rabbi listened and thought and said: 'You know what? You're also right.'

## ARTS PAGES

SEBASTIAN: Just listen to this, gentlemen. A letter infinitely superior to most. 'Whatever your decision it's bound to prove expensive. If you reject my offering, you will discover very soon, as I have already warned you, that you have missed "the scoop of the century". If you accept it and publish the articles I shall expect payment at a rate that will enable me to complete my life's work during the next two or three years.'

JOHN: Obviously we should buy them. I find it a very touching letter.

SEBASTIAN: I find it intimidating.

ERNST: I find it embarrassing. Reminds me of all those letters I used to write to editors of literary magazines offering, with great benevolence, my very bad poetry.

## IN DEPTH

JULIAN: We were at this party and this Tory bag came up to me and she asked me what I did, so I said, despite my extremely youthful looks, I said: 'I edit *The Sunday Paper*, ma'am.' And she, ignoring my youthful looks, believed me and whispered: 'Ah ha! Wanted to meet you. *I* think you've got three fully paid up members of the Communist Party on your In Depth team.' And quick as a flash I said: 'Oh no, ma'am, they're not as right-wing as all that!'

## BUSINESS NEWS

MORTY: But much more important than your controlling share-holder, your 'rentier', was your poor little swindled punter. The big boys *deserve* all they get – trying to make money work for them instead of working for themselves.

## EDITOR'S OFFICE

[PAUL *visiting*.]

PAUL: I'm not happy about our attitude to the government, Harvey. I know you feel we should be more vigorous in our comments but we do stand for something, you know.

HARVEY: Not uncritically, Paul. You can't say we're irresponsible in our condemnations of government policy. It's not the old days. We've got a first-class team, Oxbridge firsts, good, hard analytical brains who understand the problems and –

PAUL: – and nothing, Harvey. They understand nothing. *We* stopped believing in the sanctity of print long ago, but not them. You know and I know and anyone who's an old hand knows that newspapers can't deal in truths but only in facts. Not this lot though. They actually imagine they're trafficking in truth. No humility. But we *can* deal in attitudes and principles and judgements and I think we're betraying this paper's image.

HARVEY: I don't think that's fair, Paul. They're aware of limitations and very properly careful in their judgements. We'd do the same if the left were in power.

PAUL: I know that, Harvey. But not everyone else on the staff knows it. They're a bit cynical these youngsters you've gathered round you. They see *The Sunday Paper*, being an old conservative family newspaper and therefore commanding more credibility, as being the best journal through which to infiltrate radical views. True! The very words they use. 'Infiltrate radical views.'

HARVEY: Come now, Paul, don't let's get too portentous. It'll take more than a few brilliant left-wing journalists to crack the ramifications of this country's deeply entrenched and very, very competitive spirit.

## BUSINESS NEWS

ANTHONY [*reading and laughing at a newspaper report*]: We're being told here by the illustrious *Telegraph* that – and I quote: 'The Business News section of *The Sunday Paper* is like the TV power game programmes, tending to see all business as a jungle and all business men as nasty, wrangling, grinning, smooth handshaking, back-stabbing villains . . .'
DOMINIC: Except Arnold Weinstock, of course.

## NEWS ROOM

HARRY [*on the phone, but first to* MARTIN]: The Angry Brigade have struck again, a boutique. [*Into phone*] Let's get this straight. They put a bomb in the boutique, gave them ten minutes to clear out and sent this note to *The Times*? O.K. let's have it. [*Writing down.*] 'If you are not busy being born you are busy buying.' Yes. 'In fashion as in everything else capitalists can only look backwards . . .' Jesus! This is school kid's stuff. O.K. go on. 'The future is ours.' Yes. 'Life is so boring there is nothing to do except . . .' Except *what*? Spend our wages on *what*? 'Nothing to do except spend our wages on the latest skirt or shirt.' They call this political analysis? It's self pity. Yes, all right, go on. 'Brothers, sisters, what are your real desires?' Yes. 'Sit in the drug store, look distant, empty, bored . . .' Yes, I've got it. Or *what*? 'Or blow it up or burn it down.' Yes. 'You cannot reform profit, capitalism and inhumanity, just kick it till it breaks.' *What*? Revolution? It just ends like that? Revolution? 're-vol-u-tion.' Got it. No I don't write shorthand. I find most people so boring in what they say that my slow longhand is fast enough to catch what's worthwhile. Thanks. [*Replaces receiver.*]

MARTIN: A bomb in a boutique? Jesus! I wish I could distinguish between their outrage and their envy.


## FOREIGN DEPT.

[*Urgent sound of 'tick-tack'.*
MARY *and* TAMARA *are reading what is coming through the telex machine.*]

MARY: Where the hell is our fiery socialist speaking from now?
TAMARA: Hamburg.
MARY: And what's our super-star doing there?
TAMARA: Some exchange they have with New Lanark.
MARY: He's every bloody where. Read it out, there's a dear.
    [*Phone rings. It's* HARVEY.]
HARVEY: Mary? I want you to look after Peter's affairs for the month he's away.
MARY: And who'll look after mine?
HARVEY: Come on, love, you know you've always wanted to be special features editor and you've got the biggest shoulders of any of us.
MARY: Very flattering.
HARVEY: And the sharpest intellect. There! That better?
MARY: By the way, Harvey, isn't it about time Paul was pensioned off?
HARVEY: That question discredits you. I'll forget you asked it.
MARY: He's tired, sentimental and a third-rate mind.
HARVEY: He's efficient, dependable and knows the job from top to bottom. I don't like sacking old men.
MARY: If I'm to cover up for Pete he'll get in my way.
HARVEY: You're relentless, Mary.
MARY: A quality you not infrequently rely upon. Are you free?
HARVEY: No.
MARY: I want to hear your impressions of Morgan King.
HARVEY: Ten minutes. [*Phones down.*]

TAMARA: There's something unhealthy about your dislike of Morgan King.

MARY: I can't stand do-gooders. They talk with such pity.

TAMARA: Oh come now. Every politician is a do-gooder.

MARY: I can't bear to be so sorried for. Please, read it, Tamara.

TAMARA: It's difficult to see where it begins. [*Reading from long, white telex sheet.*] 'I tell you of these incidents in my private life because, if we're talking about the need for society to produce the whole man then let *us* be seen as whole men, imperfections and all, since it is an imperfect man for whom we must build a compassionate society.'

MARY: Really! Who does he think he is? Protesting his imperfections as though we wouldn't believe he had any in the first place. Don't you find something irritating about a good person?

TAMARA: Not just 'something'. It's perfectly easy to identify: their goodness, by comparison, reveals our shabbiness. Simple!

[MARY, *exasperated, leaves.*]


## SPORTS PAGES

MARVIN: I've got eight brothers and they've all, all of them got funny names. Like Jack the Corporation, James the Jumper, Willie the Woodman. And why? Because my parents were publicans and each of us was born in a different pub. Solly the Dun Cow, Chris The Mortar and Pestle, Horace the Mulberry Bush. It was Jonah The Pig and Whistle who used to object most.

RONNIE: And you, Marvin. What were you called?

MARVIN: Don't laugh? Marvin the Mermaid.


## NEWS ROOM

MARTIN: And yet, you know, I've a sneaking sympathy for The Angry Brigade. There's something about ostentation makes you want to blow it up.

HARRY: It's their warm and cosy world of small sabotage that irritates me.

MARTIN: Do you know I saw a Rolls Royce with a TV aerial on it today?

HARRY: And their weakness for simplified political platitudes.

MARTIN: Why should anyone want to watch TV while being driven through interesting streets or countryside?

HARRY: I mean they're just spit-and-run boys, aren't they?

MARTIN: Pale blue it was. And I was confused between admiration for its mechanics and disgust for its opulence. And as I was driving I got this great urge to crash into it. Irrational really. Not an urge I was proud of. Bit mean. Unworthy.

HARRY: Anyway, I think their passion for destruction is inherited from the very enemy they think they loathe. Relieves them of tiny angers.

MARTIN: Still, I did *so* want to knock it down.

HARRY: And they're no more a match for the lovely, seductive philosophical defences of capitalism than their do-it-yourself bombs are a match for tanks and nuclear toys.

MARTIN: Still, they have tried everything else without much effect. Marches, sit-downs, teach-ins, civil disobedience.


## SPORTS PAGES

RONNIE: We used to have a woman on the travel page who regularly, for two years, used to hand in stuff saying such and such a place was a lovely sunny beach until the Jews got there! Didn't care that it was never printed, she never seemed to get the message. And it took two years before management could bring themselves to sack her. She was a widow you see. Lived alone. Cruelly abandoned by kith and kin. Acid personality – but a loner. You can't fling people on the dole just 'cos they're anti-semitic can you?

MARVIN: No sense of revenge, that's what irritates me about you Jews. Understanding of everything and everyone. Not healthy, Ronnie boy. Bite! Gotta bite back.

RONNIE: That's our trouble. We're beginning to.

## BUSINESS NEWS

[CHRIS *visiting*.]

DOMINIC [*to* MORTY]: And who's your Arnold Weinstock for this month?

MORTY: Oh, he'll last, my son. Good for a reference every two months or so – at least.

ANTHONY [*to* CHRIS]: And what are our In-depth colleagues in-depthing this week?

CHRIS: The crash of boring old bridges I'm afraid.

ANTHONY: And what help can we offer you on that?

CHRIS: Not crashing bridges, old son, but crashing insurance companies.

ANTHONY: Ah! The ill-fated Atlantis company.

CHRIS: I've got a lead from a high-up on the Board of Trade.

DOMINIC [*mocking*]: 'At 08.00 hrs the shrewd and enigmatic Mr Cruikshank –'

MORTY [*taking up the mockery*]: '– a clean-shaven, handsome man, greying attractively at the temples –'

DOMINIC: '– was seen by his cleaner to arrive an hour earlier than usual at the head office of Atlantis Insurance –'

MORTY: '– Meanwhile, back at the Board of Trade, Mr X –'

DOMINIC: '– who shall remain nameless –'

MORTY: '– was heard cracking his hard-boiled, mid-morning egg –'

DOMINIC: '– four minutes, of course –'

MORTY: '– with greater anxiety than usual –'

DOMINIC: '– At that moment, 800 miles away in the Bahamas, the beautiful wife of the Swiss ambassador was sun-bathing with the even more beautiful wife of the junior partner of Atlantis Insurance and discussing the latest wines of the little known but highly sought after Château de Montaigne –'

MORTY: '– At first sight all these far flung incidents have no connection –'

CHRIS: Care to take over the column, boys?

ANTHONY: Oh, we're much too flippant for your serious investigations, Chris. Now –

CHRIS: Now. What's the percentage an insurance company must set aside to cover claims?

ANTHONY: Well, let's see. The big boys arrange that sort of thing amongst themselves, you know.

CHRIS: Good God!

ANTHONY: Yes, God is good. But, it would appear, only to them what already have. Now, at one time it was 9 per cent and then . . .


## FOREIGN DEPT.

GORDON: Of course you're growing old. We're all growing old. Especially in this profession. At 32 one's old.

TAMARA: Gordon, can you lend me a couple of pounds, please?

GORDON [*while dipping into his pocket*]: I remember when Kruschev died, there was this reporter, one of our top men, tried to phone through to the Kremlin. Didn't stop to think that neither of them would be able to speak the other's language, just automatically reached for the phone. The spark goes. Last night on TV I was watching the awful tragedy of the three Russian astronauts dying in space and I was thinking – yes, now how can we handle that? This way? Yes, maybe. That way? Yes, well – I'll sleep on it. Years ago I'd have immediately rung up people and started generating ideas.

TAMARA [*referring to newspaper*]: And the slaughter goes on. 'West Pakistan tanks fire on university students asleep in their dormitories.' We're not reporting foreign news, we're reporting madness.


## POLITICAL AND FEATURES

NORMAN *exercising with chest expanders.*]

CYNTHIA: I find your piece on futurology spine-chilling.

NORMAN: Brilliantly written though.

CYNTHIA: What's so depressing about the futurologists is their way of wrapping up the future. They define it so precisely that they obliterate it. There *is* no future. They've brought it up to the present. Nothing to look forward to or be spontaneous about.

NORMAN [*puffing*]: You miss the point. They don't define what *will* happen – only what *could* happen. Know the dangers – prevent them.

CYNTHIA: But they don't make judgements about their predictions.

NORMAN: Not their job.

CYNTHIA: Why not add a para and say that?

NORMAN [*pause in exercising*]: Because I've got a para which, if you read carefully, points out that they'd developed a unique method of formulating a question which combines science with its moral implications.

CYNTHIA: Example?

NORMAN: Example: Politicians know the potential of scientific and medical research in the field of mind control. Question: should legislation be passed to control the mind controllers before perfection of technique makes its misuse too tempting to resist? [*Continues exercise.*]

[RONNIE *enters.*]

RONNIE: What the hell good do you think you're doing?

NORMAN: Healthy body, healthy mind.

RONNIE: What great writer do *you* know who ran a couple of miles before picking up a pen?

NORMAN [*puffing*]: Walk, swim, feel fresher, prepared for anything.

RONNIE: If you're an idiot, mate, not even an Olympic medal can change that. A lovely bit of private distress, that'll sharpen your wits, not a handful of jerks.

NORMAN [*stopping*]: I'm not suggesting a healthy body *makes* a healthy mind, but given a lively mind to begin with –

CYNTHIA: – such as you've got –

NORMAN: – such as I've got, then it's enhanced by a fit body. Oh my God! I've strained a shoulder muscle.

## IN DEPTH

JULIAN: What are the lay-abouts in our business section up to?
CHRIS: Oh, trying to find a new Arnold Weinstock to write up.
JULIAN: In order to knock down –
CHRIS: – to make room for another Arnold Weinstock to build up –
JULIAN: – in order to knock down –
CHRIS: – to make room for another –

## BUSINESS NEWS

MORTY: Have you seen the new poster of Chairman Mao hanging up in the In Depth offices?
ANTHONY: It's rather like the photographs of nudes which boys hang in their rooms at public school to assert their independence while temporarily trapped by the enemy.

## IN DEPTH

CHRIS: I *do* want a cigarette. I *don't* want a cigarette. [*Reaching for phone and cigarettes.*] I *do* want a cigarette. [*Reaching for a bottle of beer.*] And a drink. Bloody bridges!

## ARTS PAGES

SEBASTIAN: You actually think Hughie Green is a genius?
JOHN: Yes, I do – and I chose the word carefully.
SEBASTIAN: And how would your article on him set about proving that extraordinary misuse of the epithet?
JOHN: Figures. His television parlour games have the highest ratings.
SEBASTIAN: Oh, I see. Impressed by numbers are you?
JOHN: *And* he's a man of the people.
SEBASTIAN: Is that his claim or your conclusion?

ERNST: But his gags are terrible.

JOHN: Which is precisely what puts him on a level with 25 million viewers who are desperately relieved to hear a famous man only able to make jokes as awful as they would themselves.

ERNST: And *that's* genius?

JOHN: There's more. He's interested in the trivia of living without attempting to counsel or instruct. He amplifies the ordinary and gives it status.

SEBASTIAN: Most interesting. You mean he's like politicians who, to curry favour and gain power, stultify the development of mind and personality by applauding the lowest instincts.

JOHN: Depends how you put it. He puts it another way. 'The people count' he says.

SEBASTIAN: Oh, they all say that, dear fellow.

JOHN: 'The people are the only patrons,' he says. 'I am the public's servant and I am there to do more or less what they want. Why defy those people who are your friends?' However, he makes a brilliant volte face when he defends the establishment. 'I sincerely believe,' he says, 'that there are certain of us who are better equipped to know what is good for us than others.' And double-thinking like that is real genius.

SEBASTIAN: Not in my dictionary it isn't.


IN DEPTH

CHRIS [*on phone*]: Professor Cobblestone? Good morning. Chris Mackintosh of *The Sunday Paper* here – yes, you've guessed it, those fallen bridges. No – all right, not now. But in fact I didn't want to go into it *now*, only check you're the right man. You are? Splendid. To be frank I don't know how to start thinking on this subject at all and – good! I'll ring you again when I've read through all this material and got a basic shape to the piece and ask you if it makes engineering sense. O.K.? Thanks. Bye. [*Replaces receiver. Closes his eyes.*] Do I want a cigarette? No! I don't want a cigarette. [*Picks up phone to dial again.*]

## SPORTS PAGES

[*Phone ringing.*]

RONNIE: Ron Shapiro here.
　　[*It's from the Editor's office.* HARVEY *has with him* MAC SMITH, *the trade union official.*]
HARVEY: Ron? Look, I've got Mac with me. They're querying the agreement we all thought we came to last week and if it's not ironed out now we'll all be in the shit again. Can you come down?
RONNIE: Coming. [*Replaces receiver.*] Who'd be bloody father of a newspaper chapel!
MARVIN: That stoppage again?
RONNIE: They may freeze the messengers. Ring round, get copy telephoned straight through to here and by-pass copy takers. I shouldn't as a union official, but fuck it! I want the paper to come out and I don't care. You agree?
MARVIN: Agreed.
　　[RONNIE *makes his way to Editor's office.*]


## IN DEPTH

JULIAN [*on phone*]: Look, I'm a layman and so if I could explain in layman's language why those bridges fell, rather than in your expertise – yes? Good. As I understand it it goes something like this: I build shelves for 15lb jam jars, test the shelves by putting 20lb jam jars on, use 15lb jam jars for 20 years and *then* return to 20lb jam jars ... what? Oh, I see. Jam jars are hardly applicable. Of course. Well, let's start again ...


## POLITICAL AND FEATURES

CYNTHIA [*on phone*]: Yes, well I think it's a very interesting story, workers *should* get a day off on their birthday, but it's hardly for us. Try the news room.

## IN DEPTH

CHRIS: As far as I can make out it's a perfectly decent feat of engineering but no one seems to have taken account of the fact that the things are built by incompetent, lumpen Irish labourers who don't care a damn ...

## EDITOR'S OFFICE

MAC: You see, Harvey, it says there that we've asked for withdrawal of the decision to close down the garage. Now you know that's not true. *We've* never ever said that. Management shouldn't go around sending notes like this to the staff misrepresenting our case. We've only asked that the *date* of closure be withdrawn to give us a chance to negotiate the men's future. That's not unreasonable, is it?

RONNIE: Hasn't that happened already, Mac?

MAC: Now Ronnie, you *know* it hasn't. They've *changed* the date. Postponed it as it were. But not actually withdrawn it.

HARVEY: Why do you want it withdrawn?

MAC: Now, Harvey, *you* shouldn't be asking questions like that. Supposing we agree to a date for closing down the garages and when that date comes we're not in agreement on redundancy compensation, eh? Come now, Harvey. *You're* an old enough hand.

HARVEY: But for Christ's sake, Mac –

MAC: Now then, Harvey, Harvey. Let's not raise our voices.

HARVEY [*softer*]: For Christ's sake, Mac, we're grown up, intelligent human beings. We've had problems like this before. Why *shouldn't* we come to an agreement on redundancy claims in good time?

MAC: Grown up, intelligent human beings – true. But 'the best laid schemes of mice and men' – you know what I mean? Besides, Ronnie, I'll tell *you* the truth. Because this document has falsified our position it's become a matter of principle for us. And for them? For management? Well, they've decided on a date and they've made it a matter of pride not to shift from it. So there's your problem. Principle versus pride. I'm taking it to my head office now and if nothing happens by the end of the week I'm asking them to make the stoppage official and I hope your men'll give us your support. Good day, lads. [*Leaves.*]

RONNIE: Doesn't look like we're going to have a paper this weekend.

HARVEY: I'll bring the fucking thing out, even if it means working the machines on my own and delivering the sheets myself. But I may need a little help from you, Ronnie.

RONNIE: When not?

## IN DEPTH

CHRIS: What I can't understand is how they *test* bridges.

JULIAN: They used to get battalions of guards to walk over them, then if the foundations trembled –

CHRIS: Our army isn't big enough, is it?

## EDITOR'S OFFICE

[MARY *visiting.*]

MARY: And what was your lunch like with comrade King?

HARVEY: I can see why you're interested in him. He's a bit too good to be true isn't he?

MARY: So you agree with me? He should be watched?

HARVEY: Oh come on, Mary. He's not a spy for God's sake.

MARY: But he's sinister.

HARVEY: He's complex.

MARY: And sinister.

HARVEY: No, guarded.

MARY: Guarded? The opposite! He's *giving*. All the time. Can't stop talking and offering his half-baked opinions on everything.

HARVEY: You underestimate him. He's got a good mind and a

generous one. Perceptive too. He sees the scale of problems and, what's more attractive, he sees them in the perspective of history – which always impresses me. No, there's something, something else. Something about the way he talks, as though he only wants to answer the questions *he* asks; as though – I don't know, as though if he stops talking he'll give someone the opportunity to ask the one question he doesn't want to answer.

MARY: As I say, sinister.

HARVEY: No, secretive. One very odd thing he said – not odd in its meaning but the words he used. He said: 'One thing I disagree with emphatically is the left's concept of the new man. Dangerous,' he said, 'misleading. It sets stout hearts on to the wrong line of action. It's not the "new man" we must *create*,' he said, 'but the original man we must *reveal*.'

MARY: Sophistry.

HARVEY: 'Clear away the undergrowth of ignorance and the rubble of fear that's gathered around him over the centuries,' he said, 'and when the dust from that job settles then,' and these are his odd words, 'when the dust from that job settles then you'll see all the patterns men can make for the pleasure of their living.'

MARY: 'The patterns men can make for the pleasure of their living.' Jesus! Harvey! Come on! They say that certain poets are bullied by a bad conscience – well this is a conscience bullied by bad poetry.


FOREIGN DEPT.

GORDON: Why don't you take a year off? Write a book? Everyone's doing it.

TAMARA: Write a book? Ha! That's very funny. I can hardly assemble words for the little bits and pieces of so-called foreign commentary they pay me to do here. A book! I'd like to resign.

GORDON: Why don't you?

TAMARA: I write letters of resignation every year. Conveyor-belt work, harsh, destructive, written in a hurry. I'm sick of first class travel and first class hotels and the quick friendships with people about whom one has finally to write something unsympathetic.

And then when there's a drive to cut expenses in all departments everyone makes a moral pitch to defend their fraudulent demands. Uch! Ugly! Sometimes I think I'm in journalism because I'm unfit for anything else.

## NEWS ROOM

SECRETARY [*on the phone*]: A union official who's *what*? Got a clause in about birthdays? No, it's hardly for the news room. Try our industrial correspondent. You'll find him in business news.
    [HARRY *rushes in.*]
HARRY: Paul? That hold-up of the supermarket in Bolton?
PAUL: Yes?
HARRY: There's been a new development.
PAUL: What are you doing with a crime story?
HARRY: It may not be a crime story.
PAUL: Not?
HARRY: Not! Three days later 97 old people living in a new development for old-age pensioners woke up and found boxes of groceries on their front door step.
PAUL: And there's a connection?
HARRY: The police aren't certain. But I've got another hunch I want to follow. Remember that factory manager kidnapped two months ago, the one that had a strike on his hands for being a bully?
PAUL: So?
HARRY: When he was released the strike was over and the men re-instated but none of us, no paper, was able to get a statement from him.
PAUL: Go on.
HARRY: Well, there's another strike in South Wales, place called Llantrisant, and this time it's unofficial and not the manager but the boss himself has been kidnapped.
PAUL: Are you suggesting the unions have become militant urban guerrillas?
HARRY: Not the unions, but someone! Now, there's something else — and here's the real break. Since the kidnapping there's been a large

bank robbery and though there's no strike pay the men have been given money.

PAUL: A local strike fund.

HARRY: No! Their *full* wages.

PAUL: How?

HARRY: Cash, in the post.

PAUL: Well that's The Angry Brigade.

HARRY: No again! The Angry Brigade are bomb throwers not soup kitchens. Besides, they'd announce themselves.

PAUL: Sounds to me as though you'd better consult the brilliant Miss Mortimer. She's got Peter's job for the month.

## ARTS PAGES

ERNST: Why do you think the devastating Mary Mortimer has it in for the King of New Lanark?

JOHN: Because she can't bear idealism anywhere but in her own column, where she calls it 'responsibility', while in anyone else it's called 'charlatanism'.

SEBASTIAN: No, no, no! You mustn't talk to him so glibly or he'll put us into one of his novels. We – and she – are much more complex than that. She suffers from the schizophrenia we all suffer from. She can't bear people who make judgements and since, in attacking them, *she* has to judge, therefore she's torn all ends up.

ERNST: But we all make judgements, surely.

JOHN: Only we fear to be seen doing so.

SEBASTIAN: Precisely! It's like a dirty act, to be done in secrecy. If you make a judgement you seem, by your choice, to be indicting those who've not chosen as you've done. *We* know about it because we work in a department where the greatest intimidations of all operate. Whether they like it or not most men regard the artist in fear, as a kind of magic man who can see the truth behind the façade, the devil in the making. And Mr Morgan King is a working-class politician who – to his credit I may add – has innocently stumbled upon the truth of art. Terrible presumption! Frightfully difficult to tolerate. Of course, to be the artist himself is the greatest presumption of all, but sometimes they let *him* get away with it. What they can't bear is lay enthusiasts like Morgan King trying to encourage *others* to pursue the bad habits of art. That's his great sin. 'Go to your artists,' he cries, 'don't listen to us, we're too jaundiced!' 'You're imposing your tastes on us,' they scream back at him from the barricades of democracy, as though social relations didn't involve impositions of some kind or another. Or their favourite paroxysm of rage: 'You're taking culture to the masses!' as though to *take* anything to people were somehow more sinister than to *sell* it to them. Capital fellow! Doomed of course. And then he confuses his enemies — and this is why Mary Mortimer can't forgive him because she'd like to have said it herself — he confuses them by making outrageous demands such as that old age pensioners should get what the national minimum wage is, and that all laws should be whittled down to the absolute essentials. Fools! I don't personally have much sympathy for the giant-killing Miss Mortimers of this world nor that 'witty, cool and deathly column' of hers.

## POLITICAL AND FEATURES

[HARRY *visiting*.]

MARY: You've done no investigating yourself?

HARRY: No, just assembled cuttings and kept an eye on it.

MARY: And the sequence is: a supermarket hold-up, distribution of food to old age pensioners, strike in Wales and a bank robbery?

HARRY: And then *full* strike pay.

MARY: And *then* full strike pay. Um. And we know it's not The Angry Brigade?

HARRY: Certain.

MARY: What's your hunch?

HARRY: It's only a hunch.

MARY: Let's hear it.

HARRY: And it's way out.

MARY: Stop covering your retreats, out with it.

HARRY: An opposition secret society.

MARY: That's not way out. There must be people in this green and pleasant land simply livid that they're not Uruguyan Tupamaros.

HARRY: Exactly! They must be intellectuals.

NORMAN: Easy! Some of my best friends are intellectuals.

HARRY: They're highly organized, sophisticated, a sense of humour and, probably, opposed to violence.

MARY: And what do you propose?

HARRY: This: I've made contact with The Angry Brigade. They're amateurs, clumsy and highly emotional. Now, if such a secret society does exist they're bound, sooner or later, to want to make contact with the Angries to tell them to lay off the bombings.

MARY: Not sure I accept the logic of that. Still –

HARRY: I just want one week free from other assignments.

MARY: I think we can spare him.

[HARRY *leaves*.]


## WOMEN'S PAGES

JANE: How about a series on people's obsessions?

ANGELA: Do *you* have obsessions?

JANE: Me? I don't know.

ANGELA: And would you confess them?

JANE: Depends what I discovered I was obsessed with.

ANGELA: No, I prefer the idea of a series on 'my best friend'. Find out what human qualities the famed and renowned look for in their closest.

[*Pause*.]

JANE: People sitting around in offices, lost, that's all a newspaper is, sitting around waiting for ideas to come, wondering what the hell to do next.


## THE CENTRE SPACE

[MARY MORTIMER's *lounge*.
Her three children – AGNES, JONATHAN *and* DESMOND – *have come for a monthly* '*family dinner*'.

MARY *is in the kitchen preparing the meal.*
JONATHAN *is reading from a sheet of copy.*
*It's a proof of* MARY's *current column.*]


JONATHAN: She's attacking him again.
DESMOND: Read it.
AGNES: But please, let's not quarrel this time?
JONATHAN [*reading*]: 'Mr Morgan-fiery-socialist-M.P.-King is with us once more. Oh what a dear, human, compassionate philosopher we have in our midst. And how thankful we must be, as he constantly reminds us, to have such a learned member of parliament guiding us through the confusions of such awful times.'
DESMOND: *Does* he 'constantly remind us?'
AGNES: It's mother's poetic licence to lie.
JONATHAN: 'We quote: "I believe," says the self-styled sage, "that the first great myth of all time was the story of the creation of order out of chaos, and all men's greatest endeavours since then have been the re-enactment of that one first myth. The universe is self-perpetuating and that means chaos. And, in it all, man has but one task: to create order and understanding if and wherever he can. And because the chaos is endless so man's task will be endless. And if there is a purpose in life *that* is it, and that is all it is." Unquote.'
AGNES: I can remember when he first said that.
JONATHAN: 'We may not know what he means,' says our O so witty mother, 'but it's certainly reassuring to have such serious sounding pontifications as this to pin by our bedside and read each night before pulling sleep over our troubled eyes in this troubled world.'

[JONATHAN *has beside him a portable tape-recorder the button of which he now presses to produce the sound of an audience whistling and applauding loudly. He throws his arms open as though presenting this extract to 'an audience' for their acclaim. The recorder is his latest 'toy' and he'll do this every so often throughout the scene.*]

DESMOND: They all write so badly, that's what's so depressing.
JONATHAN: Their biggest mistake is to quote the people they want to demolish. Always boomerangs. Much better than their own

little fifth-form farts. How about that? 'You've had the Barretts of Wimpole Street and now we bring to your screens – da-dum – The Little Farts of Fleet Street'. [*Presses tape for 'applause'.*]

AGNES [*unwrapping a package*]: But no quarrels. Jonathan?

JONATHAN: Yes, elder sister.

AGNES: We only have dinner with her once a month so no more dreary taunts about her being bourgeois. Des?

DESMOND [*deep in newspaper*]: Yes, elder sister.

AGNES: We don't think much of her column but we love her. Understood?

TOGETHER: Yes, elder sister.

AGNES [*revealing a Hogarth print in frame*]: Think she'll like it?
[JONATHAN *presses tape to applaud print.*]

DESMOND: Is that genuine?

AGNES: Not your first edition of course. From a late edition, possibly the fourth, 1838, or thereabouts. Bought it from a half-hour conversationalist.

DESMOND: A what?

AGNES: The dealer. Sweet man. But you can't talk to him for very long. He's so used to selling paintings and prints for which it's only necessary to switch on his brilliance and charm for thirty minutes – customers can't stay longer you see – that it's become a habit with him. Shines for half an hour and then he recedes. Can't help himself. Depresses him no end.
[MARY *enters in apron with a tray containing pot of 'stew', plates and cutlery. She plonks it on table, lifts lid triumphantly, and waits for response.* JONATHAN *switches on tape of applause.*]

MARY: My God! It's going to be one of those evenings.
[*They all begin to help themselves. Then –*]
Well, talk to me, my children. I know we always end up quarrelling over politics but that's no reason to be terrified of telling me your professional gossip. [*All three start at once.*] Whoa! Jonathan, 'the youngest'. You start.

JONATHAN: Directed my first concert.

MARY: Great mistake to televise concerts.

JONATHAN: Agree.

MARY: Good God! We've started with agreements.

66

JONATHAN: Have you noticed how, at concerts, there are always one or two who leap to applaud almost before the last note has been struck? And you never know whether they do it from enthusiasm or from a wish to get it in that they know the piece so well.

[*Silence. There seems nothing to add or go on to from there.* JONATHAN *presses recorder for his own applause.*]

MARY: We'll try the scientist then.

DESMOND: Three Soviet scientists – G. I. Beridze, G. R. Macharashvili and L. M. Mosulishvili have discovered gold in wine.

MARY: I beg your pardon?

DESMOND: Flowers and plants, you see, contain in their tissues residues of the metals contained in the soil where they grow. Hence bio-chemistry can trace deposits of nickel, silver, copper, cobalt, uranium, lead and other metals by pursuing, picking and analysing flowers and fruit.

[*Silence.*]

And so three Soviet scientists called G. I. Beridze, G. R. Macharashvili and L. M. Mosulishvili have discovered gold in wine. [*Pause.*] Which comes from grapes. [*Pause.*] Which grows in soils.

[*Silence.*]

Well don't I get a round of applause for that?

[JONATHAN *belatedly switches on tape.*]

MARY: Do you children rehearse your pieces before coming to dine with me?

AGNES: This is a very fine stew, mother.

MARY: There speaks the diplomat of the family. How's the foreign office?

JONATHAN: Mother, don't be so damned bourgeois. We don't *have* to make conversation.

AGNES [*forestalling friction*]: I might be posted to the embassy in Lagos.

MARY: If he calls me bourgeois again I'll –

AGNES: I'll know in a month's time.

[*Silence.*]

MARY: Bloody hell! You're not the most comfortable family to sit down to eat a meal with. Why must you always make me feel I've done something to feel guilty for?

JONATHAN: It's a change from you making others feel guilty in your columns.

MARY: That's my job. Investigation! Democratic scrutiny!

[JONATHAN *presses tape for applause.*]

And turn that bloody machine off! [*Pause.*] Oh, go home. I swear, I always swear I'll never make these dinners again and each time I relent, each time I think – no! They won't get at me this time, it'll be a happy family event. And each time it happens again. What do I need it for?

AGNES: We're sorry.

MARY: Don't I have enough bloody headaches in that bloody newspaper office and those stupid, vain, self-opinionated people I have to interview?

JONATHAN: You can't exactly deride those you interview as 'self-opinionated' when those interviews appear in a column called 'opinions'.

MARY: Oh can't I just?

DESMOND: Mary, why have you got your teeth into Morgan King?

MARY: Morgan King? What the hell do you care about Morgan King?

AGNES: Desmond, you promised.

MARY: Why Morgan King and none of the others?

DESMOND: It's just that a special kind of savagery comes out with him and it shows.

MARY: I'm a savage columnist, didn't you know?

DESMOND: We're embarrassed that's all.

MARY: Oh no you're not. There's a reason. Why Morgan King?

AGNES: He conducted a series of seminars on local authorities at Jonathan's college in Oxford and we all got to know him rather well, that's all.

MARY: Well why didn't I get to hear about him? I knew all your other friends from university.

DESMOND: Other students, yes; but we kept the tutors and visiting lecturers to ourselves.

MARY: I don't believe you.

AGNES: This is silly. Of course it's not only Morgan King, it's your column in general. We feel it's getting –

DESMOND: – bitchy –

AGNES: – no –

JONATHAN: – strident. That's the word. [*Presses tape for applause.*]

MARY: Please, please, PLEASE don't push that fucking button again.

JONATHAN: Now don't cry, mother. Tough journalists don't cry.

MARY: You're rather cruel children, aren't you?

DESMOND [*shamefaced*]: Yes, we are, you're right. I'm sorry.

AGNES: We're all sorry. Look, the stew's getting cold.

MARY: Well fuck the stew! You don't get off as easily as that.

JONATHAN: Always dangerous to apologize. The bourgeoisie has its sting in the 'tail of its tears'. Mao?

MARY: I AM NOT BOURGEOIS! Bourgeois is a state of mind not of wealth.

JONATHAN: Not in the classic sense it's not.

MARY: To hell with the classic sense. Words acquire new meanings. Think! you have to *think* about them. Your lot are so bloody mindless. [*With forced calm and mounting distress.*] I love and care for my children. That's natural, an old, old cycle, tested *long* before men began exploiting men. If I'd forced you into professions you'd've been miserable with, if I'd have given you luxuries to soften the spirit of your spine *that* would have been bourgeois. But what's my crime? To give you a home to dig your personalities in; security! Not to seclude you but to help you face an insecure world. That's not bourgeois – well is it? I'm not bourgeois if I enjoy the best that men have fought to preserve from the past – only if I allow that past to cripple the future. I'm not bourgeois if I enjoy comfort – only if comfort defuses my anger against injustice. I'm not bourgeois if I acknowledge a debt to dead men and if I'm fearful of the future. That's human. To *enjoy* being helpless about evil *that's* bourgeois, but to *feel*, to just simply *feel* helpless about evil that's human. To have loves and hates and failures and regrets and nostalgias, that's human. If I pretend order exists when it doesn't *that's* bourgeois, but if I try to create order out of the chaos of my miserable life that's human, bloody human, bloody bloody human.

[AGNES *picks up the proof of* MARY's *column and gently offers it to her.*]

AGNES: You see, mother, he also talks about order out of chaos. That's just what we mean. It's as though you're fighting yourself, and it shows. In your column it shows. [*Pause.*] Mary, we're our mother's children. [*Small laugh.*] No escaping.

[MARY *is stung but it only adds to deepen her distress.*]
Look. A Hogarth print. We've bought you a present.

# ACT TWO

## PART THREE

### THE CENTRE SPACE

[*An arbour in the grounds of the home of the Chancellor of the Exchequer,*
SIR REGINALD MACINTYRE.
*He is strolling up and down with* MARY.]

MARY: And the final question, Sir Reginald.

MACINTYRE: You won't be offended if I say, thank God!

MARY: Three days is a long time, I know. You've been very patient.
It's a very personal one. I've asked each minister this and told them
they can answer or tell me to go to hell.

MACINTYRE: I'm not very good at saying such things to ladies but
I hope your question doesn't tempt me too much.

MARY: It's this. How do you reconcile the needs of your own private
standards of living with the needs of those working people whose
standards of living you, as Chancellor, are in office to regulate?
[*Long pause.*] Please, if you think it too impertinent.

MACINTYRE: Impertinent? Yes, I suppose I do find it that. [*Pause.*]
Do you mind if I answer in an oblique way, without, I trust, being
evasive? [*Pause.*] It's a terrible problem, democracy. You see, if we
could turn round and say all the men who are dustmen are dustmen
because of their inequality of opportunity then it would be easy.
No problem. We would simply create the right opportunity. But
it's not so, is it? Make *opportunity* equal and the inequality of their
qualities soon becomes apparent. It's a cruel statement to make but,
men are dustmen or lavatory attendants or machine minders or
policemen because of intellectual limitations. There! Does that
offend you? It used to offend me. Most unpalatable view of human
beings. But all my encounters with them points to that fact. Even

71

if we automate all sewage, everything, we're still confronted with the awful fact that some men *are* born with intellectual limitations. Now, what do we do? We can't talk of these things, it's taboo. We can't say in public 'some men are less intelligent than others' – though it's part of any discussion on democracy. So what *should* we do? Help them forget by compensating them for their inadequacies with large pay packets? But what of the worker whose intellect is not so limited and who feels he should be paid higher for those abilities? Shall we tell him such distinctions are invalid? Shall we say 'a man's a man for all that?' Lovely sentiments. How I wish I could say them every day to myself, to my friends, to my constituents. But it's not even true for the dustman. Because when he strikes for more pay he may not be asking to be paid for his ability or responsibilities but he *is* asking to be paid for doing what other men *don't want to do*. For what I think should be named 'the undesirability factor'. Isn't *that* a distinction? And a very intimidating distinction I may add. In democracies those who do our dirty work have us these days by, as they say, the short and curlies. Now, government must, you'll agree, remain in civilized hands. So, whose 'short and curlies' should civilized man hold on to?

MARY: Perhaps it's the mark of the civilized man that he disdains from holding on to anyone's 'short and curlies'.

MACINTYRE: No. Only that he *appears* not to be doing so. Does that also shock you? You probably despise appearances. But wouldn't you consider me boorish if I spoke to a simple man in a way that showed him I *thought* he was simple? Wouldn't you expect of me a politeness, a civility, a humanity to show him respect by *not* discussing with him what I thought was beyond his intellect or asking him to perform duties beyond his power? Surely you'd want me to *appear* to be his equal which I could only do by not frustrating or humiliating him in that way.

MARY: But supposing your judgements are wrong? Supposing the man is capable of more than you give him credit for?

MACINTYRE: Supposing all our judgements are wrong? Yours of me, mine of you – so? Do we cease making them? We are appointed because our judgements are more often right than wrong. That too is one of the risks of democracy, unless you can find me a man

who can create a system – or a system which can create a man –
whose judgement is right, all the time, about everything. Am I
making myself clear?

MARY: Perfectly.

MACINTYRE: Do you find an answer shaping in all that? [*Pause.*]
You will, of course, let me see the typescript before going into
print?

## EDITOR'S OFFICE

[*An editorial conference.*]

GORDON: Well, do we have a newspaper this week or not?

ANTHONY: The problem, old friend, lies in the difference between
the production side and the creative side. We're prepared to work
at all hours in order to get a newspaper out and production doesn't
care a damn about the kind of journalism we think we produce.
And why should they? They don't read it.

GORDON: You think it would make much difference if they did?

HARVEY: Thirty-three garage men now, compensation, facilities for
retraining – or 2,500 losing their jobs in a few years time. Those
are the alternatives but they can't see it. That's what gets me.

GORDON: *There's* your technology versus politics problem, Harvey.
Right in your own back yard.

ANTHONY: And a back yard it *is* – *that's* the problem. We've got
Victorian machinery. Thousands to man it. Millions to buy it. Six
years to install it. And all you really need is £100,000 for a Web
off-set machine and a handful of typists to run it instead of expensive, obsolete printing men. Of *course* you'll always have stoppages.

HARVEY: Anyway gentlemen, it's in the hands of their head office
and our management boys – let them fight it out and may the best
man win. Now. The Indo-Pakistan war. What about *that* bloody
mess?

## BUSINESS NEWS

DOMINIC: Well, people who fuck up the system appeal to me.
[*Phone rings. He picks it up. It's* MARTIN *from News Room.*]

MARTIN: Dom? I've just had an earbending fink on the phone who says he's got damaging documents implicating Leonard Crafton.
DOMINIC: Head of Onyx Foods? Oh a charming man, a con but charming. Everyone wants to rubbish him.
MARTIN: Will you see him?
DOMINIC: If we must.
MARTIN: He sounds interesting if erroneous.
DOMINIC: Interesting if erroneous. I'll remember that.

## EDITOR'S OFFICE

[*Editorial continuing.*]

HARVEY: And as far as I can see we're going to be the only ones to give the cholera epidemic a big spread. The dailies have hardly touched it. Map with arrows showing its route, three nine-inch columns – front page.
ANTHONY: Don't believe in epidemic scares personally. The agencies always launch them with mortality figures in the hundreds and two days later whittle them down to ten. But if *you* think it's a real danger –
GORDON: *You* don't believe in the pollution scare either, so you're no judge.
ANTHONY: Pollution's different.
HARVEY: Which nicely brings me to my next point. I want to cover the Mersey, long diagram, showing who's pouring what into its waters and from where. Every firm named, questioned, challenged.

# WOMEN'S PAGES

ANGELA [*reading a women's magazine*]: Ooooh! Look! Moira Hartnel's entered the battle for women's liberation.

JANE: A top model gone politicking?

ANGELA: Think she's worth pursuing?

JANE: Any staying power?

ANGELA: We only have to do her once. She's not *star* quality.

JANE: Thank God for the woman's magazine. Can always rely on them to fill a hole in the column.

ANGELA: How about 'from women's waists to wasted women'?

JANE: Or 'model mauls men'?

ANGELA: Or 'from liberated fashions to fashionable liberations'?

JANE: Meeow!

# SPORTS PAGES

[DOMINIC *visiting*.]

DOMINIC: If you want me to cover your championships it'll cost you high in expenses. I'll spice it with the obligatory champagne-and-strawberries atmosphere, you pay for it.

RONNIE: You'll get what my budget will allow.

DOMINIC: A most miserly attitude if I may say so, and one not worthy of your race. Why, after all, should you not give something extra for those talented such as myself, who have something extra to offer?

MARVIN: You're not the *most* brilliant tennis reporter we have.

DOMINIC: Oh I am, I am. And you know that I am.

MARVIN: Besides, your expenses come from Business News.

DOMINIC: It's true. I can't lie. My expenses are the highest on *The Sunday Paper* on account of the terrible terrible amount of bribing I have to do among trade union officials.

RONNIE: You're a cynical man, Dominic.

DOMINIC: Cynical I am not. Spoilt, perhaps. But then we can't all have interesting backgrounds like you, Ronnie. Russian Jewish immigrants from the East End of London? Were you really born in the East End? God! How I resent my father for being so rich. All the best people were born in a ghetto. If only my father had bought *us* a ghetto, one we could go to for weekends. Now that would have been something.

## IN DEPTH

PAT: Well someone on your sodding paper ought to be interested.

CHRIS: I've tried, love, honest I have.

PAT: I mean it's more than just another abortion story, it's a story about your knotty medical problems and your callous authority.

CHRIS: That's what I said: 'Knotty medical problems and callous authority' I said. Try it on Mary. She's got Pete's job for this month.

## ARTS PAGES

ERNST: I can't review this book. I find his writing so awful and I gave his last one such a knocking that I'm beginning to feel it's unfair. Gives me guilts. No reviewer should have to feel guilty.

SEBASTIAN: Especially if he's also a novelist!

## SPORTS PAGES

MARVIN: So there I was, in Northern Ireland, soldiers shot at, civilians murdered, bombs going off everywhere, reporting on a game of golf. Jesus! I thought, what the hell am I doing covering a game of golf?

## BUSINESS NEWS

[THE FINK *is introducing himself to* MORTY.]

MORTY [*shaking hands*]: And you're the gentleman with information on Onyx Foods?

FINK [*patting his briefcase*]: Minute research. It's all here. I take it I can speak openly? Good. The basis of my information is this: that Leonard Crafton – Crafty Crafton I call him – has stated a share price since 1967 based on a false market, and that he's been able to achieve this through a complicated system of interlocking holdings which work roughly in this way: the English company takes over a French company which is then able to buy shares in the subsidiary of the English company which then buys shares in a subsidiary of the French company and so on. Clever? Ah, very clever is our crafty Crafton. Now look at these graphs of share price rises and rising profits . . .

## ARTS PAGES

SEBASTIAN: Oh my God! Another poem. We always get them after disasters or Prince Philip's birthday. Says a great deal for the soul of the British public I suppose but doesn't contribute much to British poetry.

## EDITOR'S OFFICE

[*Editorial continuing.*]

HARVEY: What's your centre piece this week?

GORDON: A finely argued piece of demolition on the myth of the silent majority which makes the very simple but devastating point that the convenience of such a concept as silence is – the silence.

HARVEY: Quite right! If you say nothing anybody can claim to speak for you. Lovely! Splendid! And the leaders? Anthony? How about one on the Persian Gulf?

ANTHONY: Do you want it to have a message? A punch line?

HARVEY: Yes, start with the joke about the Arabs.

ANTHONY: Which one?

HARVEY: Oh, that one about – how does it go? You know, showing how they can't ever agree on anything.

## BUSINESS NEWS

[*The* FINK's *story, continuing.*]

FINK: Now, I'd been following him so closely that I understood the pattern of crafty Crafton's behaviour, his psychology as it were, and of course, when his shares were at 71 I bought them because I knew, from watching his dealings, that they'd soon go up to 93 or thereabouts, which they did, and at which point I sold. And who's the Mafia, as it were, in all this? Snuff! Oh don't laugh. [*Dips into his briefcase for large foreign magazines.*] Snuff is the new narcotic. You can put your LSD into it. Kids in Germany and Sweden are doing it all the time. And so Mr Crafty Crafton and his Jewish backers are putting their money into snuff. Large profits, you see. Now, that's not all . . .

## WOMEN'S PAGES

ANGELA: Oh yes, I agree, the elegant sneer is always admired. And if it's like Pope it's very good indeed.

JANE: Problem is, it's rarely like Pope.

## BUSINESS NEWS

[*The* FINK's *story, continuing.*]

FINK: So, you're asking, where is all this leading? His saga seems endless and many vaulted, you're thinking to yourself. Nearly there. I've told you about Crafton's dealings on the continent and at home. I've told you his motives and about the habit of his Jewish brethren in helping poorer members of their community. So, we know, they stick together. And my final proof of this is from an old friend who sees these same brethren – Morgenstein the banker and Rosenthals of Town and Country Investments, big men, the biggest, you agree? the biggest! always in company with Crafton. Three of them, always together. In golf clubs, restaurants, everywhere, my friend sees them – now why?

## ARTS PAGES

ERNST: Yes, I do! I do think writing novels is more difficult than writing plays. A play is just dialogue confined to a physical space. Its canvas *can't* be large. A novel demands more attention to detail, greater psychological exploration, a richer grasp of plot. Its space and movement is unlimited and you've only yourself to rely on. No actors to fill out thinly drawn characters, no director to give rhythms which the material doesn't contain, and no lighting man playing tricks in order to create moods which the plot can't substantiate.

SEBASTIAN: Are you suggesting D. H. Lawrence is greater than Shakespeare?

ERNST: No, but I *am* suggesting Shakespeare's not as great as Tolstoy.

## BUSINESS NEWS

[THE FINK, *who has gradually become excited by his own story, allows his enthusiasm to take over from his judgement.*]

FINK: I'll be honest, lay my cards on the table. I'm obsessed by the European Jewish Mafia. Been reading about them as far back as the time Napoleon freed the Jews. And here's my point, think about it. There's the tightly knit Jewish families of Rothschilds, Mannerheims, and Herzens on the continent, and Messrs Morgen- –

stein, Rosenthal and Crafton in this country. And now [*clasps his fingers together*] with the European Common Market – click! The opportunity they've been waiting for – a highly closed plot in the traditional Jewish manner trying to dominate the important areas of food and leisure. [*Pause.*] You must not, however, think I'm anti-semitic.

## POLITICAL AND FEATURES

MARY: Shall I tell you what's wrong with your article on futurology?

NORMAN: I'd prefer you not to.

MARY: You believe them.

NORMAN: That's not true.

MARY: You ask a very reasonable question: Has technology re-arranged the genes of political issues? and then you give *their* answer: yes it has!

NORMAN: I happen to agree with them.

MARY: Have you ever asked yourself why their books are so thick?

NORMAN: Scholarship.

MARY: Balls! It's because they have to make so many allowances and qualifications for their predictions. The very size of their books contradicts their claims for accurate forecast.

NORMAN: They don't claim accuracy, just high probability.

MARY: If men were robots you'd need only a little book of graphs. But they're not. They're human, unpredictable, millions of individual wills, all different – hence, a large book of hedged bets.

[HARRY *enters.*]

Any luck?

HARRY: To be honest I changed tactics.

MARY: Meaning?

HARRY: I went to Llantrisant, where the strike was. Thought I'd get more of a lead there.

NORMAN: Do you know I was evacuated to Llantrisant?

MARY: So, if your secret society did plan to contact the angries you've missed them. And we don't even know if they exist.

HARRY [*handing her a sheet*]: I think I've got evidence to prove that.

I picked up this roneoed document which was in the latest strike pay packet. A sort of manifesto. Very flowery stuff. Not like the angries at all. Correct grammar and statements with some degree of lucidity, except the end, which –

MARY [*who's been reading it*]: Eureka! Harry, keep on to that angries cell. It may lead to something fantastic. Fan-tastic! 'Scuse me. [*She rushes out.*]


## WOMEN'S PAGES

JANE: It's a terrible confession – but my colleagues depress me. They play this great game at work and then they shuffle home on the commuter-train to suburbia.

ANGELA: Well thank God for the fantasy world, I say. Compensates for lilliputian lives.

JANE: *That's* what we are. Lilliputians! Always wanting to bring down giants.

ANGELA: *I* seem to spend my time building them up.

JANE: *They* are paper giants. But the real ones – we never celebrate the real ones.

ANGELA: Oh, I don't know. Business News celebrate Arnold Weinstock. Arts pages celebrate Hughie Green.

JANE: Fashions! Novelty! We celebrate fashions and novelties.

ANGELA: And *you're* beginning to depress *me*.

JANE: Well, do something about it.


## ARTS PAGES

ERNST: And shall I tell you why I *don't* go to the theatre? It's pampered. There's more paraphernalia attached to a first night than the appearance of a novel.

JOHN: Ah ha! Now we have it.

ERNST: Isn't it true? And there's *no* fuss at all about the appearance of a play on television and *that's* a medium enjoyed by millions!

JOHN: Demagogue!

## EDITOR'S OFFICE

[MARY *visiting*.]

HARVEY [*who's been reading* HARRY'*s document*]: It's slim, Mary.

MARY: The *exact* words, though. 'The patterns men can make for the pleasure of their living.' The same awful words. Morgan King! The man himself. Behind all those boyish Robin Hood antics.

HARVEY: Maybe they're not his words. Maybe I made a mistake and he was quoting from a poem or a Hazlitt essay or something, and he and this group – whoever they are – were using the same source, coincidentally. Have a look, Gordon.

MARY: Coincidentally! Bloody strange coincidence. Harvey, Morgan King has formed a secret society of political Robin Hoods. I *know* it. It all fits in with his shifty passions. One of my sons attended a series of seminars he gave at Oxford and from the way he describes him he sounds quite capable of seducing a small band of over-heated romantic imaginations into playing Tupamaros.

GORDON: Not good enough, Mary. I'd say you needed more evidence.

MARY: I think you're all frightened.

HARVEY: No, cautious.

MARY: So am I. I'm not asking us to print anything, but it's worth following up for God's sake.

HARVEY: You're relentless.

MARY: So you keep saying. Hell! I can see I won't get much joy here. [*She leaves*.]

## FOREIGN DEPT.

[MORTY *visiting*.]

MORTY: And suddenly I realize. This Fink's spinning me the old yarn about the Jewish conspiracy to take over the world. Poor bloody Jews. Can't do anything right can we? Jesus, Marx, Freud,

Trotsky, you, me — all part of some conspiracy or other. So I tell him about this Scotsman: sixty-five, lives in Switzerland, the only man I know who can reach into his back pocket and produce enough cash to buy a company. Started off by imagining he could make his fortune out of surgical machinery, but he did what few others bother to do — he actually took the trouble to get himself qualified as a surgeon in order to test whether his inventions worked. Strange man. Hates unions. A sort of elitist fascist, but not wholly without charm ... Anyway ...

## EDITOR'S OFFICE

[ANGELA *visiting*.]

ANGELA: Well we're staking pretty big claims as the most serious paper in the country.
HARVEY: And it's true.
ANGELA: Then let me bring the women's pages into the science versus politics issue.
HARVEY: What are you thinking of?
ANGELA: Oh, I don't know. Are women more attracted to science than politics and is there a reason? That sort of thing.
GORDON: You think women aspire to the practical rather than the empirical?
ANGELA: Could be. We just want the go ahead in principle.
HARVEY: You've got it, you've got it.
ANGELA: Hallelujah!

## POLITICAL AND FEATURES

[TAMARA *visiting*. NORMAN *has been reading the proofs of her latest piece*.]

NORMAN [*handing it back*]: It's reasonable, Tamara, reasonable.
TAMARA: That's a good word, Norman. Succinct and diminishing. Thank you.

NORMAN: Now don't sulk.

TAMARA: Oh, how I'd just like to slide around, with no purpose, having little conversations.

NORMAN: Only you can't quite give up the glamour of catching a plane and having access to important people.

TAMARA: Can't I?

CYNTHIA: None of us can.

TAMARA: *Important* people? My contempt for the Western European politicians I've had to meet is gradually extending to the whole spectrum of human beings – important or not.


NEWS ROOM

[MARY *visiting, with* PAT *at her heels.*]

MARY [*to* PAUL]: Paul, who the hell turned this away?

PAUL: It's only another abortion story.

MARY: Another abortion story? Another *abortion* story?

PAUL: I can turn you up ten stories about girls of thirteen, twelve, eleven, even ten having abortions.

MARY: That's why I have to go through everything myself.

PAUL: Look, Mary, as news editor *I* judge the kind of news story we should be printing.

MARY: Judge? You couldn't judge between a Neasden beauty competition and a Middle East war.

PAUL: It came up in the editorial, why didn't you talk then?

MARY: I wasn't there.

PAUL: Well that's hardly my fault.

MARY [*storming off*]: I want this woman hung, drawn and quartered. She's a National Health Service gynaecologist and she's not paid with my money to offer moral judgements to twelve-year-old girls in need of help . . .

PAT: Thanks!

## POLITICAL AND FEATURES

NORMAN: Well, I'm sorry – it *is* just a reasonable article because it *is* rather difficult to generate excitement about obscure Indian tribes in Latin America. I mean it may look good in print when you read a D. H. Lawrence novel, but Quetzalcoatl *does* sound funny when you actually have to *say* it.

TAMARA: Oh your bloody English upper-class wit! You can't look anybody in the face without your Empire but you still go on making pale jokes about the funny names of aliens. Haven't you heard that no one finds you funny any longer except your pudding-faced working class? They can always be relied upon to find the sound of Vladivostok good for a giggle.

CYNTHIA: Norman's hardly working-class.

TAMARA: What difference? Both classes waddle with smugness, like dogs and their owners.

CYNTHIA: True, true. We've lived with each other for so long you know, we do rather look alike.

TAMARA: And you'll never change, never! Your ruling class is so good mannered in gratitude for its privileges and your worker so brainwashed with kindness that he does everything his master does.

NORMAN: What's wrong with kindness, pray? Is every honest virtue now a form of insult?

TAMARA: Kindness as a right! but not as a payment. 'Leave me my privileges and I'll be kind to you. Honour the privacy of my mansion, I'll honour the privacy of your back-yard.' And so of course he'll mouth his master's prejudice against foreigners – a small price to pay for a pat on the head.

## IN DEPTH

[MARY *rushes in followed by a bemused* PAT.]

MARY: Right! Drop your bridges.
CHRIS: Did she say 'drop your breeches'?

MARY: I want this gynaecologist investigated.

JULIAN: Hell, Mary, it's a news story not an In Depth exposé.

MARY: It's more important than a news story. The mother herself has asked us to investigate. Problem is the doctor's clammed up. Refuses to speak to the press.

JULIAN: I don't blame her.

MARY: What we want is the story of a guilty gynaecologist. Was she married? Did she have an unhappy love affair, broken marriage? Are there any children?

CHRIS: That's Harold Robbins, not journalism.

MARY: And get a photograph, even if it's of her peering reluctantly round a door.

JULIAN: A classic news room story.

MARY: Pat, get this photostated.

PAT: How many?

MARY: About ten. Julian, you can get up there in two and a half hours on the M1.

JULIAN: Three.

CHRIS: Four.

JULIAN: And basically what you want is all the dirt I can get on her?

MARY: Yes. And get photographs of the girl and her mother. Door-step them if necessary.

JULIAN: How can you take a moral position about the gynaecologist if you start invading people's privacy?

MARY: I'll worry about that. [*She leaves.*]

JULIAN: It's too late. We go to press in twenty-four hours. Bloody news room should've handled it.

CHRIS: If we're getting other people's chestnuts out of the fire that's tough, but that's what we're paid for.


## WOMEN'S PAGES

ANGELA [*entering*]: We're in business.

JANE: He's agreed?

ANGELA: Of course he agrees. I don't know why we didn't push earlier.

JANE: Do you think the story of Lysistrata comes under the heading of science versus politics?

ANGELA: That's sex versus politics.

JANE: But the Greek girls didn't have contraception – and that's science.

ANGELA: So?

JANE: Well, the general's ladies could last out longer today by safely taking their favours elsewhere.

ANGELA: Bit of a strain on the imagination, that.


## FOREIGN DEPT.

GORDON: Now, this is what I mean about religious dogma leading to massacres. [*Reading from* The Times.] 'My dear countrymen, peace be with you,' he said in his speech announcing war. 'Our enemy has again challenged us. The Indian armed forces have launched wanton attacks on Pakistan on several fronts. India's dislike and enmity of Pakistan is well-known the world over. It has always been its endeavour to weaken Pakistan and destroy it. This fresh and grave aggression on the part of India is the greatest and last move against us. We have shown great forebearance but the time has now come when we must give the enemy a most effective answer. One hundred and twenty million crusaders of Pakistan, you have the support and blessings of Allah.'

TAMARA: Uch! Vain! Pompous! Demagogues! How I despise them.


## EDITOR'S OFFICE

[*Editorial continuing.*]

ANTHONY: Has the Chancellor read the typescript of his interview with Mary?

HARVEY: Not yet. Why?

ANTHONY: I hardly think he's going to approve of all her witty little interjections. '"It is a cruel statement to make," the Chancellor continued, "but men are dustmen or lavatory attendants or machine minders or policemen because of intellectual limitations." I resisted the temptation to ask if he had statistics on how many intellectually limited sons of the upper classes became dustmen.'

HARVEY: Heavy handed but he does need knocking.

ANTHONY: Well why didn't she simply make the point to him and get his reply?

HARVEY: Nor is the Commissioner of police going to be happy to have his force labelled 'intellectually limited'.

## BUSINESS NEWS

MORTY [*to someone off-stage*]: Yes, well I believe in the Capitalist system so I have no conflicts. Conflicts? Hah! I've been looking for them for years. Always wanted to be able to resign on a matter of principle.

## FOREIGN DEPT.

GORDON [*still reading from* The Times]: 'Your land is filled with the love of the Holy Prophet. The enemy has once again challenged our will.'

TAMARA: I just don't believe it.

GORDON: 'Rise as one for your honour and stand like an impregnable wall of steel in the face of your enemy.'

TAMARA: And on and on and on . . .

## POLITICAL AND FEATURES

MARY: I think I'm tired.

CYNTHIA: You *think* so? you're not sure?

MARY: And I've got my mother for dinner tonight. She's never tired.

CYNTHIA: Menopause?

MARY: No. Never worried me. I waited and waited, dreading all those horror stories – but it came and went, nothing! Except back-ache and other trivial reminders of creeping old age.

CYNTHIA: Don't you ever think of peppering evenings with mum?

MARY: Oh, Jason'll be there.

CYNTHIA: Your ex-husband seems to be the only man you ever see these days.

MARY: Only really intelligent man I know. Bloody fierce intelligence he's got. Puts our youngsters in their place whenever they come out with such things as [*mockingly*] 'intelligence isn't everything, you know!' God knows why I agreed to divorce him.

CYNTHIA: Why did you?

MARY: Used each other up. Why else? Some couples accept it others don't. Simple.

CYNTHIA: Oh, very.


## FOREIGN DEPT.

GORDON [*still reading from* The Times]: 'You have right and justice on your side.'

TAMARA: Always!

GORDON: 'Pounce on the enemy in a spirit of confidence and let the enemy know that every Pakistani is determined to stand up for the defence of the dear motherland.'

TAMARA: No one ever learns.

GORDON: 'The brave soldiers of our army have shown unparalleled bravery and stopped the advance of the enemy.'

TAMARA: As though history never happens for them.


## BUSINESS NEWS

MORTY [*to someone off-stage*]: And what's more, Arnold Weinstock is one of the most intelligent men we've met who's more intelligent than us, and we don't meet many of them!

FOREIGN DEPT.

GORDON [*still reading from* The Times]: 'The enemy knows that victory in war does not go to those who have numerical strength and large quantities of military hardware. It goes to those who have faith in their mission and in the ideals of Islam and who believe God helps the righteous.'

TAMARA: And who will help us? Dear God, who will help the rest of us?

## PART FOUR

THE CENTRE SPACE

[*A table in a restaurant.*
MARY *is dining with* OLIVER MASSINGHAM, *Under Secretary of State for Foreign Affairs. They are friends.*
*She is slightly drunk.*]

MASSINGHAM: I hope you're not disappointed, Mary. Lumbered with a mere under secretary rather than the Foreign Minister himself?

MARY: You think I'm drunk for that reason, Oliver?

MASSINGHAM: He hates interviews. All that personality cultifying.

MARY: Who does he think – no! I mustn't.

MASSINGHAM: Mustn't what?

MARY: I've been told by my children that my only contribution to British journalism is to have elevated the gutter question 'who does he think he is?' to a respected art form.

MASSINGHAM: And that hurt of course.

MARY: It *should* have hurt. Everything should hurt. But nothing does. Oliver – this is off the record, but here's a question I've been dying to ask one of you only I didn't dare. Your wife, I know the situation, this dinner, she'll give you hell. No, no. We're old friends. Don't protest. My question. It goes like this: you're a minister. I've watched the House in action: fights, battles of wit, of personality, intellect — but, that's not all is it? Thems not the only battles, is they? There's personality conflicts also — in the cabinet, in ministerial departments, with cantankerous old civil servants. And then — tact! Diplomacy! Different kinds, in different ways, to different people. The public face on the one hand and the private reassurance to industry, the unions, the foreign ambassadors on the other. A great juggling act, wits alert all the time. To say nothing of all you're supposed to know about the nation's affairs *outside* your particular department. And on top of all this, on *top* — of all *this*, there's the problems of being a husband, a lover, a father, a friend, uncle, brother — God wot! [*Pause.*] How-do-you-do-it-for-God's-sake? How? How don't you become overwhelmed by it all? Do certain arteries harden? Is part of you callous? Like the doctor, or the writer? Tell me.

MASSINGHAM: Mary, I think you're very drunk.

MARY: But still functioning, eh? My lovely brain still ticking — tick-tick-tick-tick.

MASSINGHAM: Perhaps I should take advantage of your lovely, drunk brain and get you to talk about yourself for a change.

MARY: Me? Oh, I had a famous father, didn't you know? Famous for what they called in his day 'thought-provoking' novels. Only his fame was media-made and his thoughts provoked very few, very shallowly, and his day didn't last long. I used to taunt him in front of my university friends about having nothing to say to my generation and he used to take notice and rush to read my required reading. I had to grow up in the growing darkness of his demission and watch his lively pleasure, at being recognized in the streets, change into a grey anonymity. He was a gentle man, made for the comforts fame brings and which the Gods gave him only a tantalizing taste of. And I, with innocent devastation, went into competition with him. I won, of course. Because good fathers never let their children lose. He stepped back, graciously, for the sake of a healthy family, following the false principle, which many half-baked artists follow, that, if he couldn't create a healthy, happy family he couldn't create a worthy work of literature. He created nothing from that moment on. Defeated! And I understood none of that.

## NEWS ROOM

[*It's a Saturday.*
*The still slide of the printing presses now becomes a film of men preparing the machines ready for use.*
*The paper is being laid out. Mainly the front page. Movement is reaching towards a height.*
(*This area can now be filled with actors who've played other parts.*)
HARVEY *is standing beside a man who's sitting drawing possible layouts on a blank sheet.*]

HARVEY: Right, we'll have the Indo-Pakistan war on the left, conductor and his baby centre space, cholera here and map over the top, here, and that leaves this area for the gynaecologist story, if there is one. Mary? Where's Mary?

NORMAN: Having a cool argument with the In Depth boys.

ANTHONY: Will someone tell me why we're featuring a photograph on the front page of a fifty-one-year-old opera conductor with his eighteen month-old baby in his arms?

NORMAN: Well, we've got a story about an outbreak of another little bloody war, one about the spread of cholera, a morbid piece about a mother urging her daughter to death in order to save her from the shame of producing a bastard and so, with a gruesome front page like that, don't you think we need a drop of human warmth? To make our millions of readers like the world just a little better on their Sunday off work?

ANTHONY: May I remind you, Harvey, that our messengers are still on strike and copy's not moving?

HARVEY: Ronnie's with Mac now.


## SPORTS PAGES

MAC: Pensions are rotten in this place, Ronnie, and you know it.

RONNIE: I know it, but –

MAC: And I'm not advising my men back until management agree to postpone the date for cancelling closure of the garage so we have time to discuss them.

RONNIE: Look, Mac. Sometimes, I've got to say it, and I can as one union official to another, sometimes you boys cut your nose to spite your face. I'd never say that to management but between you and me that's what I think.

MAC: That's not friendly, Ronnie.

RONNIE: Friendly? Do you know that your boys stopped the securicor van from bringing in the cash the other day? Now who do you think that affects? Not us, or management. We all get paid monthly by cheque, straight into our banks. No! The office girls. The poor, bloody office girls. We had to whip round in this office and pay the secretary.

MAC: All wars have their innocent casualties.

RONNIE: Cant! Don't give me cant, Mac. Look, time's pressing. Release your messengers, get copy flowing again so's we can get the paper out and I promise you I'll persuade our chapel to give two weeks notice of strike if no agreement is reached on redundancies. Agreed?

MAC: Can you guarantee it?

RONNIE: Come on, Mac. You know I can't *guarantee* a thing like that. Agreed?

MAC: If it doesn't work, Ronnie, I promise you, we'll get the whole of Fleet Street out and no one, anywhere, will have a paper.

[MAC *leaves*. RONNIE *has been dialling meanwhile*.]

RONNIE [*into phone*]: We've got a newspaper!


NEWS ROOM

SECRETARY [*yelling to* HARVEY]: We've got a newspaper!

HARVEY: Great! Mary, where's Mary?

[MARY *appears with copy*.]

MARY: All right I agree, it *is* a news story. As long as she goes on the front page I don't mind.

HARVEY: And the bridges story'll go into In Depth where it belongs. Good. Got a photograph?

MARY: Messengers should've brought one from the dark room.

HARVEY: The first interviews read splendidly, by the way.

MARY: Thanks, but don't patronize me, Harvey.

HARVEY: Cheer up, Mary. We nearly didn't have a paper this week. [MESSENGER *arrives with photo*.] My God! She looks so hounded.

MARY: It'll be a lesson to other moralizing gynaecologists. *She* hounded that poor child. [*She leaves.*]


## SPORTS PAGES

MARVIN [*on phone*]: But, Ned, we haven't got the space. We've already had to cut down on the swimming championships – it's a small paper this week. Wait, that's not a decision I can make, I'll ask Ronnie. Ronnie, Ned reporting the Arsenal West Ham match, he says the Hammers' new player is the greatest genius in the history of football.

RONNIE: That's because he's a university graduate with a 1st class arts degree and Ned's a snob. What does he want?

MARVIN: Another three hundred words.

RONNIE: No doubt it'll be full of poetry about the geometry of the game but tell him 150. It'll have to go into six-point.


## NEWS ROOM

[*The following snatches of conversation fly back and forth among the miscellaneous characters who flood this area.*]

SECRETARY [*clutching phone*]: Our copy taker is in chaos and Ian is sitting in his hotel waiting to dictate – can anyone do something about it?

SOMEONE: Right! We're going to that wedding after all. It's royalty and the chief feels a little responsible *to* them or *for* them or *something* . . .

SOMEONE: It *was* a good story until the subs got at it – inky-fingered bloody maniacs . . .

HARVEY [*to* SOMEONE]: Ring him up, tell him copy is O.K. but ask
him what he means by the top of page 7 where it says 'the secret
transcripts have been released!' *What* transcripts have been released
by whom, to whom and about what . . .

PAUL [*to* HARVEY]: Harvey, first edition of *The People*, look. They've
got an exclusive on the Prime Minister's private earnings.

HARVEY: Damn! We got anybody on to it?

PAUL: No one free.

HARVEY: I'll do it myself.

LAYOUT: Where you thinking of putting it, Harvey?

HARVEY: That's the problem.

ANTHONY: Do you really think it's that important?

HARVEY: What, after we published his diary extracts? We'd be
laughed at to miss this. Right! We'll take the cholera map out and
cut the last quarter column.

LAYOUT: And put the money story where?

HARVEY: Bit at the top here, across five columns, over the Indian
headline.

ANTHONY: Then we won't be the 'only one going to town on the
cholera epidemic'.

HARVEY: Not the moment to be facetious, Anthony.


## POLITICAL AND FEATURES

[MESSENGER *comes in with a letter.*]

MESSENGER: Letter for Miss Mortimer.
[*She reads a few lines.*]

MARY: Jesus Christ! [*She moves quickly to the door to call the* MES-
SENGER *back.*] What did he look like?

MESSENGER: Who, miss?

MARY: The man who gave you this letter, describe him, quick.

MESSENGER: Well I don't know, do I? Reception give it to me and
I just give it to you, didn't I?
[*He leaves.* MARY *whips up phone, dials. It's picked up in the*
NEWS ROOM.]

MARY: Harvey, please.

SECRETARY: For you, Harvey.

MARY: Harvey? Can I see you? Alone?

HARVEY: I'm just about to start on the P.M.'s earnings. What is it?

MARY: Something on Morgan King. I've *got* to see you.

HARVEY: Well briefly then, in my office.

[MARY *is about to rush out.*]

CYNTHIA: What's all that, then?

MARY: Morgan King and kidnappings. Tell you later. [*She leaves.*]


## BUSINESS NEWS

DOMINIC [*he's slightly drunk*]: Women! Ah, women! I love them! I mean there was this girl in Cornwall, in a pub, with a skirt just above her pubic hairs, indifferent to hostility, sublime in her sensuousness, with thighs! Ah! those thighs. Thighs which alone you'd want to spend three hours licking. And Christ! I knew the way straight through to her and she knew I knew. And when I think about it I could weep! Weep! Every time! To think it could happen to *me*. Their touch, their look, their smells. I *love* a woman who smells of action. When she works in a garage there's a smell of oil lingering around her. If she's a doctor – it's medicinal. A painter – the smell of paints. I love the smell of alcohol on her breath when she drinks; of her body after she runs. Anything that tells me she moves, is alive with decisions, agitated. Fuck your art! Fuck your politics! Fuck your conversation! Even your wine. Women! I can't bear to be without them.


## EDITOR'S OFFICE

[HARVEY *has just finished reading the letter* MARY's *handed him.*]

MARY: What do you think?

HARVEY: It's suspect.

MARY: Not to me it isn't.

HARVEY: And we'll end up with the biggest libel suit in the history of Fleet Street.

MARY: Here's what I suggest. We've got three hours till the last edition. Can the bridges hold over till next week?

HARVEY: Till eternity I should think.

MARY: This man's waiting for me across the road in the pub. I'll take Chris and see what he's got to say. If the documents he's got look authentic then we'll reproduce them and just ask questions. No comment.

HARVEY: They'll have to be bloody authentic. Can we get hold of a sample of his handwriting to check?

MARY: I've got someone doing that already. We'll spend an hour with the fink, an hour to write it and it can be on the stone in good time for the last press as an In Depth story.

HARVEY: You're rushing, Mary.

MARY: I *know*, I just know in my bones – these documents will be conclusive. I've pursued this man for a year now, Harvey, and I've warned – he's a phoney of the most offensive sort and it's our responsibility to –

HARVEY: Mary, have you thought, that if he's linked with the robbing of supermarkets for old-age pensioners, bank robberies to pay strikers, kidnapping managers to give them lessons in civility, then you'll do just what you don't want, you'll make him a martyr.

MARY: Nonsense! The English temperament can't stand martyrs.

HARVEY: Maybe. But you'll do well to remember that this nation was weaned on the myths of King Arthur, a holy grail and the merry men of Sherwood Forest.

MARY: He'll be none of those things by the time I've finished with him.

HARVEY: And there's another thing. I've got a sneaking admiration for the enterprise. It appeals to me.

MARY: Well it doesn't to me. It's the wrong tone of voice. Half-baked revolutionaries who've borrowed other people's tongues. Do you really see urban guerrillas operating in Clapham Common? The Morgan Kings of this world are ashamed of their minds like the Victorians were ashamed of their bodies, so they flirt with revolution in a pathetic attempt to be men of action. It irritates me.

Wastes energy. Misleads real fervour, real enthusiasm, real protest. It's sentimental nonsense which belongs neither to our nature, our history or our situation and I despise it.

HARVEY: Mary, some advice.

MARY: Not now, Harvey.

HARVEY: Yes, *just* now. Remember this: a journalist is only engaged in handing on fragments of information. You can spice it with comment, but don't fall into the trap of exaggerated pronouncements.

MARY: Harvey, I don't think –

HARVEY: Well I *do* think. You can't reveal, you can only inform. Don't simplify what's complex and then imagine you've clarified the truth. And it *is* complex, it's frighteningly complex. New states being born, new classes, races finding their voice, feeling their strengths. A time ripe for opportunists who can mouth the platitudes of pain and suffering, and incite the sweet taste of revenge. Anything can happen: a glorious release of all that's noble in men or a murderous unleashing of savage spites and envies. And we have the power to tip it one way or the other; not simply by what we say but *the way we say it*. The habit of knocking down Gods is very seductive and contagious and we're very good at being spiteful. I'm not all that proud of the history of journalism, Mary, but I don't want to see *The Sunday Paper* perpetuating it.

MARY: But why *this* – to *me* – *now*?

HARVEY: Because each 'God' you topple chips away at your own self-respect. The damage you do to others can boomerang and destroy you. That's why.

MARY: The duty of this paper, since we're handing out advice, is to investigate secret and well protected misbehaviour – of any kind.

HARVEY: I don't need to be told that. Nor should I need to point out that there's no institution more 'well protected' than a newspaper.

MARY: This is silly. What are we shouting at each other for? Look, Harvey, I believe passionately that there's no other country where the administration of society is carried out more honestly, humanely and conscientiously than here. But that doesn't mean we've got a society so perfect that we can afford to limit democratic scrutiny.

HARVEY: I'm simply warning you. You might want to deflate the egos of self-styled 'Gods' but be careful you don't crack the confidence of good men. We haven't got that many. Think of it.

MARY: I don't really think I needed all that. [*Leaves.*]


## POLITICAL AND FEATURES

NORMAN: She's lucky, Mary. She can insult fools. Not me. I'm damned to suffer their offensive company forever because I can see, that while the stupid man pours out his stupidity – he knows it. And I can't return the offence of showing that *I* know it. Embarrasses me. Perhaps that's why I'm a journalist, there's distance between the insulter and the insulted.


## ARTS PAGES

ERNST: Good God! What a negative piece! Ever thought of asking a critic 'not to bother this week?'

JOHN: What, him give up his precious space?

SEBASTIAN: My dear fellow, people opening their Sunday paper look forward to reading a critic's piece. Wouldn't miss it for the world. Even if it is only a bumbling on.

JOHN: Funny creatures, critics.

ERNST: Are they any good at taking criticism of their criticism?

SEBASTIAN: Most accommodating. The better they are the less they mind what you say. It's only the minor critics who go into tantrums.


## IN DEPTH

[MARY *visiting.*]

MARY: Chris, take a break and come and have a drink with a fink.

CHRIS: A gentle fink or an evil fink? My nerves are feeling frayed.

MARY: A Morgan King fink.

JULIAN: Ah! A king-sized fink.

CHRIS: Gossip or documents?

MARY: You know I never listen to gossip. Hurry, if it looks good I want to catch the last edition.

CHRIS: St George moves in for the kill.

MARY: All right, all right! He's misunderstood. *I'm* the dragon. Shall we move?

CHRIS: I fly, I fly. Watch me how I fly.

> [*They leave.*]

## POLITICAL AND FEATURES

CYNTHIA: I once knew a beautiful young boy who was like that. Everyone wanted to embrace him, me for example. And he was so sensitive to the embarrassment of refusal that he let me. Men, women – they all wanted to touch him. The more brazen seduced him outright – some people have a nose for these things, they can smell out victims. That's what he was, a victim. And so gradually he began avoiding people, shunned all contacts, withdrew. At the age of thirty he was consigned to a home, morose, confused. Born for abuse.

## FOREIGN DEPT.

> [*The urgent sound of 'tick-tack'.*
> GORDON *and* TAMARA *standing by the telex.*]

GORDON [*reading*]: 'At least 250 doctors, professors, writers and teachers, the cream of the intellectuals who could have helped create the state of Bangla Desh, were found murdered in a field outside Dacca'.

> [TAMARA *turns away.*]

'All had their hands tied behind their backs and had been bayoneted, garotted or shot.' Tamara, get this down to Harvey. It's Reuters, everyone'll have it. Tamara!

TAMARA: I –

GORDON: For Christ's sake, you're a journalist. Is this any worse than your reports on the Eichmann trial?

TAMARA: *You* see it as a bestial but inevitable tactic, don't you? It makes a morbid sense to take away your enemy's intellectual cream, doesn't it?

GORDON: It's war.

TAMARA: It's more. That bit of slaughter? It's a signpost. In that single act there's such – such darkness. You know what it is? It's the poisonous side of the sweet apple of democracy. It's Mary's 'who-does-he-think-he-is?' gone insane. It's what your lovely, ordinary Everyman would like to do in order to feel equal – massacre the thinkers.

GORDON: Don't be a bloody fool. Men have been slaughtering their thinkers for centuries.

TAMARA: How blithely you say it.


## NEWS ROOM

SECRETARY [*on phone*]: Time Life? Paul Mannering's secretary here. Yes, the same one. We can't afford two and I cost too much. It's about that article he promised you – it's my fault that it's not arrived. I forgot to give him your message about the new dateline. Will tomorrow do? Thanks. 'Bye. Holy mother of God forgive me for my sins.

MARTIN: How much are they paying you for all that, Kathy?

SECRETARY: Well they get a separate bill for every lie I tell – if that's what you mean.


## FOREIGN DEPT.

TAMARA: I don't think I can really cope much more, Gordon.

GORDON: Go home. I'll finish your story.

TAMARA: Between the oppressors and the fanatics there's the rest of us.

GORDON: Go to a cinema, or the opera.

TAMARA: Helpless.

GORDON: Spoil yourself. Buy yourself a present – records, a dress.

TAMARA: We're always so helpless.

GORDON: Or what about those antique markets you love so much. Take a stroll down Portobello.

TAMARA: Uch! Depressing! They never used to – but now antique markets depress me. Bits and pieces of cups and saucers at exorbitant prices. Cracked plates, torn lace, threadbare shawls, frail discarded toys. Old ladies' homes bought for a few pence and sold at such a profit, such a terrible profit. And all done in the sweet tones of a dear friend advising you, flattering your taste, challenging your courage to spend by saying this or that's too expensive for you. All fraudulent, cheating, such charming conmanship – and insulting. Above all insulting, and offensive, and greedy, and insulting and greedy, greedy, greedy!

## BUSINESS NEWS

[JANE *approaching* DOMINIC *with a bottle of whisky.*]

JANE: With the compliments of Women's Pages.

MORTY: And what's he done that we haven't?

DOMINIC: Gave the girls a little anecdote about the man who was refused sterilization on the National Health.

MORTY: You selling your life story again?

DOMINIC: Oh very funny. But I tell you the population explosion is serious. I can hardly park my car for people in the way.

## SPORTS PAGES

RONNIE: I mean it's like a marriage conflict, isn't it? All social conflict is like marital conflict in that only a minor incident is needed to revive the bitterness of past abuse. That's what this strike was really about. I mean what's the sacking of thirty men, comparatively? Enough of a problem, of course, but as it goes on it becomes magnified by the recollection of old enmities 'and thus the native hue of resolution is sicklied o'er with the pale cast of thought' and we're clogged by irrelevant but all too vivid memories. Do you think that when a union leader sits facing an employer he's merely confronting a man who wants to pay him less than he's asking? Never! He's confronting a personality to whom he needs to show how he too can argue, be firm, tough, wield power. Have you ever seen the conference rooms in trade union offices? Replicas of city board rooms. What you might call 'Jewish baronialism'. And when he confronts a really aristocratic employer it's even worse. He's confronting a whole class whose life style of monied elegance – no matter how civilized, cultured and courteous – is a criticism of his own, a challenge to be matched in other ways. Win your five pounds a week extra for your men and that'll show you where all your fine culture'll get you and what you can do with it. It makes sense, I understand it, I can explain it and, as a trade union official myself, I even defend it. But, frankly, between thou and I, I loathe its spirit, its mean I'll-knock-you-down-spirit.

## ARTS PAGES

JOHN: ... It was Beethoven's violin concerto and Carl Orff's 'Carmina Burana' and our music critic overheard one of the musicians saying, in a very loud voice: 'now that we've buggered up Beethoven we'd better fuck Orff ...'

## BUSINESS NEWS

MORTY: Tell me, Jane. That feature on dressing fat ladies, your model, where did you find her?

DOMINIC: Thinking of modelling fat men's wear are you?

JANE: The less we talk of that little fraud the better, I think.

MORTY: But she was beautiful. Fat, beautiful, happy and well dressed. Tremendous morale booster for stout ladies.

JANE: But what those photographs didn't show, and we only discovered it afterwards, was that the clothes she was given to wear
didn't meet at the back and had to be kept together with safety
pins. She got hundreds of offers of marriage though.


## NEWS ROOM

HARVEY: Right! My copy's gone down. [*To* LAYOUT] Sam, you
laid out the new shape yet?

LAYOUT: It'll look like this. What's your headline?

HARVEY: Any ideas?

ANTHONY: How about 'Earnings I ain't got'?

HARVEY: He had earnings all right.

LAYOUT: How about 'Earnings: P.M. tells all'.

HARVEY: No. We'll keep it straight. 'P.M. I've still got an over-
draft'. That's what he said. Will it go in?

LAYOUT: I think we can fit *that* in.

[MESSENGER *arrives with proof sheets.*]

HARVEY: Anthony, do me a favour and sub that for me, please.


## SPORTS PAGES

MARVIN [*slamming down phone*]: Thank you very much! Another
bloody adviser. Why do they always come through on a Saturday,
the day when we're the only office working our balls off.

RONNIE: Occupational hazard, mate. Unlike the other departments
in this autocratic establishment we have democracy forced on us.
*Everyone's* an expert on sport and every Sunday morning spiteful
little eyes race down our columns in the 'let's-catch-'em-out-
game'.

## NEWS ROOM

MORTY *arrives on the scene.*]

HARVEY: Morty, your Fink's story. Anything in it?

MORTY: The problem is, if a company like Onyx declares an overseas profit of £1 million they don't have to say where it comes from.

HARVEY: On the other hand don't you always do business with your friends?

MORTY: Right. That's what business is about, and Crafty Crafton was only going about his business.

HARVEY: Good. So we forget it.

MORTY: And a plague on all their houses.

HARVEY: Tony, that piece Chris did on Atlantis Insurance.

ANTHONY: All true, Harvey. Every word of it. But no documents.

HARVEY: We'll print it but it weakens the story without names.

ANTHONY: The old problem, loyalty to sources of information.

HARVEY: I bet there'll be a tribunal to investigate the collapse.

ANTHONY: Bound to be. And no doubt Chris'll have to appear and no doubt they'll ask him where he got his information from and he'll refuse to tell them and then, no doubt, they'll dismiss it all as hearsay. But what can we do?

HARVEY: My piece O.K.?

ANTHONY: O.K.

HARVEY: Good. We'll push out the first edition.

[*Now the film on the backscreen becomes a film of the machines beginning to roll out the first edition. And with it comes the full blast of their noise which, though subsequently reduced for the remaining dialogue, continues till end of play.*]

## IN DEPTH

[ANGELA *visiting.*]

JULIAN: And so our ex-prime minister, Hotspur Hoskins as he was fondly known to us all, said of her, in one of his more jovial and confiding moods: 'Political commentator? Huh! That bitch'd get a scoop wrong if you gave it to her at dictation speed.'

ANGELA: Did he actually use the word 'scoop'? Jesus!

## NEWS ROOM

[HARRY *rushes in.*]

HARRY [*calling* HARVEY *aside from main table*]: Harvey?

HARVEY: What is it, Harry?

HARRY: I was right. There does exist a secret society.

HARVEY: Let's have it.

HARRY: It's hot.

HARVEY: Maybe, maybe.

HARRY: So prepare yourself for a burn because this one you won't want to print.

HARVEY: Well let's have it for God's sake.

HARRY: There's three people to a cell.

HARVEY: Yes, yes.

HARRY: And I'm sitting on top of an Angries cell when in bursts three youngsters, nylon stockings over their faces, one carrying a gun, and they tell the Angries to lay off the violence.

HARVEY: With one of them carrying a gun?

HARRY: It turns out to be a water pistol.

HARVEY: Go on.

HARRY: So I trail the three rivals –

HARVEY: Make it short.

HARRY: And one of them turns out to be Mary's youngest son.

HARVEY: Oh no! Bloody hell! no.

ANTHONY: You're looking harrassed, Harvey.

HARVEY [*to* HARRY]: Tell him.

## BUSINESS NEWS

JANE [*reading a letter*]: 'And what's more,' she writes, 'I think you should not only be urging people not to have babies but you should encourage them to save our resources. Water for instance. I mean, soon the world will run out of water. Forgive the personal touch but *I've* stopped pulling the chain on my urination.'

DOMINIC: I see. Save our water and start a dysentery epidemic.

## NEWS ROOM

ANTHONY: You can't tell her, Harvey.

HARVEY: Not in front of this lot, I can't. And it can't be *her* story either.

HARRY: You bet it can't. I've stood in the cold for days on this one.

ANTHONY: Don't be a fool, Harry. Yours is only half the ditty.

HARRY: Half?

ANTHONY: At this moment Saint Maria Mortimer is out gathering dirt which she believes will topple the dragon of Lanark.

HARRY: I don't connect.

ANTHONY: You should, my boy, you should. 'Only connect,' says Forster.

HARRY: I didn't go to university.

ANTHONY: I thought everyone went to university. She's in a pub, across the road, talking to an evil fink, who's offered her documents proving a link between Morgan King and your so-called secret society.

HARRY: Jesus!

ANTHONY: Well, Harvey?

HARVEY: I'm still thinking.

## IN DEPTH

JULIAN: And so I walked into El Vino's for the first time in my life, 'cos everyone assured me I had to do my drinking there or I wouldn't know what was going on in the world, and I was thinking to myself: what a sad, grubby place this is, full of disappointed men and not a woman in sight to console them, and perhaps I'd come into the wrong profession after all, when a bloke comes up to me, pissed out of his mind, and says, as though he'd read my thoughts, he says: 'Pssst. A journalist is a man who possesses himself of a fantasy and lures the truth towards it – remember that and you'll go to the top.'

## NEWS ROOM

HARVEY: Right! The bridges story comes back. [*Picks up phone.*] Frank? Don't hold that last edition. Yes, *don't* hold it I said. The bridges story stays in. Yes, in! In, in, IN!

ANTHONY: Harry my boy, what you now do with your story is your own decision. Can you believe it?

## FOREIGN DEPT.

[MARTIN *rushes in.*
Urgent sound of '*tick-tack*'.]

MARTIN: There's something coming through on the telex. Jesus Christ! Listen to this. 'The most horrific episode carried out by the Mukti Bahani guerrillas of the newly formed state of Bangla Desh, took place today in the midst of celebratory prayers which turned into cries of revenge for the 250 murdered Bangla Desh intellectuals. The rally ended with Islamic prayers in which five prisoners, whose crime was alleged to have been an attempt to abduct two women from a Dacca street, joined their captors in offering praise to Allah. The crowd began to beat the trussed up men until a group of the Mukti Bahani, wearing black uniforms, pushed them back, fixed bayonets and began to charge the prisoners themselves. They stabbed them through the neck, the chest, the stomach. One of the guards, dismayed at having no bayonet, shot one of the captors in the stomach with his Sten gun. The crowd watched with interest and the photographers snapped away. A small boy of ten, the son of one of the prisoners, cradled the head of his dying father, which act infuriated the crowd who proceeded to trample on the child.'

## NEWS ROOM

[MARY *and* CHRIS *rush in.*]

MARY: They're authentic. I knew it. Look.

CHRIS: True, Harvey. Front page material.

HARVEY: It's too late.

MARY: Too late? You've held the last edition haven't you?

HARVEY: It was too late I tell you.

MARY: Too late? Too late? Whose nonsense is this? We agreed.

HARVEY: It came from the top. The bridges story had to stay.

MARY: Bloody hell! Didn't you tell them we had an important story coming up?

HARVEY: They wanted to see the evidence first. Too risky.

MARY: What cock and bull story is that, Harvey? *You're* the editor aren't you?

HARVEY: And that's *my* decision.

MARY: But I promised I'd bring him down.

## BUSINESS NEWS

JANE: Do you know, I never ever see any of you working. You're always standing around reading magazines with incomprehensible graphs and tables.

DOMINIC: Not work? My dear lady. First of all it's Saturday and our work's all done. Secondly I'm reading the opposition, and that's work. But that apart, do you realize the scope of our sphere of activity? Industry: sub-divided into heavy, light, state-owned and private. Economic management. Industrial relations. International monetary control. The stock market, take-overs, interpretation of balance sheets, the impact of new technology. And *then*, all those headings are multiplied, and hence complicated, when we deal with them on an international scale. Not *work*?

## NEWS ROOM

MARY: I demand a better explanation, Harvey. That man's a politician and in the running to be on the party's executive. That makes him dangerous, a national risk.

## BUSINESS NEWS

JANE: Surely you can't possibly attend to all those headings, there's not enough of you.

DOMINIC: Ah! *That's* a different question. What we *should* do is one thing, what we're *able* to do is another. I tell you, the cigarette packets carry a notice saying: 'Warning! Smoking can damage your health!' But what about all newspapers carrying a notice, on the front page, just below their names, saying: 'Warning! The selective attention to data herein contained may warp your view of the world!' What about *that*, eh?

## NEWS ROOM

MARY: But I could have brought him down. I promised you I'd bring that man DOWN!

## ARTS PAGES

SEBASTIAN [*on phone*]: No, no, dear fellow, you know it's much better to cut an entire paragraph rather than re-arrange it. The printers invariably make a balls of it.

## SPORTS PAGES

RONNIE [*on phone*]: I can't help it. It'll have to wait over till next week. It's a small paper this week and fishing's a small sport – NO! I don't care if it does feed multitudes . . .

## NEWS ROOM

HARVEY [*to* SOMEONE]: Get me some pulls of the News Digest, the bloody idiots have cut the wrong story.

MARY: He doesn't even listen to me now.

## BUSINESS NEWS

JANE: I like it. 'Warp your view of the world.'

DOMINIC: Just below the name. Imagine it. '*The Sunday Paper* – Warning! The selective attention to data herein contained may warp your view of the world.' Po-pom!

## ARTS PAGES

SEBASTIAN [*still on phone*]: Yes, yes. Your air tickets are in the post and they'll reach you in good time, now concentrate on the paragraph you're going to cut for me. How about the one comparing his playing to a 'flight of homeward flying fleas'? Yes it may be accurate and funny but we do try to discourage our distinguished critics from being gratuitously offensive.

## NEWS ROOM

SOMEONE [*to* HARVEY]: The bridges story, Harvey, with the cartoon across four columns, it's too big.

HARVEY: What else is on the page?

SOMEONE: Look, here. Photo, diagram, cartoon, ad –

HARVEY: Cut the story.

MARY: Harvey, answer me!

## IN DEPTH

JULIAN [*on phone*]: Yes, the Atlantis story is going in, it's a big story – very eye-catching – pretty diagrams and all that – most impressive. No! of course no names are mentioned.

## BUSINESS NEWS

JANE: '*Daily Mirror*' – warning –
DOMINIC: '*The Times*' – warning –
JANE: '*Private Eye*' – warning –
TOGETHER: 'May warp your view of the world!'

## NEWS ROOM

MARY: HARVEY!
ANTHONY: Mary, my dear, look, I've got a problem . . . [*He takes her, consolingly, from the scene.*]
MARY: But why isn't he listening? He's not even listening.
[*Now, as they move off, everyone in all departments talks at once, a babble, a crescendo of voices melting into the full blast of the machines. The sound continues but – the stage darkens – except for the bright image on the screen of the presses turning – turning.*]

*The Wedding Feast*

A play in two acts and a prologue freely adapted
from a short story called *An Unpleasant Predica-
ment* by Fyodor Dostoevsky

FOR NIKKI AND BOB GAVRON

WITH LOVE AND GRATITUDE

*The Wedding Feast* received its world premiere at the Stadtsteater, Stockholm, on 8 May 1974, directed by Gun Arvidsson.

It received its British premiere, greatly revised, at the Leeds Playhouse on 20 January 1977, with the following cast.

| | |
|---|---|
| LOUIS LITVANOV | David Swift |
| KATE WHITE | Fiona Walker |
| DAVID LOWERY | Noel Collins |
| STEPHEN BULLOCK | Brett Usher |
| MR HAMMOND | Michael Egan |
| BONKY HARRIS | Andrew Jarvis |
| KNOCKER WHITE | David Troughton |
| TOSH WHITE | Dickie Arnold |
| EMILY WHITE | Barbara Atkinson |
| TINKER WHITE | Nigel Gregory |
| DAPHNE DAWSON | Stephanie Fayerman |
| MR DAWSON | Ted Morris |
| MRS DAWSON | Mary Ann Turner |
| MAUREEN DAWSON | Carol Leader |
| MARTIN DAWSON | Michael Troughton |
| RINGO RAY | Sebastian Abineri |

Directed by John Harrison and Michael Attenborough
Designed by John Halle
Lighting by Mo Hemmings

# CHARACTERS

LOUIS LITVANOV, *a shoe manufacturer*
KATE WHITE, *his secretary*
DAVID LOWERY, *his manager*
MR HAMMOND, *managing director of chain of shoe shops*
KNOCKER WHITE, *Kate's brother, a shoe operative*
TOSH WHITE, *their uncle, a shoe operative*
EMILY WHITE, *Tosh's wife*
TINKER WHITE, *their son, regular in the army*
DAPHNE DAWSON, *Knocker's bride, a shoe operative*
MR DAWSON, *her father, a shoe operative*
MRS DAWSON, *her mother*
MAUREEN DAWSON, *her sister, a shoe operative*
MARTIN DAWSON, *her brother, a building worker*
RINGO RAY, *Martin's friend, a shoe operative*
STEPHEN BULLOCK, *Kate's friend, a journalist*
BONKY HARRIS, *a shoe operative*

(MR HAMMOND and MR DAWSON can be played by the same actor)

# PROLOGUE

---

*There are four small sets for the Prologue to suggest:* LOUIS's *lounge,* LOUIS's *bathroom,* LOUIS's *office, streets of Norwich. All could involve the use of a screen with projected slides and/or film, though this is not essential. There is one main set for Acts One and Two: interior of the* WHITES' *house for the wedding.*

## SCENE ONE

[*Lounge of a large country mansion in the outskirts of Norwich in Norfolk. Four people, three men and a woman.*
*A drinks trolley, four chairs around a small table. Late evening. Behind, a huge screen.*
*The host,* LOUIS LITVANOV, *is serving and chatting with his guests:* MR HAMMOND, KATE WHITE, DAVID LOWERY.]

LOUIS: And *why* do you think I make my office of glass? To be *seen* working! And why do you think that office is on the shop floor? To discuss business where work is done! Noise! Activity! I'm a worker. I work hard.

[STEPHEN BULLOCK *steps forward.*]

STEPHEN: This – uncomfortable story occurred about the time our elected representatives decided bravely that we should take our fortunes into the European Common Market.

LOUIS: My operatives see me work hard. They respect me!

STEPHEN: A courageous time when our cool captains of industry streamlined their factories, sacked superfluous labour – albeit with a touching impetuosity – and, fortified by high hopes of new destinies, struggled firmly to calm the anticipated though unreasonable industrial unrest which followed. A time of optimism and regeneration owing much to men of high commercial idealism. We think, ourselves, that such men have been a little unjustly castigated for the harsh measures they were forced to take: prosperity, after all, has its price and in the beginning must always take a sad toll of victims. Or must it?

LOUIS: When the men get there at eight in the morning who do they see? The night-watchman? No! Me! The first to arrive, the last to go. And they respect me.

STEPHEN: And so you see, not every businessman was ruthless when faced with the challenge of streamlining for entry-into-Europe-day. This tale adjusts the balance, a little at least. And if for the moment capital has failed to find a modus vivendi with labour, well – it will not have been, as we'll show, for the want of trying. However, before the main story – the preamble, a filling-in, a few – vivid brushstrokes.

DAVID: Mr Litvanov –

STEPHEN: – is our central character.

DAVID: – I don't think you're being very honest.

STEPHEN: Honest, in the formal sense of the word, that is.

LOUIS: Not honest? Have you ever known me do a crooked deal, break a contract, abuse my workers?

STEPHEN: But we're talking about –

DAVID: – the private sense, Mr Litvanov –

LOUIS: Louis, please, it's out of office.

DAVID: – the private sense. You won't face the lessons of experience.

LOUIS: Experience! Experience! What, what, what experience?

STEPHEN: What experience? We'll soon hear. To begin, then [*flicks switch of control which projects interior on to screen*], a country mansion in the outskirts of Norwich in the county of Norfolk. Four people. One Sunday evening. No! To begin with: me! Name: Stephen Bullock. Education: Norwich Grammar and the London School of Economics. Profession: journalist. For whom? The local daily press. Ambition? To tell good and ordinary men good and ordinary stories about good and ordinary people. [*Self-disgustedly*] Yeach! Temperament? Unreliable. Achievements? Mediocre. Vices? self-pity when drunk. Virtues? Honest – when drunk. But now, the story in which, later on, I play a not too worthy part, though I wouldn't have missed it for worlds! So, a country mansion in the outskirts of our lovely city of Norwich in the county of Norfolk. The county – rich in agriculture; the city – a centre for shoe manufacturing industry; the epoch – one of softening class barriers with the Alps two hours away and the moon a mere thirty-six hours away. Next, background –

LOUIS: One thing I was brought up to be and to be absolutely: honest! I can remember my father telling me that when he was a boy in Russia he saw a pogrom – houses burning, peasants looting – you know what I'm talking about? And he got angry, my father, and wanted to go in there and fight – a boy of fourteen with drunken peasants! But his father, my grandfather, grabbed him and shouted 'Take no notice! TAKE NO NOTICE!' So my father told me the same, 'Take no notice! Don't learn the wrong lessons! That's the way *they* want to behave? Let them! But not you. Honest! Always be honest and peaceful. Don't learn the wrong lessons.'

STEPHEN: And so Louis Litvanov, son of an impoverished Jewish cobbler and grandson of an impoverished Jewish cobbler, came with his poor, bewildered parents to our hospitable land and became one of its grateful, prosperous sons. But not a –

LOUIS: – millionaire! I could have been a millionaire, but no! I love my workers and they love me and because they love me they trust me and because they trust me I can run a factory. A simple philosophy.

STEPHEN: Louis's guests –

KATE: A simple guilt!

STEPHEN: – are not in agreement with him.

KATE: You're like a man who couldn't ever be a doctor – you'd associate too much with the patient's pain. You look at your operatives, you watch them do the same monotonous job every day and it hurts you. Guilt! You should have grown out of it by now.

LOUIS: You see how they talk to me?

KATE: But he enjoys it.

LOUIS: What other employer would let his secretary talk to him like that?

KATE: See how he enjoys it?

LOUIS: No! I say. It's her right. Every human being's got the right to talk to his, or her, employer as an equal.

KATE: How he enjoys himself in the act of tolerating his – to use an indelicate word – employees.

DAVID: He'll never understand the nature of British democracy.

HAMMOND: And what's that?

DAVID: You can only tolerate those who know their place.

STEPHEN: That's David Lowery –

LOUIS: – My tough, matter-of-fact Scottish manager. Listen to him. You're not interested in people, that's your trouble. You're not even interested in shoes, are you?

DAVID: Frankly, no! I'm interested in making money. That's what you pay me for and that's what I'm good at. Shoes bore me.

LOUIS: Pretending he's tough. Playing at big business. And you'll fail. People aren't stupid, you've got to *earn* their trust. The public *and* your workers. Respect them and earn their trust. It pays dividends. Both ways! In profits and human dignity. Believe me!

KATE: You're shouting.

STEPHEN: That's Kate White –

LOUIS: I'm Jewish. I shout!

STEPHEN: – his attractive secretary, my dear school-friend, my school girl-friend, and the teacher's dearest, brightest pupil.

KATE: Louis can never resist the sensation of standing alone in defence of a principle.

STEPHEN: I nearly married her.

KATE: Especially one so seasoned with a touch of evangelic fervour.

STEPHEN: But she is cursed with divine discontent: she is right for most men but not one is right for her. Kate, a tired Marxist, who learned her Marxism from me but her tiredness from the world, and whose affectionate bullying Louis explains away as the behaviour of a [*delicate pause*] getting-on-in-years-woman needing to be saved from sex-starvation. But Louis is prone to clichés. My own view is that he accepts her bullying because he once contemplated running off with her, and she bullies because she would have liked to have gone but didn't, couldn't, as none of us can do what it's not in our nature to do. He was older and she was younger.

He was married and, though he was married to an ageing coquette with a small brain supporting too much energy, and Kate knew it and Louis knew Kate knew, yet Kate was no home-breaker! Not that Louis's *politics* weren't a substantial appeal. He'd also once been a Marxist. As we all had once been. In our brave youth. In 1936, during the fascist riots in the East End of London Louis was a young communist messenger taking instructions from headquarters to strategic field positions. On roller skates! But – it *was* in his brave youth.

HAMMOND: And what, tell me, is the experience that Mr Litvanov won't face?

STEPHEN: That's Duncan Hammond –

LOUIS: Louis, please. I'm at home now.

STEPHEN: Managing director of a chain of shoe shops. An honourable man whose company is specially gratifying to Louis Litvanov, for his presence – as a weekend guest, no less – is a sign that Louis has mastered those rough sides of his peasant origin which he prefers to keep apart from those rough sides of his peasant origin which he finds it wise to boast of on occasions.

HAMMOND: Mr Litvanov –

LOUIS: Louis –

HAMMOND: Louis has always struck me as a pretty practical man. Can't really see him not learning from experience.

STEPHEN: But listen –

DAVID: We'll tell you then.

STEPHEN: Just listen to this.

DAVID: Where shall we begin?

STEPHEN: A real roll-call of honour, this.

KATE: At the beginning.

STEPHEN: Oh, I'd better add –

DAVID: In the beginning?

STEPHEN: This little gathering is to celebrate Louis's very youthful fifty-second birthday –

DAVID: You start then.

STEPHEN: – and they're all a little drunk.

KATE: When he first bought over this ailing factory and I was a little girl and a bit –

DAVID: – Mr Litvanov said, right! Huge bonuses for everyone in the first year of profit.

KATE: And Louis, being an honest man, kept his word. We reorganized, the workers responded, and in two years we were making profits.

DAVID: Handsome bonuses all round.

KATE: In the third year bigger profits still.

DAVID: Even handsomer bonuses all round.

KATE: In the fourth year still bigger profits.

DAVID: And up again went bonuses.

KATE: But, Mr Hammond, as you and every good Marxist knows, nothing stands still in capitalist society. You don't expand, bor, you stagnate. So, he added a wing, bought more plant, employed more men.

DAVID: Good for the business, good for employment, good for the country but – profits were down.

KATE: Inevitably –

DAVID: – and quite properly, as any good businessman –

KATE: – or Marxist –

DAVID: – will understand –

KATE: But the workers being neither good businessmen nor Marxists instantly sent deputations.

STEPHEN [*but to us*]: Excuse us, Mr Litvanov, but why are our bonuses down?

DAVID [*still to* HAMMOND, *of course*]: We've expanded, we explained. Profits are down.

STEPHEN: Excuse us, Mr Litvanov, but *you've* expanded, *your* profits are down, that's not our fault. Us've worked hard as any we worked 'afore an' we've come to rely on it.

LOUIS: I understood their arguments.

KATE: And Mr Litvanov –

LOUIS: Louis –

KATE: – understood their arguments.

DAVID: So, we had a discussion and agreed to a *fixed* bonus *not* geared to profits.

LOUIS: I'm sure Mr Hammond is familiar with all this . . .

HAMMOND: Oh, I'm not so sure.

KATE: Story number two. One day one of the wives visited Louis.

STEPHEN: Excuse me, Mr Litvanov, but could I borrow some money? My husband's bin ill five weeks, look.

DAVID: 'What?' cried Louis. 'Doesn't this firm pay sick pay?'

KATE: And up he jumped, called in David here, and the accountant – everyone! and asked with child-like amazement: no sick pay?

DAVID: We pointed out that no one in the industry pays sick pay.

LOUIS: I spoke to the federation of shoe manufacturers – no! It would be abused, they said. Spoke to the union – no! Other demands more important, they said.

KATE: So, Louis went ahead alone and instituted sick pay –

DAVID: – and a very, very interesting situation arose. As you know, a long time ago we had machines requiring three men to run them and so, because workers have a fine sense of history, they insisted that even though technology had produced a machine operable by one man yet, for historical reasons, of course, they should continue using three.

STEPHEN: And good luck to them I say.

DAVID: Now, what happened when one of those three was ill? Not only was he paid sick pay but the remaining two insisted that the third man's wage be divided between them, *and* that they should be paid the overtime needed to catch up on the backlog which the third man's absence created.

KATE: And what backlog was there?

DAVID: None! Because the machine only needed one man anyway.

KATE: And where was the sick man?

DAVID: Temporary work! In another firm!

LOUIS: But reasons! There were reasons! Behaviour like that has historical reasons.

DAVID: We appealed to the unions who said don't pay sick-pay then. But Mr L, being a humanitarian, paid the price of over-manning *and* sick pay, and illness rose from fifteen days a year to thirty.

LOUIS: But profits rose. You've got to keep pointing out that profits rose also.

KATE: And so Louis felt he had to humanize relationships even more. He had an idea. Hire the Blue Suite of the Royal Hotel at Christmas and have a party.

DAVID: For everyone!

LOUIS: Down to the messenger boy –

KATE: – and his girl-friend.

LOUIS: And why not! It was a new experience for them. Big band, big cabaret, drink unlimited. Hired it for the whole night.

KATE: So's they could stay for breakfast.

LOUIS: *I* used to make a funny little speech, then one of *them*'d make a funny little speech. Everyone was happy.

DAVID: Until one day a union leader came to visit us. A new man.

STEPHEN: Excuse me, Mr Litvanov, but that were a great party, that really were a great party. I reckon a party like that must've set you back a penny or two.

LOUIS: Who knows, I said. £4,000, £5,000. One year it cost us £7,000.

STEPHEN: £7,000! [*Whistles.*] Now, let's see. You divide a figure like that atween us that'd give us each about £50, wouldn't it? Why not do that instead, Mr L? Most on us could use that extra money.

LOUIS: Now *that* I didn't like. *That* I thought was not nice. And I refused. They loved that party, the men. Used to come to me to tell me, loved it!

DAVID: But pressure was brought to bear.

LOUIS: Not *pressure*. Arguments! Money which *they* needed for essential living *we* were spending in order to buy ourselves *their* goodwill.

KATE: Terrible thing!

LOUIS: Mr Hammond, I mean, Duncan, you could see their point. It was like taking their money in order to buy their respect for us.

HAMMOND: There aren't many men in business would interpret it quite like that. Still . . .

LOUIS: But if you buy goodwill, even with your own money, isn't that corruption? They were right!

KATE: Louis understood their arguments. Next?

DAVID: The football saga?

KATE: Ah! The football saga!

DAVID: One day, I remember the very day, a Friday, we were together in the packing room, looking outside where the men were playing football in their lunch hour.

LOUIS: How about a match between the men and the management I suggested.

STEPHEN: Smashing! One Saturday afternoon. Crates of beer. Sandwiches. Beat them seven-one, of course.

DAVID: Then it grew.

STEPHEN: What about a regular team, Mr Litvanov?

LOUIS: Splendid, I said. Great idea. I'll hire the grounds, pay for refreshment –

KATE: – until one day one of them came and said –

STEPHEN: – excuse me, Mr Litvanov, but we play a team the other day, and they had a special kit paid for by their management.

LOUIS: Don't worry, I said, we'll have a team kit, best money can buy –

STEPHEN: – and boots, Mr Litvanov, we get through helluva lot o' boots in a season.

LOUIS: Nothing easier, I said.

STEPHEN: And can we hev Wednesday off for the league matches?

LOUIS: Now wait a minute, I said.

STEPHEN: Can't stay in the league otherwise, y'see, Mr Litvanov.

KATE: So Louis agreed, didn't you, Louis?

DAVID: And then we found they weren't coming in on Thursdays because of bruises to their ankles –

KATE: – and that they had to have time off on Tuesday for training sessions –

DAVID: And that they needed supporters which meant time off for other workers –

KATE: – and always these veiled threats about leaving if each new demand wasn't met.

LOUIS: Which I didn't like. No! *That* I didn't like. *I'd* encouraged the idea in the first place and that wasn't nice. But I tell you what –

KATE: – he understood.

LOUIS: If you have a deprived upbringing, a job that's monotonous, you grab at all the recreation you can get. I know. I did it myself.

KATE: And therefore Louis Litvanov understood their motives.

HAMMOND: Tell me, Mr Litvanov –

LOUIS: Louis, please.

HAMMOND: Louis. Tell me, are all Jewish businessmen as paternalistic as you?

LOUIS: That's what you call it? Give everything a name and dismiss it. All right! So I'm paternalistic. You think my workers care if it means good wages and a pleasant atmosphere?

HAMMOND: Pleasant atmosphere? That's interesting now. And it doesn't occur to you that because you insist on putting your office on the shop floor it might disturb your operatives?

LOUIS: Disturb them?

HAMMOND: Disturb them, for example, to watch you giving us drinks, as you so kindly do before we visit your collection? And it's in the middle of the morning, don't forget.

LOUIS: Disturb them? Why should that disturb them? They know why it's happening. Buyers come to look at a collection you've got to give them a drink. The operatives understand this. More, they want it! The more I sell the more they earn. What *should* they say?

HAMMOND: What *could* they say? They're on your territory. You confuse their diplomacy for honesty. Am I correct, Miss White?

LOUIS: Don't ask her. She's an old-fashioned Marxist. It annoys her that I get on so well with my workers. Confuses her. Right, Kate?

KATE: You *imagine* you get on with them.

HAMMOND: Yes, what about when they're *not* on your territory?

KATE: And he's planning to expand into Europe.

LOUIS: I'm a European, of course I'll expand. The European business community needs men like me. The worker must be loved, cared for, respected as a human being. How else can you make an Industrial Relations Act work, or a Treaty of Rome or any other of those agreements which, we all agree I hope, are only aimed at the benefit of all?

HAMMOND: Oh we agree, we agree. But your theories, Mr Litvanov, the men of Europe are tough and hard and won't so easily respond, I fear.

LOUIS: Then we must teach them, mustn't we, Kate?

KATE: Yes, Louis. You, me and David here. We'll do a lecture tour of company board meetings. 'Mammon and manual worker: how to love both and survive!'

LOUIS: She's beautiful when she's witty.

HAMMOND: But what about the worker *outside* his work situation? They like to keep their distances, you know. I mean, supposing you went to their homes. There. Where they live. What then? Would your sense of equality stand up there do you think? Between four dreary working-class walls? Stand up? Would it?

DAVID: Ah ha! Now there's a question.

KATE: I bet that'll give Louis something to think about.

DAVID: To keep him awake at nights.

KATE: Poor Louis.

   [*The guests leave.*]

STEPHEN: Poor Louis! The party came to an end. [*Switches off slide.*] It had been a good way to celebrate a fifty-second year. Civilized. They'd been frank, witty, flattered each other's intelligence. Louis Litvanov had cause to feel pleased with himself.


## SCENE TWO

[*A bath, many tall mirrors, a handsome dressing gown, bathroom boxes.*]

STEPHEN: And so, man of habit that he was – for habit is not, as some men think, the outward form of a reactionary mind, but rather the discipline necessary for progress – and so, with a discipline born of an impoverished childhood, Louis undressed, meticulously folded his clothes in neat piles and laid them on one of his tapestry covered chairs [*switches on suitable new slides of tapestried chair*] in one of his oak panelled bedrooms [*switches on slide*] alongside one of his mirrored bathrooms [*switches on slide*] in this, one of his two country homes, and prepared to soak in that hot bath all hard-working bodies need in preparation for sleep and tomorrow's enterprise.

Yet, something irritated him. The little party, for all the expansive attention he'd given to it, had left some vague uneasiness in his soul. What?

   [*Sound of telephone.*]

His wife, telephoning from their London flat.

[*It is a machine necessitating a mere button so that he can talk to and hear it from any part of the room. This enables him, now, to undress and look at himself in the mirror while talking.*]

WIFE'S VOICE: Louis?

LOUIS: I'm here.

WIFE'S VOICE: Where are you?

LOUIS: In the bathroom.

WIFE'S VOICE: You alone?

LOUIS: No!

WIFE'S VOICE: Who's with you?

LOUIS: Everybody. You finished with the Inquisition?

WIFE'S VOICE: What you so irritable for?

LOUIS: I always think maybe this time you'll ask me first how I am, how's the factory.

WIFE'S VOICE: I hate the factory.

LOUIS: Or happy birthday.

WIFE'S VOICE: Oh, Louis, I forgot.

LOUIS: So why you ringing?

WIFE'S VOICE: You asked me to ring – I'm ringing.

[*He grimaces at his wife – the telephone machine.*]

LOUIS: How are the boys?

WIFE'S VOICE: They also hate the factory.

LOUIS: I know. And you teach them to hate me too. I'm a very lucky man. Blessed.

WIFE'S VOICE: For goodness sake, what are you doing there?

LOUIS: Undressing. What else should I be doing in a bathroom?

[*She is silent.*]

[*To himself* Not only am *I* a peasant but I'm married to one.

STEPHEN: Ah ha! The words slipped out. Was this the reason for the vague uneasiness that had slowly overwhelmed what he'd thought were his good spirits? Had the effort to be especially gracious with his oh so English week-end guest been too taxing for our little 'peasant'? Louis was an honest man. Strange tensions tugged at his hard-won equanimity.

WIFE'S VOICE: I can't hear you. Stop undressing and come nearer to the phone.

LOUIS: Tell me something. Tell me something interesting. Tell me a beautiful story, something beautiful you've done.

WIFE'S VOICE: Hurry up, Louis, please. I'm late for an appointment.

LOUIS: An appointment? This hour?

WIFE'S VOICE: I'm in London, remember? The big city? We don't die with the sun here you know.

LOUIS: Go, go.

WIFE'S VOICE: I'll buy your present tomorrow.

LOUIS: I'm much obliged.

WIFE'S VOICE: 'Bye!

LOUIS: [*mocking her tone*] 'Bye, 'bye!

　　[*Switches off contraption. Looks at himself in the mirror.*]

You're growing old.

　　[*Confronts another mirror.*]

You're growing fat.

　　[*Falls to floor and attempts press-ups. Collapses and gives up after four.*]

And you're a peasant.

　　[*Slowly rises. Takes up a magnificent dressing gown over his shoulders. Again sees himself in a mirror. Draws himself up to his full height.*]

No! You're a tycoon.

　　[*Defiantly throws open his arms. Dressing gown falls off.*]

No! You're a peasant. [*Pause*] Who the hell needs so many mirrors? And so many doors? And so many rooms? And so many houses and so many cars? [*Mimicking, shouting*] Louis, you're shouting.

　　[*Takes off pants, finds himself confronting another mirror – naked and vulnerable.*]

　　[*Softly, sadly*] I'm human, I shout!

　　[*He enters bath, slowly crumbles, sinks, dejected.*]


## SCENE THREE

[*The factory.*
*To begin with, the sounds of machines from the shoe factory. Then –*
*Film or articulated slides of morning on the shop-floors of* LOUIS's *factory.*
*Visuals match sounds:*

*first – the hum of the electric current revving up;*
*then – the first large sound of the enormous 'clicking' (cutting) machine called*
*'the revolutionary press';*
*then – the 'in-sole moulder' moving up and down;*
*then – the machine for bevelling the sole's edges, spinning round;*
*then – the long rows of girls at the machines which stitch the uppers together*
*and the linings to the uppers.*
*A symphony! a visual poem! Ah!* ]

STEPHEN: Poor Louis Litvanov, husband, father, idealist, factory
owner on the threshold of big, European industry, and if such
responsibilities were not enough to confuse a man's loyalties there
were the conflicts of old ideals fighting present realities, and creeping age at odds with the stubborn enthusiasms of a reluctantly
fading youth. Who would dare pass judgement on a man's actions
when such awful contradictions are passing through his soul?

[*Glass office is set up.* LOUIS *inside.*]

But 'stubborn' is an admirable word to apply to our hero.

LOUIS: Harris!

STEPHEN: The next morning brought fresh energies, and all doubts
were drowned in dreams where, they say, most unsolved problems
settle themselves.

LOUIS: Harris!

STEPHEN: He found time, on his way to work, to pause and climb a
tree, which action – though it irritated his sceptical chauffeur –
boosted his own morale. His chauffeur, besides, was a slothful un-
imaginative man who, for example, failed to appreciate the need to
drive to work in a modest Ford rather than the ostentatious Rolls
which was only reserved for week-end visiting. And so, fortified
with new resolves, Louis began a new day with special bounce.

LOUIS: Harris! Harris!

[BONKY HARRIS, *an operative, appears.*]

LOUIS: Bonky? I've got something special to discuss with you. But
first, this. You've made a good job of it. [*He's referring to a wooden
model of a new style shoe and drawing from which it was made.*]
Excellent! But this line, from the sole to the heel. Look [*pointing
to drawing*], a little steeper.

BONKY: Do you really think it can rise so sharp?

LOUIS: I know it can rise so sharp. Apart from that you've copied it beautifully. An artist! You're a real artist! Which brings me to my special thing: your secret hobby.

BONKY: Who told you about that?

LOUIS: No matter who. It's true, isn't it?

BONKY: My hobby is my hobby, Mr Litvanov.

LOUIS: You paint, don't you?

BONKY: My hobby is my —

LOUIS: And I want to see them.

BONKY: I don't show —

LOUIS: I mean, *may* I see them? Please?

BONKY: I don't show no one what I do.

LOUIS: I want to buy some.

BONKY: I don't sell —

LOUIS: I mean I'd *like* to buy some. Please.

BONKY: But I don't do them for selling, Mr Litvanov.

LOUIS [*impatiently*]: Oh, come on, Bonky. Let me see them.

BONKY: Yes, Mr Litvanov.

[BONKY *moves off. Employers must be indulged.* KATE *enters.*]

LOUIS: Good morning, Katherine.

KATE: You're shouting.

LOUIS: I'm in good spirits, I shout. [*But softer*] Good morning.

KATE: Good morning.

LOUIS: You think I made a fool of myself last night?

KATE: I have a favour to ask you.

LOUIS: You did, didn't you?

KATE: It was your birthday.

LOUIS: Drank too much.

KATE: Your hearty concern —

LOUIS: Talked too much.

KATE: — it irritates me.

LOUIS: Made a fool of myself.

KATE: You were at your worst.

LOUIS: What favour?

KATE: My brother is getting married. There's some wedding shoes —

LOUIS: Take. Now, ask me a real favour.

[BONKY HARRIS *enters with some paintings on hardboards.*]

BONKY: Oh, sorry, Miss White. I'll come back later.

LOUIS: Come in, come in. Look, Bonky's paintings. Did *you* know one of our operatives painted in his lunch hour? You didn't did you? No! You're so busy criticizing my black sins that you miss the jewels around you. [*Pause.*] I like them. [*Pause.*] Bonky, tell me, help me solve a little argument we've been having. When the buyers come, to look at our collection, and I bring them into this office for drinks, and you can all see us – does it upset you? To watch us? You know, in the middle of the morning and all that? You mind? You? Any of you?

BONKY: No, sir. Don't worry me none, Mr Litvanov, no sir. Drink yourselves to death for all I care, if you'll pardon the joke.

LOUIS: And the others?

BONKY: Can't talk for the others, master; no one can't talk for no one else can they?

LOUIS: But what do you think?

BONKY: Well, reckon they might some on 'em want a pint watching you, but they don't think on it much. They know it's not their time o'day, see. They think you people gotta drink then. They think it's your way, don't they? Not the same way as them, is it?

LOUIS [*he's scored*]: You're a wise man, Bonky. [*Holding up paintings for* KATE] Look! Good, yes? I'll buy them. How much?

KATE: For God's sake, you're embarrassing him.

LOUIS: You embarrassed, Bonky? Miss White's ashamed to talk about money matters; are *you*? [*Pause.*] See, wrong again. So. Five pounds each? Ten? Twenty? Tell you what, fifty pounds for the three of them. [*He proceeds to count out notes to an oppressed-looking* BONKY HARRIS.]

[*The film of the operatives working is now full stride into its rhythm.*]

STEPHEN: When a good man's determined to do good there ent no stopping him, there ent. Fired by principles he'll defy all scorn. And that was only one of Louis's generous actions that day. The present of the wedding shoes for Kate's brother – who, incidentally, was one of the operatives in his factory – was another. And, for a third, the brother's wife-to-be who, not surprisingly, was also an employee of Louis Fashions Ltd, was given a bottle of champagne to drink the boss's health that very day. The word spread quickly through the factory which buzzed with grateful and admiring comments, all of which a delighted Louis was well aware of from the looks cast at him as he did his daily rounds of the shop floors. It even seemed to him that the work went faster and better, and what greater proof does a visionary need of the efficacy of his ideals? It is said by men of mean spirit and short sight that it is only greed which drives the working man to harder work. But such a view ignores the subtle paradox that, in order to satisfy this so-called greed, men must cooperate! They must! One man don't produce a car do 'ee? No! Takes a whole lot on 'em, cooperating together. And is not cooperation a worthy human aspiration?

[*To prove which the rhythmic sound of the machines intensifies and the visuals showing men and women 'cooperating' are even lovelier and, somehow, holier.*]

## SCENE FOUR

[*The streets and landmarks of Norwich projected on the screen as and when* STEPHEN's *continuing story indicates.*]

STEPHEN: And how happily that next week passed; for leadership *is* an important attribute of the human personality. When Louis was enraged – which to his credit was rare – then misery fell upon all his operatives and mistakes were increased tenfold. But with such a week as we now talk of, ha! Old enemies on the shop floor ceased snarling and found time to make jokes with one another; the quality of factory teasing was gentle rather than vicious; men opened doors for women and not one shoe was thrown aside into the rejects bag. Louis's benign good humour was everywhere and piece rates really proved themselves in Thursday's eagerly awaited pay packet. When the next Saturday came his good humour persisted and Louis took his chauffeur, the chauffeur's wife and their children into the colourful market of Norwich, bought them presents, fed them lunch, took them to admire the city's castle and cathedral and walk the old delightful cobbled Elm Hill Street. And when teatime came fed them cream and jam squashed between soft scones, after which he whipped them into a late afternoon film showing of *Nicholas and Alexandra*. Whew! What a purring troupe it was that spilt out from the celluloid world of regal living into the cold, brisk, starry night of a Norfolk sky and, laden with parcels and giggling when their Ford was discovered to be hooked bumper to bumper to a Rolls-Royce, finally drove out of the city centre through the suburbs towards fields and a sort of home. [*Pause.*] Until –

CHAUFFEUR'S VOICE: Don't worry, Mr Litvanov. Be fixed in five minutes.

[LOUIS *walks into a background of a projection of a starry night.*]

STEPHEN: Not even a puncture can disturb the good humour of our munificent manufacturer. The night air is fresh and good. The sky is razor keen with sharp stars, and from round about come the domestic sounds of families, alive with their week-end pleasures and pastimes. A baby cries, momentarily frightened out of sleep; a dog barks at an owner's return; children play hide and seek in the shadows and, why – there's even the sounds of music; a party, a wedding, a birthday feast? Can there be so much misery in this world if settings of such charm are possible? But wait! Who's this? Those voices are familiar.

[*A* FATHER *and* SON, *arguing, walk past.*]

SON: And I tell you Knocker said *one* more crate.

FATHER: What in hell do 'ee know. 'Is sister say two crates an' two crates is what I'm buyin'.

SON: But he'll be riled. He say to get only one.

FATHER: Never mind what 'ee say. 'Ee say many things what no one wanna take notice of. She say two, and two it'll be.

[*They pass by.*]

STEPHEN: Crates of beer? Knocker? Can it be? Kate's brother's name is Knocker. Surely not. Everyone's got a nickname like that in these parts. Still, it is a coincidence. But no! The wedding wasn't today. Or was it? Perhaps it was. Perhaps he'd forgotten.

[FATHER *and* SON *return. A crate to each.*]

SON: Well, I'm telling you, that's all, just warnin'. He'll be riled.

FATHER: Oh give over. You ben't afeared of Knocker White, surely?

SON: Me afeared of Knocker White? Him? That accident-prone lump of merchandise?

FATHER: He is that. Narthin' what stand is safe when he's talkin'. Ole Knocker White.

[*They pass by.*]

LOUIS: Knocker White. It is. The wedding.

STEPHEN: It is well known that whole trains of thought sometimes pass through our brains instantaneously. However, we'll try to unscramble our hero's thoughts, at least to give you a kernel of them, as they say, the most essential and nearest to reality. 'Why,' flashed through his mind, 'Hammond's right. I talk and talk and only test my notions in the factory, but not in their houses. Here, for example, is one of my workers, Knocker White . . .

LOUIS [*taking over*]: . . . just returned from a moving ceremony, full of hope, excitement, looking forward to his wedding feast. One of the most blissful days of his life – sharing it with his nearest and dearest, thanking them, with a banquet. Modest naturally, poor but gay. Full of genuine gladness.

What, what if he knew that outside, at this very moment, I, his boss, someone *he* felt was his superior, was toying with thoughts of coming in? What would he say? What would he feel if suddenly I *did* walk in? [*Thinks.*] Ha! Dumb! He'd be dumb with embarrassment. Stands to reason! I'd be in his way, upset everything. [*Thinks.*] Or would I? With anybody else, perhaps. But with me? A man who's known poverty half his life? How I'd transform that embarrassment into a sweet pleasure, a real human moment. [*Pause.*] What would happen? I'd go in. Silence. They're amazed. Anxious. Dancing stops. They back away. Understandable. But, I go straight to the groom. A smile. Simple words. Tell him about the puncture, the voices going for crates of beer, the sounds of music I heard, the coincidence. 'I don't suppose you'll turn me out,' I say. Turn me out! Ha! He'll be ecstatic! He'll take my coat – rush to get me an armchair – trrrremble with delight. And one by one I'll make the acquaintance of the guests, the bride, compliment her, tell jokes – about coming again in nine months time to be godfather. I'll beg them not to stand on ceremony . . .

But not for self-honour. I won't be looking for special attention, laurels, flattery, servile humbleness. No! My actions will evoke nobler feelings. Our conversation will be modest, natural, men facing men in a human situation. For only a half-hour, just to offer respects, or perhaps an hour, and one or two or maybe three drinks. But no more! Before the food comes I'll leave. 'Business,' I'll say. And they'll understand that.

Then I'll leave, with a joke about the wedding bed which'll make them roar with laughter, and then I'll kiss the bride, gently, on the forehead, and I know how they'll all look at me, because it's a beautiful gesture, in the right proportion, at the correct moment, everything correct, most important. For to every action is a time and place and they see that I know that. And then, in the factory, next week, the efficient industrialist, kindly but firm. Not the place to remember weddings and kisses. Work! The world must turn on. Men must be fed, houses built, shoes cut out and sewn up. Two sides! They'll see two sides of me. And when they're old they'll tell their children and I'll be spoken of with affection, honoured, remembered.

STEPHEN: These, or thoughts something like these, flashed through Louis's mind. Though, it must be remembered, that the most virtuous and honourable intentions felt in the heart take on a shade of vulgarity when actually put into words. So that it was more the *sensation* of his intentions rather than their crude articulation, such as we have had to record for you, that spurred him on to his final decision which, with his star carrying him, was to walk confidently in through the gate, along the pathway, push open the front door – which the happiness of the occasion left ever open – and . . .

[*Dance music! Screen lifts to reveal interior of the* WHITES' *house, guests dancing. On his way through the passage,* LOUIS *trips over a heap of coats, steadies himself by placing his hand into a large blanc-mange, draws back in horror and covers his coat with the white mess –*

*– in which state he finds himself drawn inexorably into the room where –*

*– guests see him and freeze.*

*And our hero seems to have recognized, with a chill of certainty, that he's about to embark upon one of the most mortifying episodes in his life.*]

END OF PROLOGUE

# ACT ONE

[*As at the end of the Prologue.*
*There is no longer need for* STEPHEN *to help keep the story going – it has its own inexorable momentum! Background has been established and now no 'plot' need hold up the rhythm of the disastrous wedding scene about to be enacted.*
*Inside the* WHITES' *house.*
*We see the passage, the stairs up, the area under the stairs, possibly the kitchen, or part of it.*
*The dividing doors between front room and dining room have been parted for the dancing. In the dining room area are set up trestle tables and the beginnings of 'the spread'.*
*The wedding scene. Frozen. Then –*]

KNOCKER: Well go t'hell! The master!
　　[*A buzz of mumbling 'Liftoff, Liftoff, Liftoff'.* LOUIS *smiles, weakly. Raises his arms.*]
LOUIS: Knocker White, don't you recognize me?
　　[*Silence.*
　　LOUIS *reaches for a paper serviette to brush away his accident. The mess is multiplied.*]
　　Blancmange! [*Another dead smile.*] You won't turn me out, will you? I mean even if you're not pleased to see me. [*An even deader smile.*] We-have-to-welcome-our-guests, don't we? [*Not even an attempt to smile.*] If I've stopped anything, interrupted, disturbed – please, I'll go away.
　　[KNOCKER *makes a dash to grab a chair which he plonks in the middle of the room.*]
KNOCKER: I'm sorry, Mr Liftoff – er – Litvanoff. Sit you on a chair, look.
　　[*Gratefully, though it's in the middle of the room, attached to nothing, to no one, he sits.*

*And he sits.*
*And he sits. Then –*]
Your coat.
[LOUIS *stands to be relieved of his coat, and again sits.*
*And sits.*
KATE *and* DAVID *enter from the kitchen – and freeze!*]

LOUIS: Just fancy, on my way home, a puncture, here, near here, on the way back from town. Shopping. With the housekeeper and their family. I took them out for the day. Do it frequently. Lunch, tea, pictures, the lot. [*Pause.*] Beautiful city, Norwich. [*Pause.*] The market. Those coloured stalls. Back streets. The Castle. [*Pause.*] The Cathedral. [*Pause.*] Bought a pair of wellingtons. For country walks.

KATE [*at last*]: Well, well, well! Mr Litvanov, how unexpected.
[DAVID *steps forward to end* LOUIS'S *lonely stand in limbo, and take him to another less conspicuous seat.*]

DAVID: And welcome. Bring yourself over here and be a bit more comfortable.
[*A grateful* LOUIS *allows himself to be led and now talks torrentially to relieve his tensions.*]

LOUIS: And then this puncture came and my chauffeur – Hoppy Johnson, you know, who helps me drive this old Ford I've got – he says 'I'll mend the puncture.' Because you know I'm useless with mechanical things. And while I wait I hear this music and I see these two men carrying big boxes of beer – these two, over there [*pointing*], am I right? And they talk and I hear the name 'Knocker White' and so I know, I guess at once, the wedding of one of my workers – there can't be two Knocker Whites. What could be nicer? Share his joy, drink his health, that's what friends are for, am I right? You can't *not* look in to drink a toast I say to myself. What sort of man would that be? He won't turn me out, pleased or not pleased, Knocker White won't do that. We have to welcome our guests. Excuse me, if I'm in the way I'll GO! [*He's suddenly aware that everyone is listening.*] I'm shouting, aren't I?

KATE: Knocker! The first thing you do is introduce your wife and then you offer Mr Litvanov a drink.
[KNOCKER, *who's stood holding* LOUIS'S *coat, thrusts it unceremoniously away, grabs* DAPHNE *and storms on his guest.*]

KNOCKER: This-is-my-wife-Daphne-what'll-you-have?

LOUIS: Of course we know each other, Miss –

DAPHNE: *Mrs* White.

LOUIS: Mrs White. Congratulations. I'll have a whisky, Knocker, and your wife must come and sit with me and point out who all the other guests are, and everyone must carry on as though I wasn't here.

[RINGO *seems to oblige. Very seriously he begins to catch flies, but creeping around the room, calling to them gingerly more as if they were cats.*]

RINGO: Here, bluebottle, bluebottle, bluebottle! Here, bluebottle!

MRS DAWSON *pulls him aside for a silent reprimand. It was not what* LOUIS *had intended.*]

LOUIS: Please. The music. Dance. Carry on dancing.

[*An attempt to regain balance is made. Pop music had been coming from a tape recorder which is again switched on.*]

DAPHNE: Well, you could've blowed me down with a feather. When I see you, you could've blowed me down with a feather.

DAVID: I'm sure everyone is delighted you've come, Mr Litvanov.

MR DAWSON [*to* MRS DAWSON]: Who *is* that?

MRS DAWSON: Thaas Liftemoff, what own the factory.

MR DAWSON: Who?

MRS DAWSON: Liftemoff!

LOUIS: Er – excuse me, it's Litvanov, Litvanov.

EMILY [*to* TOSH]: Did we invite the owner?

LOUIS: I'll stay for half an hour or so –

EMILY: Why didn't you tell me we invited the owner?

LOUIS: – then you can relax.

EMILY: I didn't know we invited the owner.

KATE: I'll get you some appetizers.

[KATE *moves to get a tray of 'canapés' from the other side of the room. On the way* KNOCKER *bumps into her and spills the whisky on her frock.*]

KATE: What fly – you bring down! What stand – you knock down! What's knocked down – you tread on!

[*In the confusion* KNOCKER *hands* LOUIS *the empty glass.*]

DAPHNE [*to* LOUIS]: Knocker hev this tendency to bump into things.

KNOCKER [*to* KATE]: Look at her.

DAPHNE: Or hev things bump into him.

KNOCKER: Ent she making a fool on herself?

DAPHNE: He trip and knock the vicar so's we nearly didn't hev anyone to bring us together.

KNOCKER: I bet she's making a right ole fool on herself.

[KATE *leaves him for the 'canapés'.*]

EMILY [*raising a glass*]: Would you do us the honour, Mr Liftoff, now you've come?

[LOUIS *raises empty glass,* KNOCKER *dives to fill new one.*]

Can't 'spect no big feasts like what you're used to, but a little ole drink, to the health o'bride and groom.

DAPHNE: Thaas already done a hundred times, look.

EMILY: No matters. Not by 'im it ent, and you be a little more respectful.

LOUIS: Now let's see, you're whose mother?

EMILY [*pointing to* TINKER]: His, sir. He's mine, and [*pointing to* TOSH] Knocker an' Kate are nephew an' nieces to him who be brother to their mother what's bin dead these last few years. She die of a broken heart she did, when their father die –

MRS DAWSON: She's off!

EMILY: – an' he die of cancer which were just the same as what his father afore him die of an' thaas no good saying it ent heredity 'cos I knowed it were an' you're not going to convince me otherwise 'cos look here, look, I had a friend what live up along side me an' she died –

TOSH: '*Course* she didn't wanna live a'ter he'd gone, their mother, she didn't, that she didn't. 'Tosh,' she say to me –

MRS DAWSON: Now he's off!

TOSH: – 'Tosh, I don't think I want t'go on anymore,' she say. 'I hed 'nough!' She'd made up her mind, see. Made it up, she hed. So she took to her bed, refused to eat an' just died. Like that. Two hours later the doctor he come an' he put a stethamething on her an' I ask him: 'Doctor, what you looking for? The woman's bin dead two hours, look.' But he didn't listen to me, no, he had to make sure hisself.

[*During all this* KNOCKER *has tried to hand over a new drink to* LOUIS. *The chattering defeats him, he drinks it himself!*]

KATE *has returned and moves in with 'canapés' to save a bamboozled* LOUIS.]

KATE: Now that you've honoured us this far, Mr Litvanov, you'll share our humble table, won't you?

RINGO [*piss-taking and mumbling his question here and there*]: Is ours a humble table?

LOUIS: U-uh-uh! No bullying, Kate.

RINGO: A humble table?

LOUIS: You know very well yours won't be a humble table.

RINGO: Ours, is it, a humble table . . .?

DAVID: No office quarrels, they'll not be understood, Mr Litvanov.

RINGO: . . . humble, humble, humble?

LOUIS: Well tell your girl-friend this is no time for silly sarcasms.

DAVID: She's not, alas, my girl-friend.

LOUIS: She's not, alas?

DAVID: Alas, not, proposition her though I have.

LOUIS: Then if you can be here, I can be here. What are you doing here anyway if you're not her boy-friend?

DAVID: I've been asked for moral support and by popular request.

LOUIS: And I'm neither moral support nor popular request I suppose?

KATE: Right!

LOUIS: Now that's rude, Kate. You know you'd've been very upset if I'd told you I walked right past your brother's wedding, wouldn't you?

KATE: I would, would I?

LOUIS: She never approves my decisions.

DAVID: I'm not sure it's your wisest decision.

KATE: You won't convince him.

LOUIS: On principle she never approves my decisions.

KATE: Once he's convinced – nothing! I've learned.

[TINKER *has been making faces at* DAPHNE *of the 'Oh-so-you're-mixing-with-the-hoi-polloi-now-are-you' sort. She's giggling.*]

LOUIS [*irritably*]: What are you laughing at, young woman?

DAPHNE: It's him, Mr Litvanov, look at 'im, the ole fool.

KATE: Daphne, stop it!

DAPHNE: Oh you don't wanna mind me, Mr Litvanov. Anything

make me giggle, and that Tinker White, he's their cousin you know, he tell me this funny story –

TINKER: Go on, tell 'im!

DAVID: Here we go.

KATE: Shut you up, Daphne. Mr Litvanov don't wanna hear no Tinker stories.

LOUIS: Of course I do. Where else would you want to tell stories if not at weddings? I'm listening. [*But with trepidation.*]

DAPHNE: Well, there was this field mouse, see, an' she've a date wi' her bor what live the other side o' the field, and she doll herself up for him, you know [*she titters*], lipstick an' powder an' special dress an' ribbon – an' then [*titters again*], an' then she go 'cross the field to her bor friend. But on the way [*tittering becomes less easy to control*], on the way she stumble right into a threshin' machine what was gathering the harvest an' she go in at one end [*long titters*], an' she get mauled an' scratched [*now* TINKER *joins in the laughter*] an' battered an' beaten, but she still go to her bor friend an' he open the door an' see her all bleedin' an' torn an' a right ole mess, an' he say [*she has great difficulty in getting the last part out*], he say – 'Blimey, gal [*great laughter*], blimey, gal,' he say, 'what happened to you?' An' she say [*now everyone except* KATE, LOUIS *and* DAVID *are laughing*], an' she say 'I – I – I bin REAPED!'

[*Everyone is convulsed.*]

LOUIS [*to* KATE]: I been what? [*She refuses to answer, then to* DAVID] What did she say, I been what?

DAVID: Reaped.

LOUIS: Reaped?

DAVID: When you gather in the harvest you call it reaping.

LOUIS: I know. So?

KATE: Leave it alone, for God's sake.

DAVID: The word 'reap' sounds like the word 'rape'. [*Blank.*] I wouldn't pursue it too hotly, Mr Litvanov. Just laugh.

LOUIS: Oh! Reaped! I see.

[*He laughs, loudly. But everyone else has finished. Silence. Embarrassment.*
*Suddenly –*]

MR DAWSON: You'll look after our children, 'ont you?

DAPHNE: My father.

MRS DAWSON [*loudly in his ear*]: Well, 'course he will, father.

DAPHNE: My mother.

MR DAWSON: I mean you're master and they be young and thaas not an h'easy life. Not afore and not now, no time. No matters what any on 'em say. Not an h'easy life.

MRS DAWSON: Don't you fret, father. 'Course he'll look after them.

MR DAWSON: Well thaas all right then, 'cos thaas none on it an h'easy life, an' –

MRS DAWSON: An' don't start goin' on an' on an' –

RINGO [*still piss-taking, as though working it out for himself*]: The word 'reap' sounds like the word 'rape'. Reap, like rape, Rape, rape. Reap reap.

[*The other young ones pick it up and chorus with him.*]
The word 'reap' sounds . . .

TOGETHER: The word 'reap' sounds like the word 'rape'.

MRS DAWSON [*taking over. To* LOUIS]: 'Course, they hed to hev their bachelor's night out. [*Shouting over to* KNOCKER] I said you hed to hev your bachelor's booze-up, didn't you? [*Back to* LOUIS] I said to Daphne I said, 'do you take a hold on him or you'll find him a sketch in the mornin'.' An' he were. Didn't I tell you, Daphne?

DAPHNE: They were so plastered, look, that even though they were round the corner in Flowerpot Lane they took the map out to find their way home.

TINKER: Plastered? Us plastered?

MRS DAWSON: Jimmy Leist went, Arthur Shanks went, John Jolly went, Ernie Holland, Harry Nunn, Eddie Bush, Herbie Kay, Dickie Pemberton, Arthur Calton, John Bally.

MR DAWSON: She know a lot o' people don't she?

DAPHNE: I reckon if they'd bin given the breathalyser the bugger'd've disintergrated.

MRS DAWSON [*to* DAPHNE]: Like your father. He once went on a shopping trip for me in an' old pony and trap an' stopped on the way to get so drunk, look, that he fell asleep at Long Stratton and when he woke up he didn't know whether he was goin' t'Norwich or 'ad just bin!

[*Silence.*]

LOUIS: What about this toast? I'm here to drink their health so why not now? And I'll do it Jewish style.

MRS DAWSON [*distantly*]: I met a Jew once.

LOUIS: Three whiskies, please.

MRS DAWSON: *I* didn't see narthin' wrong wi' him.

TOSH: Comin' up. [*Gives three glasses to* LOUIS.]

LOUIS: Good. So. First. I – er – I'm particularly, no – specially, yes, specially glad of this opportunity that I can express, that I may with this express thought – er – wish, as your employer, as your fellow worker, extend to you, the bride – the very pretty bride of this lucky man who will, no, who must – er – let's see now – who – er – [*gives up*] in short, your very many good healths for the future.

[LOUIS *quickly swallows first whisky to cover failure.*
*Silence.*]

DAVID [*rescuing*]: The bride!

EVERYONE: The bride!

[KATE *joins in but very half-heartedly, hating this circus.*]

LOUIS: And next I'm particularly – [*thinks twice*] – the groom!
[*Swallows second whisky.*]

DAVID: The groom!

EVERYONE: The groom!

LOUIS: And lastly [*desperately searches for another excuse to toast. Sees* EMILY.] – the mothers. No! in this case it's aunts, yes? And, of course, the bride's mother, I forgot the bride's got a mother – and so – mothers and aunts – that old generation of ladies we'll see no more, tough like we could never be. God bless them, I love them.
[*Downs third to mixed and bewildered murmurs of 'aunts', 'mothers', 'mothers and aunts', 'aunts and mothers'.*]

TOSH: You missed out the real mother, if you'll pardon the correction, Mr Litvanov.
[TOSH *reaches for a full glass of beer each, for the two of them.*]
She [*pointing to* KATE] be mother of this family. Keepin' us together, rememberin' birthdays, sortin' out tax claims, explainin' me to her, and her to him. She be the tough'n. Tough as any what we were, if not tougher. And we'll drink it Norfolk style. [*Hands* LOUIS *full pint of beer.*] Kathy, to her!

LOUIS: Of course. Miss White. How could we forget? Katherine!

EVERYONE: Katherine!

[TOSH *drinks his glass in one and urges* LOUIS *to do the same. While they drink –* EMILY, *a compulsive talker who doesn't really care if anyone's listening to her or not, will simply chatter on. Every so often we hear the beginning of her utterly inconsequential chattering which after the first seconds settles to become an inaudible background drone. One such begins now,* EMILY *addressing herself to whoever is nearest, they – ignoring her.*]

EMILY: Now you were talking about freezers, I'll tell you this: there's lots they say can be bagged up for freezers but you gotta know how t'do them. You have! My neighbour she've got one but she don't know how to bag up apples, she don't. She ask me! She ask me how to bag up apples an' I tell her . . . [*Drones on.*]

[LOUIS *finishes his long draught to round of cheers from youngsters.*]

LOUIS: Oh good God!

[*He's away! Eyes glowing. A pint in one. On top of three whiskies! Anything can happen.*]

Please. I beg you. Music. Dancing. You mustn't stop for me. It's a wedding. Dance. Sing.

[*The tape which had come to an end is now turned over.*]

DAPHNE: Oh excuse me, won't you? When I hear music I just gotta go.

[*She kisses a surprised* LOUIS *with a too wet and too familiar kiss on the lips. He takes out handkerchief to wipe away lipstick.* KATE *takes over.*]

KATE: And are her kisses sweeter than wine?

LOUIS: Why haven't you been helping me, Kate?

KATE: Did you need it, then?

LOUIS: She can be really cruel when she wants.

KATE: I'm not cruel. I'm pragmatic.

LOUIS: And I'm Jewish!

DAVID: Were those toasts really Jewish style?

LOUIS: No, but I needed three whiskies quickly.

KATE: Well now you've had them.

LOUIS: Look at her. Angry all the time. Just because I'm getting on with her family and friends.

KATE: Stop deceiving yourself.

LOUIS: Thinks the class-struggle goes on all the time.

KATE: Stop deceiving yourself and go home.

LOUIS [*hurt*]: I'm not deceiving myself and I won't go home till respects have been paid and you're proved wrong.

KATE: Louis, I'm warning you. You're a dear man, but don't depend on my affection to see you safely through social experiments with my family.

[*He kisses her, a defiant peck.*]

I'm issuing no safe-conduct passes.

LOUIS: She's beautiful when she's determined.

KATE: None!

LOUIS: Isn't she beautiful?

KATE: None!

LOUIS: Beautiful!

KATE: I'll go and lay the table for food. Mrs Dawson, we'll lay up, shall we?

MRS DAWSON [*to* MR DAWSON]: I'm goin' to lay up.

MR DAWSON: Lay who?

KATE: Aunt Emily, you and Uncle Tosh work on those serviettes.

[MRS DAWSON *follows* KATE, *who moves towards the kitchen just in time to be swept up into a dance by the swiftly entering* STEPHEN.]

STEPHEN: Sorry I'm late, shall we dance?

KATE [*dancing*]: How many times must I tell you not to use the side door?

STEPHEN: I want to feel one of the family.

KATE: And this is not a waltz.

MRS DAWSON: Who's he? I ent never seen him before.

STEPHEN: Kate and I went to school together to learn how to change the world. And who are you?

MRS DAWSON: Only the bride's mother, me.

STEPHEN: The bride's mother! Shall we dance?

[STEPHEN *dances away from* KATE *to sweep up* MRS DAWSON *in a dance. She protestingly whirls with him till he sees* LOUIS, *at which he stops dead.*]

I don't believe it.

[KATE *leaves him to figure that one out and takes off* MRS DAWSON *to lay up the food. Meanwhile,* KNOCKER, *who's retreated, glares at his wife, who's dancing closely with his cousin,* TINKER.]

KNOCKER [*to* TOSH]: See 'im.

TOSH: See who?

KNOCKER: 'Im. See 'im?

TOSH: I see 'im.

KNOCKER: Well look at 'im.

TOSH: He's your cousin, you look at 'im.

KNOCKER: Oh yes, I'm lookin' at 'im.

TOSH: Thaas all right then.

KNOCKER: Yes, I'm looking at *h*im all right. I see *h*im.

[STEPHEN *introduces himself to* LOUIS.]

STEPHEN: Excuse me, Mr Litvanov. I'm Stephen Bullock, friend of Kate's, reporter on the local press. Mind if I mention that you came to Knocker's wedding?

LOUIS [*relieved*]: Mind? Of course I don't mind. I'd like you to. Tell them – Louis Litvanov came to drink the health of one of his workers, uninvited, unprompted, came and sat among the guests, like one of them. Go ahead. My pleasure.

STEPHEN: I won't be using quite those words, but thank you.

LOUIS: Any words. Use any words. You know better than I how the reader thinks.

STEPHEN: None of us knows how the reader thinks. One of the reasons newspapers are always running opinion polls is that they don't know what the reader thinks.

DAVID: I thought journalists claimed to know –

STEPHEN: – nothing! We claim nothing except the moral right to expose those whose moral righteousness we suspect.

DAVID: And who, sir, will be left to expose your moral righteousness?

STEPHEN [*bouncing away*]: Ho, ho! Hum, hum! There's always the readers' letter column, isn't there?

[LOUIS, *who'd anticipated a longer interview, is abandoned in mid-flight.*]

LOUIS [*calling vainly after him*]: I say! What about –?

[*Every moment is undermined, seems menacing, unnerving.* DAVID *tries to help.*]

DAVID: Have you noticed Bonky Harris's painting on the wall?

LOUIS [*relieved once more*]: Ah! Bonky Harris!

[*They begin a tour of inspection.* RINGO, *showing a disquieting interest, follows respectfully behind as if to see what knowledge he can pick up.*]

Lovely colours. Good sense of colours. I bought some you know. Brighten up the home.

DAVID: Colours? You think he's colourful? Funny, I'd have thought colour wasn't his strong point.

LOUIS [*undermined*]: Wasn't?

DAVID: Atmosphere. Good atmosphere.

LOUIS: Atmosphere? [*Looking*] Ah! Yes.

DAVID: This lake with the trees. Very tranquil, don't you think?

LOUIS: Tranquil. Yes.

DAVID: Only look at the way he does reflections on water. It's more like a polished surface than a wet surface. Wet surfaces quiver more.

LOUIS: I see. [*Amazed his manager can talk about painting.*]

DAVID: Still, that's the charm of the primitive. As in this one here. Or that. Nice sense of shapes but no sense of textures.

RINGO [*to* LOUIS]: Nice sense of shapes but no sense of textures.

[DAVID *takes* LOUIS *out of range, back to his seat.*]

DAVID: Now sit there, Mr Litvanov. Relax. I promised to help Kate. I'll try not to leave you too long. [*Leaves.*]

[*Meanwhile,* RINGO *has beckoned* MARTIN *to look at the paintings. They go back over the tour.* LOUIS *anxious, overhearing, as they intend. As always in Norfolk the irony is dry, not raucous or savage.*]

RINGO [*to* MARTIN]: Nice sense of shapes, no sense of textures.

MARTIN ['*learning*']: Nice sense of shapes, no sense of textures.

RINGO [*moving on*]: Charm of the primitive.

MARTIN: Charm of the primitive.

RINGO [*moving on*]: Lovely atmosphere. Very tranquil.

MARTIN: Very.

[*Both turn to* LOUIS *and raise friendly glasses.*]

Glad to have you with us.

[LOUIS *acknowledges their greeting but is very alone. Nothing has happened quite as he'd fantasized. Every encounter stretches him on the rack of his foolish impulse.*

STEPHEN, *who can't take his eyes off* LOUIS, *approaches* KNOCKER. *Meanwhile –*

EMILY *at her serviettes, or whatever.*]

EMILY: Now you talk about transport. I can remember when it was all bicycles and buses. These days you need cars! You haven't got a car you can't get nowhere. You can stand waiting all you like an' no bus'll come an' pick you up. I know! I stood! You talk about transport . . .

[*Drones on.*]

STEPHEN [*to* KNOCKER]: How long has he been here?

KNOCKER: Come about half 'n hour ago.

STEPHEN: And *wasn't* he invited?

KNOCKER: No! That he weren't! Invited!

[MARTIN *and* RINGO *decide to approach* LOUIS.]

MARTIN [*to* LOUIS]: Good on you to come. [*Pally faces.*] I'm Martin Dawson. Daphne's brother. Soon get warmed up, won't we, Ringo?

RINGO: Yerp!

MARTIN: You got something wrong with your motor-bike, he'll take it to pieces and put it together again before you can say Louis Liftoff – er – vanov. [*Pause.*] Even though that *do* take a long time to say. Right, Ringo?

RINGO: Yerp.

MARTIN: He work in your factory, don't you, Ringo?

RINGO [*going after it*]: Here bluebottle, bluebottle, bluebottle.

MARTIN: Not me, though. Everyone work in shoes 'cept me. No shoe factory for me I ses. An' I tell Ringo he shouldn't waste time there neither, don't I, Ringo? More money on building sites. More money on building sites, Ringo, I keep telling. An' money count. Money count, don't it, Mr Liftoff?

[MAUREEN *has approached and is now sitting in* RINGO's *place.*]

MAUREEN: You boastin' o' your wage packet again, an' your ole buildin' sites again, an' your being cleverer than us again?

MARTIN: An' this be our Maureen, Ringo's girl-friend an' my sister.

MAUREEN: Hev 'ee bin showin' you photos o' his big manly body heavin' bricks an' pushin' cement yet?

MARTIN: She also work in your factory an' I tell her too, no money in shoes – 'cept for you, that is. I tell everyone, only they don't listen. 'Fact no one don't listen to narthin' I say. [*Pause.*] We all growed up together, see. Thick as thatchin'. Same village, same school, same school choir.

LOUIS: School choir?

MARTIN: Angels. We was angels.

LOUIS: Angels?

MARTIN: Only no one don't listen to narthin' I say.

MAUREEN: Come on, Ringo. Leave them ole bluebottles alone. I wanna dance.

MARTIN: Go an' dance wi' my ole sister, Ringo. Neglecting your woman! Won't do. Won't do, will it, Mr Liftoff?

RINGO [*moving away with* MAUREEN, *to* LOUIS]: Nice sense of shapes, no sense of textures!

MARTIN: Now, Mr Liftoff. How would you like to see an art exhibition? [*Takes* LOUIS *by the arm on a second 'tour'.*] Did you know this here mansion was an art gallery. Yes! Very high-class house our Knocker lives in.

LOUIS: Oh I know, I know. You see, young man –

MARTIN: Martin.

LOUIS: Martin. You see, the painter is one of my – er – he works in my factory.

MARTIN: In shit grow roses, they say.

LOUIS [*totally at a loss how to respond*]: They say that? Yes, well, of course – er – I was saying, Bonky's paintings, I even bought some.

MARTIN: Did you now?

LOUIS: Talent must be encouraged.

MARTIN: Must it now?

LOUIS: In workers. Encouraged. And by who if not the employer.

MARTIN: If not.

LOUIS [*not getting anywhere*]: Lovely atmosphere they've got.

MARTIN: Atmosphere? Don't know about that, but he can paint bricks.

LOUIS [*again undermined*]: Bricks?

MARTIN: Bricks. Look on 'em. You can tell he've had to build a wall some time or other. May only hev bin the wall in his garden but he've had a brick in his hand. You can tell it. [*Leaves* LOUIS. *Suddenly*] Soon warm up. [*More pally faces.*]

> [LOUIS, *again left alone, wanders back to his chair, until* —
> DAPHNE *and* TINKER, *exhausted, giggling, settle on either side of him, and sit, and sit, and sit.*
> *Meanwhile,* STEPHEN *grabs* MARTIN.]

STEPHEN: What's he done since he's been here?

MARTIN: Done?

STEPHEN: Done. Said. Happened. Since he's arrived?

MARTIN [*feeling* LOUIS *is threatened, defends him*]: He've drunk three toasts.

STEPHEN: Who to?

MARTIN [*raising his glass to* LOUIS *across the room*]: Bride, groom, and the mothers and aunts. Very good on him.

STEPHEN: What were you saying to him just now?

MARTIN: I tell him there's more money to be earned on building sites than in shoe factories.

STEPHEN: What'd he say to that?

MARTIN: Narthin'.

STEPHEN: Then?

MARTIN: Then I took him round the art gallery.

STEPHEN: And?

MARTIN: And he tell me he've bought some from Bonky Harris.

STEPHEN [*getting what he's been looking for*]: Boasted about that, did he?

> [KNOCKER, *his eye on what* DAPHNE *and* TINKER *are up to, takes a drink over to poor, abandoned* MR DAWSON.]

MR DAWSON [*taking drink*]: We got a thrashin' last week.

KNOCKER [*but looking at his wife*]: So I heard.

MR DAWSON: Couldn't double out.

KNOCKER: Yerp.

MR DAWSON: Played two of their worst darts players and we got a thrashin'.

KNOCKER: Yerp.

MR DAWSON: Couldn't double out, see!

> [*Meanwhile, the awkward silence between* DAPHNE, TINKER *and* LOUIS *is breaking.*]

TINKER: Shoes – them difficult things to sell, Mr Liftoff?

LOUIS: Excuse me, I don't really care what people call me but in fact the name is Litvanov. Russian. Not Liftoff but LIT-VAN-OV. Not difficult really.

TINKER: Liftemoff, yes. Well, you mustn't mind me. In Norfolk we soon find a handle for people. Me, I'm Tinker. Not much like Derek, is it? Derek's me real name, only they call me Tinker on account I always had lots o' gals an' I keep ringing them up, see? Ringling, tingling, Tinker? Here, your glass is empty.

DAPHNE: So 'tis. We'll soon change that won't we, Tinker, bor?

TINKER [*filling up* LOUIS's *glass*]: Shoes.

LOUIS [*confronted with another full pint glass*]: Shoes? Well, let's see. [*Pause.*] Everybody wears shoes.
[*Silence.*]

DAPHNE: Well thaas true 'nough. Everybody wear shoes, Tinker.

TINKER: Yes, they do. Everybody do that.
[LOUIS *catches sight of* KNOCKER *glaring at them.* KNOCKER *backs away, falls into an armchair near* MR DAWSON *and in which lies* LOUIS's *coat still, and drops tray. The clatter disturbs* MR DAWSON.]

MR DAWSON: Blast bor! There you go again. There ent never no tellin' where you'll end up. [*Directly at* KNOCKER] I say there ent never no telling where you'll end up.

DAPHNE: Well hang it up, Knocker. [*Pause.*] Go on. [*Pause.*] SHOO!
[KNOCKER *flees.*]

TINKER: Daphne! You shouldn't be leaving your employer to drink beer – that's for the proles. Whisky! Get the man some whisky as befits his station in life.

LOUIS: I didn't come here to drink you know. It wasn't my intention to –

TINKER: Thaas all right, thaas all right, my mannie.
[*At the other end of the room, where* KATE *and* MRS DAWSON *are laying out food, have collected a knot of* STEPHEN, DAVID *and* KNOCKER.]

KNOCKER [*who's just turned off the tape*]: Well he've done it, ent 'ee, eh? He've really put the last touch to my matrimonial festivications, that 'ee 'ave.

MRS DAWSON: You should be proud, Knocker. That ent everyone has 'is boss come to 'is wedding.

STEPHEN: There's not everyone has a boss so presumptious.

KNOCKER: Proud? They're gettin' 'im drunk in there! Anythin' can happen. But she don't care. [*Indicating* KATE] She's his pet an' she's laughin'.

KATE: She's not his pet and she's not laughin' and you listen to me. You're on your own now, bor. I made you this weddin', I'm leavin' you this house, but you're host. That ent my fault he've come but he have come, so you be civilized and look after him and learn to take your own decisions. There ent no more *I* can do for you.

KNOCKER: I'll lose my job, you see.

KATE: I sometimes wonder we're in the same family.

KNOCKER: There's men out of work an' women ten a penny. Who'll pay the mortgage then?

DAVID: You won't lose your job, Knocker, don't be an ass. But he's right, Louis is getting drunk. He shouldn't be left.

STEPHEN: He's a pompous ole fool. What in hell does he imagine he's doin' any road?

DAVID: Kathy, use your wits.

KATE: What wits do I have left? Wouldn't have happened ten years ago. But we fought to change the times and the times they've changed! We kept saying we're equal to any man! Right? Some've been listening and now they've come to eat at our table to prove it and we're going to be gracious about it. [*Pause.*] For as long as we can. [*Pause.*] We'll keep our creepy, crawly spites and envies to ourselves, shall we? Please?

STEPHEN: What you looking at me for?

KATE: We went to school together to change the world, remember? So I know you, Stephen.

STEPHEN: Poor Kate, straddling two worlds. In love with both, and none of you in either, is there, my love?

MRS DAWSON: Well I don't know what all you clever people is on about but I do know I'm the bride's mother an' there ent no one takin' a blind bit o' notice o' me. There ent no one bin bothered to introduce me to him nor narthin'.

KATE: We've all been a bit put out, Mrs Dawson. Once we're sittin' eatin' it'll be better, look.

MRS DAWSON: So you say, my gal, so you say. But I reckon I bin made a fool on, that I do. You took over all the arrangements for the weddin' an' I weren't asked about narthin' an' I bin quiet all this time but I hevn't bin any too happy about what's bin happenin' no! that I hevn't. All the cookin' *you* done. All the invitations *you* sent out –

KATE: There weren't anyone to invite. All our family is dead, you don't speak to yours – who's left?

MRS DAWSON: No matters. I should've bin asked. An' now he've come an' I'm left lookin' like a bloody skivvy.

[DAVID, STEPHEN *and* KNOCKER *try, discreetly, to disappear.*]

Yes, that's right, you go my mannies – bloody little mice.

[LOUIS *is high in conversation with* TINKER. *Others have gathered round.*]

LOUIS: What's an employer's responsibility? To provide work and not care about his employees? That's all? I say no! I say an employer's got to show an interest in his workers. The days of fighting between management and labour are past.

TINKER: Well I'm impressed to hear it, 'cos thaas what I say too. Workers is men like others an' no one should push them around. There's unions an' there's rights an' no one's gonna tell me to do things I don't want.

MARTIN: You ent got much choice bein' in the army hev you, bor?

TINKER: Thaas different. Thaas a question of discipline. Everyone know you gotta hev discipline. Besides, I volunteered for the army. My own free choice. No one pushed me into it. I chose.

MARTIN: Well there you are then.

TINKER: There you are, 'what' then?

MARTIN: Thaas what I say. You chose once, now you can't choose!

TINKER: Bit monosyllabic your brother ent 'ee?

MARTIN: We all choose once, then we can't choose no more. We give ourselves up to discipline. In factories, offices, everywhere.

LOUIS: Don't make it sound like God, young man. Employers have their disciplines as well. Employers, unions! Balance of forces!

RINGO: Here bluebottle, bluebottle. Here bluebottle.

LOUIS: What *are* you chasing?

RINGO [*to* MARTIN]: Did you notice there was funny grating under where they stood for the ceremony?

TINKER: Lots o' rings fall down there, bor.

RINGO: What's it for?

TINKER: Parson always carries a spare. Grooms shake so. Ring can't reach the finger, see. [*Shows shaking hand.*]

MARTIN: That grating, my lad, is where the groom can dump the bride if he changes his mind at the last minute.

RINGO: Here bluebottle, bluebottle. Here bluebottle.

MARTIN: Flies. He catches them, trains them an' sells them, you know?

[*But* LOUIS *doesn't know. Is blank.* RINGO *sees* KNOCKER *gloomily alone.*]

Knocker! Come on, lad, join us.

[*He refuses to budge.*]

LOUIS: What's wrong with you? It's your wedding isn't it?

KNOCKER: Beginnin' to wonder, I am. I'm really beginnin' to wonder.

LOUIS: So join us.

[KNOCKER *sulkily moves forward.*]

Knocker, Knocker, Knocker. Look at you. You feel uneasy I'm here, eh? But I understand. What can you do when your boss suddenly comes to your wedding? You feel you need a special behaviour because he must be a special kind of boss who can find the time to come to an employee's wedding and sit and drink and talk naturally. Of course, I know other bosses come to their employees' weddings but – they just pop in, kiss the bride, pop out. Would it be easier if I were that kind of boss? Is that what you're thinking? In, out, quick? [*Affectionately*] Knocker, Knocker, Knocker. You all got funny names. Tosh –

[EMILY '*descends*'.]

EMILY: You talk about Tosh and his eating?

LOUIS: Tinker –

EMILY: 'You hev sandwiches all day,' I tell 'im –

LOUIS: Knocker –

EMILY: 'Get you that inside you,' I say, 'you want something hot when you come home!'

LOUIS: Knocker, Tinker, Tosh!

EMILY: He complain but I tell 'im, 'Tosh you get that inside you . . .'

LOUIS: Funny names!

MAUREEN: You know what I'm called?

LOUIS: No, what're you called?

MAUREEN: Skirts.

LOUIS: Skirts?

MAUREEN: Skirts Dawson, on account I like showin' my legs.

[*To a slow 'woooah' she draws up her skirt to show a leg.* LOUIS *is embarrassed.*]

DAPHNE [*during the 'woooah'*]: Maureen Dawson, stop that, blame fool! Drawin' attention to yourself. Blame fool!

MAUREEN [*with Slavic passion*]: I WANT MUSIC!

KNOCKER [*to* MAUREEN]: You do that too often I'll be sacked and he'll hev a heart attack!

[*She ignores him and switches on tape. The crowd disperses leaving* LOUIS *alone again.*

*The deaf old man,* DAWSON, *passes by.*]

MR DAWSON: 'Course, them used to be rough ole times, the ole days. My father, he used to flog me when he were riled, used to flog me an' then used to cry a'ter he'd done it, used t'cry. [*Pause.*] Never flogged *my* chil'un, though. But them's still rough ole times. *I* can't see no improvement, no, I can't. They keep tellin' me there is an' maybe there is, but I can't see it. There's none on it gotten a great deal better.

[*He wanders off, leaving* LOUIS *again in mid-air.*

*Then, for no reason, except presumably taking advantage of* LOUIS'*s philosophy that all men are equal,* MARTIN *makes another of his faces and screams a loud 'cock-a-doodle-doo' into* LOUIS'*s face.*

LOUIS *jumps, uncertain whether to be angry or not.*]

LOUIS: Now that's not nice. That's taking liberties. I didn't like that at all.

[*But* MARTIN *does it again and others take it up in merriment.*

LOUIS *offers a weak smile and a weak 'cock-a-doodle-doo' of his own.*

*But* MAUREEN *saves him.*]

MAUREEN: Wanna dance? Come on, Mr Litvanov. I'll show you how.

LOUIS: I'm not very good at this you know.

MAUREEN: Ent narthin' to it. Make it up for yourself. Just hop, jump, sway, twist – anythin' anyhow.

[*Slowly at first, self-consciously, but gaining confidence, he tries.*]
Smile, then, thaas not a funeral.

LOUIS: I'm concentrating.

MAUREEN: Relax, loosen up, flop.

[*He tries to do just that. Then, to his horror, he realizes that* MAUREEN *is swaying seductively and slowly sliding her skirt up to reveal a suggestively rotating pelvis.*]

MAUREEN: Thaas right. Very good. Good boy. Yes. Mmmm!

LOUIS [*stopping*]: Stop that. No. Really. That's not nice. Stop it. Stop doing that.

KATE: THE FOOD IS READY!

[*He's saved and everyone moves to help arrange the half-laid-up tables.*]

EMILY: Tinker! Get these tables away from the walls. You and Martin get hold on this one. You and Stephen or someone get hold of this other one.

[*Now follows a set of 'table-setting' lines. Other lines in other productions may be needed instead of, or additional to, these. They should be discovered in an ad-libbing situation but once found should be firmly planted and uttered as bold text.*]

KATE: Mr Dawson, can you get me a couple of chairs from the kitchen?

MRS DAWSON [*to* STEPHEN *and* DAVID]: Will you put that little table down here.

KATE [*anxiously*]: Not you, Knocker. Don't you touch the tables.

KNOCKER: OK, I'll get the chairs from upstairs.

STEPHEN: Which way does it go?

DAVID: Bottom of a 'T' – this way, I think.

TINKER: Where does the big table go?

KATE: That's the top of the 'T' – with the four best chairs.

KNOCKER: I got three chairs here.

DAPHNE: You would have to carry three! Why can't you carry two at a time?

KNOCKER: I can manage. [*Drops one.*]

DAPHNE: So I see!

KNOCKER: Who needs these chairs?

TINKER: Give me one before you break them.

KNOCKER: I got two chairs here.

MARTIN: I'll take one.

KNOCKER: I got one chair here.

[*No one calls for it so he places it himself. In the midst of this re-shuffling,* BONKY HARRIS *appears with a painting.*]

MARTIN [*standing on a chair*]: The artist himself to honour us.

KATE: Why, Bonky! You said you couldn't come.

BONKY: No more couldn't I. The wife's still queasy but her mother's there to sit awhile so I brought over this wedding present.

[DAPHNE *goes up to take it from him.*]

DAPHNE: Oh, Bonky! Thank you. [*Kisses his cheek.*] Look everyone! Bootiful, ent it? [*Holds it up to them. Everyone applauds.*]

RINGO [*to* DAVID]: Nice sense of shapes, no sense of textures!

LOUIS: What a touching wedding present. Very original. Look at that house. You can tell you've handled bricks at some time in your life, eh?

BONKY [*incredulous to see him there*]: Never! Never touched a brick in my life, Mr Litvanov.

[LOUIS, *again undermined, is also ignored while* BONKY *is fussed over as* LOUIS *wasn't.*]

KATE: Stay and eat with us, Bonky.

BONKY: I can't, Miss White, honestly.

KATE: I'm Kate in this house and I insist.

MARTIN: We all insist. Here's a chair, Maureen! Another plate and things.

MRS DAWSON: There's plenty of food, look, plenty of it.

KATE: That's settled.

EMILY: You can eat and then you can go, so long as you eat first.

KATE: Come on now, settle everyone. Mr Litvanov, will you sit in the centre here? Be the guest of honour?

[*Turn to* LOUIS. *But in the general melée it hasn't been noticed that he's put on his coat.*]

LOUIS: Now really, it wasn't my intention to impose on you – not eat as well as to –

EMILY: Thaas not what you might call a banquet but it's wholesome an' plentiful an' you're welcome.

MRS DAWSON: Now then, Mr Liftoff, I'm the gal Daphne's mother an' I say you're very welcome to share with us our daughter's celebration. Had us knowed you was comin' we'd've laid on something special, I'm sure, but howsomever we've not done badly for ourselves so do you take you your seat in the middle an' we'll begin. [*Pulls out chair for him.*] If you please, sir.

[KATE, *feeling she's perhaps overdone her stern reproach, extends a friendly, reassuring arm of 'peace', and takes his coat.*]

LOUIS [*relieved somewhat*]: In that case it'll be a privilege to join you.
[*General approval.* TOSH *appears.*]

TINKER: Where *you* bin?

TOSH: I reckoned with an important guest like the one we got it's only right to have a little champers.

TINKER: How far you reckon thaas gonna go, Poppy?

TOSH: That ent for you for a start. This here's so's we can do the right thing by the bride an' groom an' the guest of honour. Watch out! [*Pops bottle.*]

TINKER: You don't pour champagne into beer glasses, dad.

KNOCKER: Well we ent got no champagne glasses so shut you up.

DAPHNE: Oh, real champagne!

KNOCKER: Don't say it like that – haven't I ever bought you the stuff?

DAPHNE: You! You did your courting on a single gin or half o' bitter.

KNOCKER: Now thaas not fair, Daphne Dawson.

DAPHNE: White – remember?

KNOCKER: Daphne White. You give people the wrong impression about me.

LOUIS: Another toast, then. To the happy couple.

TINKER: I can't stand this. What sort of toast is that with only three on you able to drink the stuff? No one's gonna say I was ever mean. I'm gonna buy a coupla more o' these.

LOUIS: Good idea, Tinker. Here, buy two for me. No, four – make it six!

[*He peels off four £5 notes from a big bundle.* KATE *glares,* DAVID *winces.* STEPHEN *smiles.*]

EMILY: Oh, we're going to have such a lovely time, real posh.

MRS DAWSON: Well, I think we oughtn't to forget it's Mr Liftoff here what caused it. So I've got a toast also – Mr Liftoff!

EVERYONE: Liftoff! Liftoff!

KNOCKER [*loud whisper*]: LITVANOV! LITVANOV!

LOUIS: Thank you. Now, no more formalities or I'll feel guilty for coming. Let's eat.

[*Everyone tucks in.*]

Mmm! Who made this beef?

DAPHNE [*nodding towards* KATE]: Her!

MARTIN [*to whoever is near him*]: Glad thaas not lamb.

DAPHNE: She do everything.

MARTIN: 'Cos I'd've bin sick.

DAPHNE: She go away to all them foreign places an' she come back wi' strange, newfangled ideas for food.

MARTIN: I pass by lambs every day an' they smell.

MRS DAWSON: 'Course, anyone can make a thing if they hev the mind an' time.

MARTIN: I can see pigs up to *here* in shit an' I can still eat them, but lambs smell so.

MRS DAWSON: No one don't ever complain about *my* Sunday joint.

MARTIN: I *should* really *like* eating sheep 'cos they're so stupid, but –

DAPHNE: But Knocker 'ont get no fancy stuff from me though, not that I can see 'im eatin' half-done beef anyways.

KNOCKER: No, it'll be fish an' chips or Kentucky Fried Chicken from little boxes for us.

DAPHNE: Knocker White, I don't ever eat fish an' chips from boxes. I make it. 'Sides, even if we did it'd be 'cos I'm out workin' an' such.

[KNOCKER *in his agitation is eating quickly and reaching out wildly for this and that and exchanging anxious, resentful or apologetic looks with* LOUIS.]

KATE [*loudly*]: Mr Dawson. You're not eating.

[MR DAWSON, *at the other end of the table, sits before an empty plate.*]

MR DAWSON: What she say?

MRS DAWSON: She say eat up, look.

MARTIN: Every time you talk, look, you miss a mouthful.

MR DAWSON: What'd he say?

MRS DAWSON: You ent eating.

MR DAWSON: Tell her there ent narthin' I recognize.

[MRS DAWSON *ignores her husband and fills up his plate.*

LOUIS *points to the new painting that's been leant against the wall.*]

LOUIS: Now *that* painting, Bonky, you may never have laid bricks, but that new painting has atmosphere. You've got real talent, believe me.

BONKY: Atmosphere, Mr Litvanov?

LOUIS: Yes. Er. Atmosphere. You paint good shapes. [*But he's not really confident any longer.*]

BONKY: Don't know about shapes, Mr Litvanov, I just paint the earth.

LOUIS: Earth?

BONKY: Earth! In everything, ent it? Everything you touch –

MARTIN: Earth!

RINGO [*musically, as though joining in a search for the right note. High*]: Earth! [*Low*] Earth!

MAUREEN [*middle*]: Earth!

[*All the young ones take it up. A game but – a raucous noise.*]

LOUIS [*silencing them*]: Now seriously, everybody, seriously. You do like your jokes about everything, don't you? Let's hear what Bonky has to say. Bonky?

BONKY [*slowly, shyly*]: Well. I love earth. That's all. I mean – everything you use in this world comes from the earth. Your own self comes from the earth, don't it? The water you drink comes from the earth. The food you eat in some shape or form, the bricks you use, the tools you use, the wood you use, the match you use, the chairs you sit on, they all come from the earth. [*Pause.*] And when you die – you go back there. Don't you? [*Silence.*] I mean – don't you?

[*Then, at last, the youngsters seem to have found the right note, and a sweet chord rises, as if the table is singing; comes, dies away, to the old ones' 'mms' and 'aahs'. Till –*

KNOCKER, *whose agitation never really subsides, rises to reach for a sauce bottle and knocks a glass of champagne over* LOUIS, *who jumps up.* KATE, MRS DAWSON *and* EMILY *all jump up with him.*]

MRS DAWSON: Knocker, you clumsy oaf, Mr Liftoff's expensive suit ruined. I'm sorry, Mr Liftoff.

LOUIS: LITVANOV!

MRS DAWSON: Liftemoff, yes. Now don't you fret, we'll have it

cleaned, the firm's expense. That ent too bad. Knocker, you're a
real burden.

KATE: Don't get excited, Mrs Dawson. I'll get a cloth.

LOUIS: Please, sit down. It's all right. It's only a suit.

STEPHEN: I'm sure Mr Litvanov has many suits.

[TINKER *returns.*]

TINKER: Here she is, my lovelies. A crate of the best. Martin, you
open up one. Knocker, you struggle with another. Ringo, one for
you. And Mr Litvanov, you must be used to this – one for you.
I'll pop this beauty.

KATE: Please, now let's eat and get it over with or it'll be time to go
before we start.

TINKER [*to* MR DAWSON]: Champagne, look.

MR DAWSON: What?

TINKER: Champagne.

MR DAWSON: What?

TINKER: CHAMPAGNE!

[*The bottles go 'pop, pop', the glasses clink, the voices rise in sounds of
real pleasure, and –*]

THE FIRST ACT ENDS

# ACT TWO

[*Post-banquet torpor.*
*The dishes are washed. The left-over food placed on the trestle table now lying along the wall to make more room.*
*The tape is low.* DAPHNE *dances with* TINKER. KATE *with* DAVID. MAUREEN, RINGO *and* MARTIN *sitting it out, listening, sprawled. All are in various stages of drunkenness and watched by a sober and miserable* KNOCKER.
*In a corner sits* MR DAWSON, *deaf to everyone, if not asleep. Sitting beside him, eyes closed, is his wife singing an old song, totally at odds with the taped music.* KNOCKER *moves to them.*]

KNOCKER [*to* MRS DAWSON]: Ent that time you took him home?
MRS DAWSON [*singing*]: And though I grow too old to dream,
  Your song will live in my heart.
  Kiss me and then, until we meet again . . .
    [KNOCKER *moves to where his aunt,* EMILY, *is ecstatically and with glazed eyes watching the dancing and clapping her hands out of rhythm with the music.*
    *From the kitchen comes the sound of an argument between* STEPHEN *and* LOUIS.]
STEPHEN: You don't know how the other half lives.
LOUIS: I *was* the other half!
KNOCKER: No one don't think o' me, do they?
EMILY: Oh, Knocker, thaas a lovely wedding.
KNOCKER: What about me, though?
    [*She is beyond caring.*
    STEPHEN *and* LOUIS *stumble through from the kitchen. To* KNOCKER'S *consternation they're quarrelling violently. Both are very drunk.*
    TOSH *is struggling with a last bottle of champagne.* BONKY *is sitting, melancholic and drunk, near by.*]

165

LOUIS: And how do you imagine I started? You think *my* parents had money?

TOSH: Here she comes.

LOUIS: Fill me up. So don't tell me I don't know about workers and hardship and how the other half lives.

STEPHEN: That's not my point.

BONKY: I mean, everything come from the earth, don't it?

LOUIS: I know what your point is.

STEPHEN: Workers' control that's what my point is.

BONKY: Your own self come from the earth.

LOUIS [to STEPHEN]: I know, I know! Think I'm a fool? I can't follow a dialectical argument?

STEPHEN: Workers' control, not to be confused with silly ole participation.

LOUIS: Well, I'm not a fool. I was debating things like that when you were a twinkle in your mother's eye.

STEPHEN: My father's. I studied business management.

LOUIS: While I actually managed business.

STEPHEN: And I've studied reports on participation experiments.

LOUIS: While I actually carried out those experiments.

STEPHEN: And I've studied –

BONKY: I've studied rocks. Earth! It's all earth.

STEPHEN: I've studied –

LOUIS: And did you study how two thousand workers can *each* have a say in how to manage a large factory? Did you do that?

STEPHEN: I know –

LOUIS: You know nothing.

STEPHEN: Oh yes I do.

LOUIS: Oh no you don't.

STEPHEN: I do!

LOUIS: You don't!

STEPHEN: I do! And if you'd stop going on so much and didn't commandeer the bloody discussion I might be allowed to make my point.

KNOCKER [*trying to pull* STEPHEN *away*]: Why must you always go an' start quarrels?

STEPHEN: Now you keep your hands off me, Knocker White, 'cos you know nothing.

KNOCKER: If you write about any o' this in your newspaper I'll –

STEPHEN: You'll what?

KNOCKER: Never mind what I'll do, you just don't, thaas all.

BONKY: Everything at your wedding, Knocker, all on it, come from the earth . . .

LOUIS: And another thing, young man, another thing.

STEPHEN: What other thing?

LOUIS: I don't like the way you talk to me.

STEPHEN: Ah ha! There we have it. That's it.

LOUIS: No respect.

STEPHEN: I knew you'd give yourself away if I just let you carry on, Mr Liftoff.

LOUIS: And you call me by my right name. You know it, don't you? It's Litvanov, L–I–T–V–A–N–O–V. Litvanov.

STEPHEN: Yes, Mr Liftoff, that's what you'd really like, wouldn't you? No answering back.

LOUIS: That's distortion. I didn't say that –

STEPHEN: Know thy place.

LOUIS: Always win by distortions.

STEPHEN: *That's* what *you* call respect.

LOUIS: What am I doing sitting here talking to a little fool like this for? [*Tries to stand but finds his legs unsteady.*] Oh my God, no. No! How did *this* happen?

[*Tries to stand once more and fails.*

STEPHEN, *to press his point even more, shows he can not only stand but can mount a chair from which he continues.*]

STEPHEN: Yes, Mr Liftoff. We can see you'd like us just to love you –

[KNOCKER *shifts uselessly between them, threatening* STEPHEN *and pacifying* LITVANOV.]

KNOCKER: I'm sorry, Jesus, I'm sorry, Mr Litvanov. [*To* STEPHEN] An' you shut up, get down an' get out.

STEPHEN: You came here to court popularity, didn't you? Good ole Liftoff. Just one of the boys.

LOUIS: I said remember who you're talking to, young man.

STEPHEN: I'm talking to you and I'm not a young man. You spoilt everyone's enjoyment. Do you know that? You came, they *had* to buy champagne, and then you humiliated them by buying not one but six bottles yourself. Good ole Liftoff, yes. I'll write about you all right. This wedding and you. The event of the year. One of the boys . . . [*But the effort is too much and he comes crashing down, throwing his drink over* LOUIS *on the way.*]

KNOCKER [*rushing to dry his employer*]: Oh, my sainted aunts. Take no notice on him, Mr Litvanov, leave him now. [*But his employer pushes him away.*] Well, come you out to my sister an' the others then.

[LOUIS *struggles to take control of himself. The sight of* STEPHEN *stretched out on the floor helps restore some of his dignity. He does up his collar and tries to straighten his tie.* KNOCKER *attempts to help him.*]

LOUIS: Get the hell out of it, you. You've been no help right from the start.

KNOCKER: I know what, Mr Litvanov, Bonky Harris's paintings! You like his paintings, don't you? We got them all over the house. Kathy had 'em framed. I'll show 'em you.

LOUIS: Paintings? [*Savagely*] I hate paintings.

[BONKY *sadly rises at this and moves away, out of the room.* LOUIS *stretches his arms out in apology, but too late. Now angrily he struggles to put on his jacket.* KNOCKER *attempts to help, and with his employer resisting and pushing him away, a minor lunatic battle ensues. Still, poise is regained, of a fashion, and with a smile* LOUIS *staggers into the other company.*

KATE, *tipsy herself, has now grown used to the situation.*]

KATE: Ah, our guest of honour. We bin neglectin' him. Louis, come here.

TINKER: Louis? Ah! Looooouis! Welcome back, Louis.

[*Everyone mockingly picks up the name and calls it out at varying levels of the harmonic scale.*]

Come on, Louis, take your jacket off. Tape's finished. Besides, the neighbours, noise you know, so we sorta gotta 'muse ourselves.

[KATE *unbuttons* LOUIS's *jacket. Their faces are close together.*]

KATE: Enjoyin' yourself Louis?

LOUIS: Not 'Louis', Kate, have pity.

KATE: So, you want to get on with my family, do you?

LOUIS: I wish I could be sick.

KATE: It's a family only a member of which could love.

LOUIS: What you unbuttoning me for?

KATE: Not even I ever really got a foothold in it.

LOUIS: Don't unbutton me, I'm going home.

KATE: Look at this house. All my life, my home.

LOUIS: What you loosening my tie for?

KATE: But what of me do you see in it?

LOUIS: Don't loosen my tie, I'm going home.

KATE: What – what of me?

LOUIS: I wish I could be sick.

[TINKER *from behind whips off his jacket.*]

TINKER: Now then, friends, party games! Thaas forbid to dance so we're left to our own natural resources.

LOUIS [*trying to put his jacket on again*]: I must go now. Please. You've been very hospitable, all of you. Not my intention to stay and intrude – and outstay – by intrusion – my welcome – must say – goodnight – [*But he can't make it and staggers collapsing into a chair.*]

TINKER: Ringo, give us a hand.

[*They lift* LOUIS *in his chair and set it to one side.*]

DAVID [*to* KATE]: I don't think we should let this go on you know, Kate.

KATE: Well, I think we should 'let this go on you know, Kate'. The lesson will 'enrich' his character.

DAVID [*warning*]: People who play God are . . .

TINKER: Now sit there, me ole son an' we'll show you a game we play in these parts, an' when we've done one round you'll join in, right? [*Pause.*] Yes, well, you'll be all right in a second or two, never fear, my mannie. Now –

BONKY [*returning, presumably from the lavatory*]: Earth! The water you drink comes from the earth –

[STEPHEN, *recovered, staggers around with a soda syphon in his hands. He's douching himself with it.*]

STEPHEN: Look! Lovely! Refreshing! I'm awake all over again.

[*He squirts some at* DAPHNE *who giggles, and then at* TINKER *who's less amused.*]

TINKER: Now cut that out, ole son, we're going to play games.

STEPHEN: I am playing games. [*Turning to* LOUIS] Now here's a man who needs waking up.

[*He's about to squirt soda at* LOUIS *but* KNOCKER, *who's been keeping a wary eye open, rushes in the way and takes the blast.* DAVID *steps forward to take the syphon away.*]

KATE: All right. Enough now. It's time to go home.

KNOCKER: You bin dyin' to do that all evenin' haven't you?

KATE: Mrs Dawson, your husband's asleep, look.

KNOCKER: I see you. I watched you. You done it – now you go home. This party's finished for you.

KATE: Uncle Tosh, look at Aunt Emily.

STEPHEN: The little men rise up at last –

[KNOCKER, *though smaller, rushes to hoist the drunk* STEPHEN *in a fireman's lift. The action is greeted with cheers – except from* KATE.]

KATE: Put him down, Knocker White, this instant, now – put him down.

KNOCKER: This is my house, you tell me? Right – I'm making the decisions then, startin' from now, an' this is my first decision. He be your friend? Now you take him to *your* home.

[KNOCKER *wants to carry* STEPHEN *to the front door but has lost his sense of direction and is swinging and staggering about in all directions. This enables* STEPHEN *to retake the soda syphon and fire his weapon in a swinging circle at everyone.*

*Pandemonium! Which is increased as* KATE *and* DAVID *try to pull him down – which battling quartet lumbers on through the passage.*

*But* KATE *and* DAVID *have to reach for their coats which leaves* STEPHEN, *still on* KNOCKER's *shoulder, free to pick up the syphon again and squirt it on* KNOCKER's *backside.* KNOCKER *staggers so far back into the room that he's even able to squirt it, finally, over* LOUIS, *before he's dumped in the street and wanders off, chanting –*]

STEPHEN: I woke him up, I woke him up, I woke him up.

KATE [*rushing back into room to* LOUIS]: Don't go. I'm coming back. [*To* KNOCKER] If it weren't for Litvanov I'd let you finish this party on your own, Knocker White, and not bother coming back. [*She and* DAVID *go off.*]

KNOCKER [*calling after them*]: Well, were it my fault? Did I invite the master? Did I make him stay?

[*Nevertheless, he's quite pleased with his feat and returns in triumph to the company.*

*The women are tidying up, men putting chairs and bottles away.*
TINKER *is attentive to* LOUIS.]

LOUIS: My jacket, I want my jacket.

TINKER: Your jacket, ole son? You want your jacket? You shall have it. His jacket, where's Mr L's jacket?

[*But* LOUIS *has already succeeded in putting it on.*]

TINKER: Why, you've got it on, my mannie. You got me all confused, look it's on you.

LOUIS: Oh yes, well, that's kind of you, you're a good man, very kind.

TINKER [*helping*]: Thaas right, you button yourself up an' sit there an' it'll all be civilized again, you see. We're going to have a nice party an' we're goin' to send you away with good impressions and pleasant memories.

[*Seated,* LOUIS *now sinks into reverie to sort out this mess.*]

LOUIS: That's what I came for, pleasant memories –

RINGO [*draped over a chair, dreamily*]: I think Litvanov's right.

LOUIS: – to wish you all good health, show I'm human, you're human, everyone's human –

RINGO: I think he's right – very praiseworthy, Litvanov.

LOUIS: – good intentions, pleasant memories, human contact –

RINGO: An' very noble 'tis, too, Mr Litvanov.

LOUIS: You're very kind to me, I'm very grateful.

RINGO: Very praiseworthy, Litvanov is, very praiseworthy indeed.

LOUIS [*woken, irritated*]: What the hell's the matter with him? He silly or something? You silly or something?

TINKER: Now you don't wanna take any notice of Ringo there.

LOUIS [*still exploding at* RINGO]: I mean even mockers get tired of their own voice.

TINKER: He's only a boy.

LOUIS [*calming down, returning to reverie*]: Yes, I know, only a boy. I mean – what I want to say was – was –

[*Long pause. Everyone waits.* LOUIS *is very drunk.*]

– not one of you love me, do you? Not one. Whereas me – I – I love you all – and – and –

[*Acute embarrassment.*]

BONKY: The food you eat in some shape or form, the bricks you use,

the tools you use, the wood you use, the match you use, the chairs
you sit on – they all come from the earth. [*Pause.*] Don't they?
[*Silence.*]

TINKER: Now then, everyone – the shoe game.

KNOCKER [*confidently*]: Oh no, Tinker White. No games. We bin
at it a long time and I reckon we're all fit for our beds. I am least-
ways.

TINKER: Knocker! You were marvellous. Weren't he marvellous? –
You picked that snotty nose up like he were a feather.

DAPHNE: Who'd've thought.

TINKER: A feather!

DAPHNE: My Knocker.

TINKER: I ent never seen 'im do anything like that before, have you?

DAPHNE: He deserves a drink.

TINKER: Did you see 'im, Mr Litvanov? That loud-mouthed little
journalist what squirted soda on you? Well, our Knocker here soon
showed him.

KNOCKER [*disarmed and taking drink*]: Soon ever I see 'im do that I
weren't hevin' any on it. I wanted to throw him out afore but you
seemed like you was coping wi' 'im nicely. Nicely I thought. All
his daft ideas. I don't know anyone what read what he write, that
I don't.

DAPHNE: But him being a friend o' your sister's –

KNOCKER: No matters! No one's gonna go insultin' my guests –

TINKER: You married a hero!

KNOCKER: – an' now it's all peaceful an' we can sit, talk an' drink in
peace –

TINKER: – an' play the shoe game.*

KNOCKER: Oh well, I don't know about that. Mr Litvanov here
don't wanna play our silly ole games, Tinker.

TINKER [*plying* KNOCKER *with drinks*]: Mr Litvanov's all right now,
aren't you, Mr Litvanov?

*Note : as this is the dramatic high point of the play, precise (though not
mechanical) orchestration is essential. It's advisable, after the first week of re-
hearsal, to rehearse these three rounds of the shoe game for half an hour every
day before rehearsals begin – a good way to warm up! Or for half an hour at
some point in the day. If it's left to be worked out towards the end of rehearsals
then the result will be sloppy instead of electrifying.

[LOUIS, *completely melancholic, offers a confused smile – rather like a reluctant and crippled old king confronting a mob he despises and wishes had his ailment.*]

He's goin' to sit there an' watch us an' then he's gonna join in, ent you, ole son? It's very simple.

[*As he talks the action takes place with everyone except* MR DAWSON *and* BONKY *forming a circle round him. The following positions are taken.*]

NOTE: *This layout is based on the Leeds production which took place on an apron stage confronted by a high raked auditorium. In a proscenium stage* KNOCKER *and* DAPHNE *would probably need to be to the fore.*]

|   | DAPHNE | | KNOCKER | |
|---|---|---|---|---|
| RINGO | | | | MRS DAWSON |
| | | TINKER | | |
| EMILY | | | | MARTIN |
| | TOSH | | MAUREEN | |

Someone's blindfolded, see? I'll do it first, this handkerchief here, round my eyes, can't see a thing, an' everyone forms a circle around me an' then, someone takes off his shoe. [TOSH *does so, throws it to* MRS DAWSON.] I don't know who 'tis. So I've got to follow the sound of the throw. Then they hev to hit me on my backside an' I gotta turn round quickly to see if I can lay hands on them.

[*Someone swipes at him, he turns, but fails to grab them.*]

Like that! see? They can't hit you anywhere but your backside 'cos thaas the point of the game. You gotta turn the moment you think someone's comin' up behind you, like this [*he turns*] – then, of course, he can't wallop you so he hev to throw the shoe to someone else or just pass it along. Passing it makes less noise, of course. Sometimes you stick your backside out to tempt them, slowly, and then – spring!

[TINKER *springs and catches* MAUREEN *who had just tapped him but couldn't escape in time. She's blindfolded. But while he was talking, the following was happening:* TOSH *threw to* MRS DAWSON. *The sound made* TINKER *turn to* MRS DAWSON.

*But then* MRS DAWSON *passed to* DAPHNE
*who passed to* RINGO
*who passed to* EMILY.
TINKER *held his attention to* MRS DAWSON *and had not heard the
swift and silent movement of the shoe back to* EMILY. EMILY *swiped
successfully,* TINKER *turned but failed to grab her. Then –*
EMILY *threw to* MAUREEN *who*
*threw to* DAPHNE *who*
*threw to* MARTIN *who*
*passed to* KNOCKER *who*
*passed to* MRS DAWSON *who*
*passed to* DAPHNE *who*
*passed to* RINGO *who*
*passed to* EMILY *who*
*passed to* TOSH *who*
*passed to* MAUREEN *who swiped and*
TINKER *caught her.*]

See? Simple. Now, Mr Litvanov, you can play that, can't you? Up
you get.

[*He hands over a jelly and staggering* LOUIS *to* KNOCKER *and*
DAPHNE.]

That's it. You'll manage.

### 2nd Round

|                  |          |               |
|------------------|----------|---------------|
| DAPHNE           | LOUIS    | KNOCKER       |
| RINGO            |          | MRS DAWSON    |
|                  | MAUREEN  |               |
| EMILY            |          | MARTIN        |
|         TOSH     | TINKER   |               |

[MAUREEN *seems to enjoy offering her bottom for a 'whack', though
no one slaps hard. She moves slowly round, seductively.* TINKER
*throws to* DAPHNE *who*
*throws to* MARTIN *who taps* MAUREEN *and*
*throws to* EMILY *who*
*throws to* MRS DAWSON *who*

*passes to* LOUIS *who*
*gaily and too obviously is about to swipe and walk straight into*
MAUREEN'S *arms but is held back by* DAPHNE *and* KNOCKER.
DAPHNE *shows* LOUIS *he must wait till back is turned, then she*
*swipes and*
*passes to* RINGO *who*
*passes to* EMILY *who*
*throws to* KNOCKER *who taps* MAUREEN *and*
*passes to* MRS DAWSON *who*
*throws to* LOUIS *who taps* MAUREEN *with slow relish and is caught.*
*They begin to blindfold* LOUIS.]

KNOCKER [*loud whisper*]: No! Not the master!

[*But he's outvoted.* LOUIS *is blindfolded, placed in centre.* KNOCKER *folds his arms stubbornly.*]

KNOCKER: Well, *I* ent goin' to hit 'im!

[*The circle is the same as before, only* MAUREEN *is between* MRS DAWSON *and* MARTIN.

### 3rd Round

*This round begins in a friendly spirit. Nothing menacing.*

MRS DAWSON *throws to* TOSH *who*
*throws to* KNOCKER *who obviously is terrified to handle it, it's his*
*boss! and passes the shoe on like a hot potato to* MRS DAWSON *who*
*throws to* TINKER *who taps* LOUIS *and*
*throws to* RINGO *who*
*throws to* MAUREEN *who taps* LOUIS *and*
*throws to* TOSH *who*
*throws to* KNOCKER *who quickly wants to pass it on to* DAPHNE *but*
*realizes how eager she is and instead*
*passes it to* MRS DAWSON *who*
*passes to* MAUREEN *who*
*passes to* MARTIN *who*
*throws to* EMILY *who excitedly taps* LOUIS *and passes to* RINGO *who*
*becomes badgered by an irritated* DAPHNE *who has not had a go at*
LOUIS.

RINGO *teases her and finally*
*throws to* MARTIN *who*
*throws to* RINGO *who taps* LOUIS, *again teases* DAPHNE, *and*
*throws to* MARTIN.

*In exasperation* DAPHNE *snatches off her own shoe, her wedding slipper.* EMILY *gasps.* MAUREEN *gives a little hysterical giggle. Everyone freezes. Two shoes? Is that fair? She wouldn't dare. Surely. But she does. And what's more it's a slightly harder, more vicious whack. The sound stings through them.* DAPHNE *defiantly holds on to her slipper. They all look at each other, sheepishly at first.*

*Then the mood changes. There's still no menace but there is a heightening of tension and excitement.*

MAUREEN *with a nervous laugh takes off her shoe and taps* LOUIS. *Then* RINGO *takes off his shoe and taps* LOUIS. *Then* TINKER *takes off his shoe and taps* LOUIS.

*What's happening?*

TINKER *raises his shoe like a triumphant sword above his head. The other three follow. Defiance, however futile, is contagious in a crowd, and so the remaining ones take off their shoes and all stand with shoes poised high.*

LOUIS *is alert. Something's in the wind. One by one they each step forward to tap him. He's confused. They become intoxicated. The beating grows. It's no longer a game. A mob mentality takes over and each tap becomes more malevolent, the sound of the whack more frequent, until all control is lost and they simply crowd in and beat him about the body. (Not the face.)*

LOUIS *realizes he's being beaten. He wrenches off the blindfold with a profound howl of great rage. Then –]*

LOUIS: WHAT ARE YOU DOING TO ME? I came here
– I wanted to – it was my intention –

[*He sways, reaches to sit on a chair by a table and lays his head to rest – in the remains of the blancmange!*

*The shock temporarily revives him. He pulls himself up, striving for dignity, and like a huge, tragi-comic clown, staggers about, falls and passes out.*

*The aggressiveness of the company turns to sheepishness, shame and a touch of fear.*]

BONKY: It all comes from the earth. And when you die – you go back there.

[*Is he dead?*]

KNOCKER: Oh, bloody hell! Oh, creeping, jumping, bloody hell. Well thaas it. Thaas done it. Thaas my lot, ent it?

[*Silence. Then – the sound of snoring.*]

TINKER: I go t'hell! Listen to him, then. [*Pause.*] Knocker, ole son, the night has come – that great special moment. Precious to every man. An' thaas all yours.

[TINKER *and others move for their coats.*]

DAPHNE [*unbelieving*]: Tinker?

MR DAWSON [*passing prone figure, mumbling*]: They keep telling me there's an improvement but I can't see it. There's none on it gotten a great deal better. None on it ... no ... none on it ... none on it ...

KNOCKER: You can't leave him like that. What – us up there an' 'im down here? That'll kill my first night's activities, hell if it won't.

TINKER: Well, what you wantin' of us?

KNOCKER: Call a taxi, take 'im 'ome. That's what I'm wantin' o' you.

TINKER: An' put 'im to bed? Not likely, ole son. He's your boss.

DAPHNE: An' you got 'im like it.

KNOCKER: An' I'm left wi' it. Thaas me. Thaas my luck all right. Born wi' it I was.

TINKER: Good night, Knocker. Daphne, look after 'im.

DAPHNE: Tinker White, if you go now, us like this, I'll not speak to you ever again. Thaas true that is, not ever again.

TINKER: I'll hev to spend my leave in foreign parts then, won't I?

DAPHNE: Mother! Do something.

MRS DAWSON: No one don't ask my advice for narthin' an' I ent givin' it. Ask her. [*Referring to* EMILY.]

EMILY: Don't be daft, Tinker, we can't leave 'im like this.

TINKER: Well what am I supposed to do? What you all looking at me for? Did I lay 'im out? You all wanna pass the buck so quick, don't you? 'Sides, he wouldn't spoil my first night's activities. In the mornin' he'll wake up, give hisself a wash, phone for his

chauffeur – that man what 'help me drive my little ole Ford' – an'
go 'ome. What's the panic for?

[KATE *has returned and at the sound of the door slamming they all turn
to her. She is furious.*]

They think it's all my fault.

KATE: Go on home now. We'll see to him.

[*All move homewards.*]

EMILY: Lovely wedding, Knocker.

MARTIN: This is it then, bor.

TOSH: We'll leave you to it, Knocker.

MAUREEN: Leave you to it, Knocker, Knocker. Thank you, Knocker.
Treat her well, my sister, treat her well ...

RINGO: Better'n what she did.

EMILY: Lovely wedding, Knocker.

MR DAWSON: Good on you, Kate. I enjoyed all that.

KATE: Not you, Tinker. You ent gettin' away without some help.

[*The four remaining stand around the heavily-breathing body.*]

He's ill. He can't be taken home. Take him upstairs to the bed.

KNOCKER: The bed? *Our* bed? An' where do *us* sleep? You took your
bed away to your new flat. Where do *us* sleep?

KATE [*pointing to narrow divan*]: There!

DAPHNE: There? Two on us?

KATE: For one night, you'll manage.

KNOCKER: It's got a broken leg.

KATE: It'll last.

KNOCKER: On my wedding night?

KATE: He's gonna feel rough enough when he wakes up after all
you've put him through and I aren't lettin' him wake up to find
himself in all this mess. Knocker, get me a flannel. Daphne, go make
up that divan. Tinker, take off his shoes.

[*Each sets about their task. When the jacket is removed* KATE *gently
wipes* LOUIS's *face.*]

Now Louis, you must take a long holiday, restore your spirits.
Perhaps you'll listen to me from now on. Just give them the rate
for their work and the sweet, sweet *illusion* that they're equal to
any man. Stop pretending it's a reality. [*Pause.*] And don't be kind
**or** ashamed or apologetic for your money. You go around behaving

like that, how shall we be able to hit you when the time comes, bor? [*Pause.*] There! You're ready for your bed, I reckon. In the morning I'll bring flowers, make you coffee and nurse your wounds. Huh! Wounds! You won't think you've got any will you? Tinker, Knocker – carry him up – and gently.

[KATE *turns to see* DAPHNE *struggling to make up the divan. She helps.* KATE *is systematic, folding in the corners hospital-style.* DAPHNE *is chaotic, shoving them under. When it's done the two men have returned.*]

KATE [*to* TINKER]: Come on, you. You can walk me home. Goodnight, you two. I'll be here before you're up in the morning. [*Gently, to a brother she's leaving.*] Sleep well.

KNOCKER: Huh!

KATE [*washing her hands of him*]: Or not well, as you please!

[*They leave.* DAPHNE *throws a hateful look at* KNOCKER *and storms past him.*]

KNOCKER: Where are you goin'?

DAPHNE: And what do you reckon I should sleep in?

KNOCKER: What you wanna sleep in anythin' for?

[*She ignores him, contemptuously. Leaves.* KNOCKER *undresses, not without some last remaining vestige of excitement and anticipation, and gingerly creeps into bed. Soon* DAPHNE *returns in a night-dress and lunges onto bed.*]

KNOCKER: Careful!

[*Though angry, she too gingerly creeps into bed, reaches to switch off remaining bedside light, and slams heavily down. In the darkness there is a crash.*

KNOCKER *puts on light again to reveal them lying in a collapsed divan.* DAPHNE *is hugging the blankets and whimpering.* KNOCKER, *rigid and wide eyed, returns to a prone, horizontal position, resigned.*]

A sacred night *this* is gonna be. Oh yes! Witch-cursed White, thaas me. Howsomever, this is only the beginnin'. Tomorrow the pipes will freeze and burst. I know it! Pneumonia! And then next week the chimney'll catch fire. Burn to death! Or those stairs. What lunatic built them? Someone who hated my ole Nanny White, sure to fall down them. Or there'll be a war, or I'll get knocked over by a car, or cut me fingers off in the machines, or lose a winnin'

pools coupon, or be assassinated by mistake. Every day! Somethin'
new! Some lousy, rotten, little accident, some great, black tragedy.
For the rest of my life an' ever an' ever amen! Thaas me!

[KNOCKER *turns off light and hugs himself back to sleep.*
*The night passes. A slow dawn light filters into the room.*
*The wreck of* LOUIS *shambles downstairs. Stands in centre of room,*
*surveys the mess. Walks to get overcoat, then across the room to pick*
*up his shoes.*
*He surveys the mess and memory of the evening before, clenches his*
*teeth, hardens his face.*]

LOUIS: Yes, that's the way it has to be.

[*And a great melancholy settles upon his heart.*
*He shuffles off. Lights fade, and –*]

CURTAIN

# The Merchant

## A play in two acts

This is the eighth draft of the play, based on the Birmingham production of 1978, and differs from the version world premiered in Stockholm in 1976 and the English-speaking version premiered on Broadway in 1977.

'I do not use despair, for it is not mine,
only entrusted to me for safe-keeping.'
*Wisława Szymborska,*
*Polish poetess*

# ACKNOWLEDGEMENTS

I have always depended upon my friends for comments and criticisms of early drafts of my plays but with *The Merchant* my gratitude also extends to many scholars whose works provided the background to a period and setting I only barely knew.

Of those friends and scholars three must be mentioned for my especial debts. Dr D. S. Chambers, lecturer in Renaissance Studies at the Warburg Institute, who read the third draft and made many helpful observations, and whose book *The Imperial Age of Venice* I continually raided. Similarly the books of the late Dr Cecil Roth whose *History of the Jews* everywhere-all-the-time must be invaluable for any creative writer in need of Jewish historical detail. Lastly, the incredible persistence and patience of my friend and German translator, Nina Adler, whose scrupulous intelligence questioned so much that some of the logic and fine detail of the play would not have been as clear without her.

None other of my works have acknowledged such debts – perhaps they should have – but that this one does I'd like taken as a measure of how real and not merely polite this acknowledgement is.

A. W.

*The Merchant* received its world premiere at the Royal Dramaten-theater, Stockholm, on 8 October 1976, directed by Staphan Roos.

It received its English-speaking premiere at the Plymouth Theatre, New York, on 16 November 1977, with the following cast.

| | |
|---|---|
| SHYLOCK KOLNER | Joseph Leon |
| JESSICA | Julie Garfield |
| RIVKA | Marian Seldes |
| TUBAL DI PONTI | John Seitz |
| ANTONIO QUERINI | John Clements |
| BASSANIO VISCONTI | Nicolas Surovy |
| LORENZO PISANI | Everett McGill |
| GRAZIANO SANUDO | Riggs O'Hara |
| PORTIA CONTARINI | Roberta Maxwell |
| NERISSA | Gloria Gifford |
| SOLOMON USQUE | Jeffrey Horowitz |
| REBECCA DA MENDES | Angela Wood |
| MOSES OF CASTELAZZO | Leib Lensky |
| GIROLAMO PRIULI | William Roerick |
| ABTALION DA MODENA | Boris Tumarin |
| MAID/SINGER | Rebecca Malka |
| SERVANTS/SENATORS | Russ Banham |
| | Mark Blum |
| | Philip Carroll |
| | James David Cromar |
| | Brian Meister |
| | John Tyrrell |

Directed by John Dexter
Designed by Jocelyn Herbert
Lighting by Andy Phillips

N.B. Zero Mostel was originally cast as Shylock but tragically he died after the first night out of town in Philadelphia – 8 September 1977.

*The Merchant* received its British premiere at the Birmingham Repertory Theatre on 12 October 1978, with the following cast.

| | |
|---|---|
| Shylock Kolner | David Swift |
| Jessica | Julia Swift |
| Rivka | Hana Maria Pravda |
| Tubal di Ponti | Aubrey Morris |
| Antonio Querini | Frank Middlemass |
| Bassanio Visconti | Tim Hardy |
| Lorenzo Pisani | Greg Hicks |
| Graziano Sanudo | Timothy Spall |
| Portia Contarini | Angela Down |
| Nerissa | Margi Campi |
| Roderigues de Cunha | Teddy Kempner |
| Solomon Usque | Roger Allam |
| Rebecca da Mendes | Judith Harte |
| Moses of Castelazzo | Alfred Hoffmann |
| Girolamo Priuli | Andre Van Gyseghem |
| Maid/Singer | Joanna Foster |
| Servants/Senators | Peter Evans |
| | Christopher Gillespie |
| | Ian McFarlane |
| | Raymond Savage |

Directed by Peter Farago
Sets designed by Christopher Morley
Costumes designed by Ann Curtis
Lighting by Mick Hughes

NOTE: During this production Angela Down suggested that Portia's solitary Scene Two in Act One should be moved to become Scene One in Act Two. It was too late to make this change in this text but I think it's an admirable idea and strongly advise it in future productions. A.W.

# CHARACTERS

SHYLOCK KOLNER, *a Jew of Venice*
JESSICA, *his daughter*
RIVKA, *his sister*
TUBAL DI PONTI, *his partner*
ANTONIO QUERINI, *a merchant of Venice*
BASSANIO VISCONTI, *his godson*
LORENZO PISANI, *Bassanio's friend*
GRAZIANO SANUDO, *Antonio's assistant*
PORTIA CONTARINI, *an heiress of Venice*
NERISSA, *her maid*
RODERIGUES DE CUNHA, *an architect*
SOLOMON USQUE, *a playwright*
REBECCA DA MENDES, *daughter of Portuguese banker*
MOSES OF CASTELAZZO, *a portrait painter*
GIROLAMO PRIULI, *Doge of Venice*
MAID IN SHYLOCK'S HOUSE★
PATRICIANS AND OTHERS
(at director's discretion)

★ Who should also be singer at end of play.

# ACT ONE

## SCENE ONE

[*Venice, 1563. The Ghetto Nuovo.* SHYLOCK'*s study. It is strewn with books and manuscripts.*

SHYLOCK, *a 'loan-banker', with his friend,* ANTONIO, *a merchant, are leisurely cataloguing.*

ANTONIO *is by the table, writing, as* SHYLOCK *reads out the titles and places them on his shelves.*

*They are old friends, and old: in their middle sixties.*]

SHYLOCK [*reading out*]: 'Guide to the Perplexed'. Author, Maimonides, Ram-bam, known as the Great Eagle. Cairo. Twelfth century.

   [ANTONIO *writes.*]

Hebrew/Hebrew Dictionary. Author, R. David Kimhi. England. Twelfth century. Not too fast for you, Antonio?

ANTONIO: It's not the most elegant script, but I'm speedy.

SHYLOCK: And I'm eager. I know it. But here, the last of the manuscripts and then we'll begin cataloguing my printed books. Such treasures to show you, you'll be thrilled, thrrrrrilled! You'll be – I can't wait ... just one more –

ANTONIO: Do I complain?

SHYLOCK: – and then we'll rest. I promise you. I'll bring out my wines, and fuss and – the last one. I promise, promise.

ANTONIO: Shylock! Look! I'm waiting.

SHYLOCK: I have a saint for a friend.

ANTONIO: And what does the poor saint have?

SHYLOCK: An overgrown schoolboy. I know it! The worst of the deal. But –

ANTONIO: I'm waiting, Shylock.

SHYLOCK: Deed. Legal. Anglo-Jewish. Twelfth century. Author –
I can't read the name. Probably drawn up by a businessman himself. [*Peering*] What a mastery of Talmudic Law. I love them, those
old men, their cleverness, their deeds, their wide-ranging talents.
Feel it! Touch it!

ANTONIO: The past.

SHYLOCK: Exactly!

ANTONIO: And all past.

SHYLOCK: Antonio! You look sad.

ANTONIO: Sad?

SHYLOCK: I've overworked you. Here. Drink. Why should we wait
till we're finished? [*Offers wine.*] Drink. It's a special day.

[*They drink in silence.*]

ANTONIO: So many books.

SHYLOCK: And all hidden for ten years. Do you know what that
means for a collector? Ten years? Ha! The scheme of things! 'The
Talmud and kindred Hebrew literature? Blasphemy!' they said,
'burn them!' And there they burned, on the Campo dei Fiori in
Rome, decreed by Julius the Third of blessed origin, August the
12th, 1553, and followed swiftly by our very own and honoured
Council of Ten in Venice. The day of the burning of the books.
Except mine, which I hid, all of them, even my secular works.
When fever strikes them you can't trust those warriors of God.
With anything of learning? Never! That's what they really hated,
not the books of the Jews but the books of men. I mean – MEN!
Their spites, you see, the books revealed to them their thin minds.
And do you think it's over even now? Look! [*Pushes out a secret
section of his bookcase.*] The Sacred Books. The others I can bring
back, but still, to this day, the Talmud is forbidden. And I have
them, the greatest of them, Bomberg's edition, each of them,
starting 1519 to the last on June the 3rd, 1523. Aren't they
beautiful?

ANTONIO: So beautiful.

SHYLOCK [*referring to others*]: I've friends who buy for me all over
the world. I'm a hoarder of other men's genius. My vice. My
passion. Nothing I treasure more, except my daughter. So – drink!
It's a special day.

[ANTONIO, *looking at this and that, reads from something pasted to the side of the bookcase.*]

ANTONIO: 'July 12th, 1555. Forasmuch as it is highly absurd –' What is it?

SHYLOCK: Read it, read it. A papal Bull. Another mad edict. I kept it. I'm a hoarder, of other men's genius, remember? 'Cum Nimis absurdum', forasmuch as it is highly absurd –

ANTONIO: 'Forasmuch as it is highly absurd and improper that the Jews, condemned by God to eternal slavery because of their guilt, should, on the pretext that they are cherished by Christian love and permitted to dwell in our midst, show such ingratitude to Christians as to insult them for their mercy and presume mastery instead of the subjection that beseems them . . .' Oh! I can't go on. The malicious use such pompous language to proclaim their righteousness.

SHYLOCK: Cardinal Caraffa! He's fortunate it *is* my God in charge or he'd be in hell by now. Oh, forgive me. An arrogant joke. First I tire you, then I depress you, then I insult you.

ANTONIO: I'm not tired, Shylock, except to go looking for insults where intelligence is.

SHYLOCK: Look! A present to cheer you up. One of my most treasured manuscripts, a thirteenth-century book of precepts, author Isaac of Corbeil, with additamenta made by the students. I used to do it myself, study and scribble my thoughts in the margin. We all did it. We had keen minds, Antonio, very profound we thought ourselves, commenting on the meaning of life, the rights and wrongs of the laws, offering our interpretations of the interpretations of the great scholars who interpreted the meaning of the meaning of the prophets. 'Did the prophecies of Daniel refer to the historic events or to the Messianic times, or neither? Is the soul immortal, or not? Should one or should one not ride in a gondola on the Sabbath?' Money lending was never a full-time occupation and the Ghetto rocked with argument – ha! I love it! [*Pause.*] There! I *have* tired you.

ANTONIO: I assure you –

SHYLOCK: Depressed you, then. I've done that.

ANTONIO: Not that either. But –

SHYLOCK: But what? What but, then?

ANTONIO: Those books. Look at them. How they reminded me
what I am, what I've done. Nothing! A merchant! A purchaser of
this to sell there. A buyer up and seller off. And do you know, I
hardly ever see my trade. I have an office, a room of ledgers and a
table, and behind it I sit and wait till someone comes in to ask have
I wool from Spain, cloth from England, cotton from Syria, wine
from Crete. And I say yes, I've a ship due in a week, or a month,
and I make a note, and someone goes to the dock, collects the corn,
delivers it to an address, and I see nothing. I travel neither to
England to check cloth, nor Syria to check cotton. I haven't even
the appetite to visit the lovely island of Sante to inspect the raisins,
or Corfu to see that the olive oil is cleanly corked, and I could
steal time for myself in such places. It never worried me, this
absence of curiosity for travel. Until I met you, old Jew –

SHYLOCK: Not so old then, old man, only just past fifty –

ANTONIO: – and I became caught up in your, your passion, your
hoardings, your – your vices!

SHYLOCK: Is he complaining or thanking me?

ANTONIO: You've poisoned me, old Shylock, with restlessness and
discontent, and at so late a time.

SHYLOCK: He's complaining.

ANTONIO: A lawyer, a doctor, a diplomat, a teacher – anything but
a merchant. I'm so ashamed. There's no sweetness in my dealings.
After the thrill of the first exchange, after the pride of paying a
thousand ducats with one hand and taking fifteen hundred with
the other – no skill. Just an office and some ledgers. It's such a
joyless thing, a bargain. I'm so weary with trade.

## SCENE TWO

[*Belmont.* PORTIA's *estate outside Venice.*
*The estate is in great disrepair.* PORTIA *and her maid,* NERISSA, *both in
simple, hardwearing clothes, have just arrived to view the neglect.*]

PORTIA: Decided! The speculating days of the family Contarini are
done. The goods warehoused in our name at Beirut and Famagusta

we'll sell off cheaply to cut our losses, I shall raise what I can from the sale of our properties on Crete, Corfu and the Dalmatian towns which are too far from Venice and not worth their troubles, but –

NERISSA: – but agriculture, my lady, what does my lady Portia know of agriculture?

PORTIA: Your lady Portia will learn, Nerissa. The famines are cruel and constant visitors. We must reclaim the land. Besides, the competition for the trade routes is too devious a task for my taste, and –

NERISSA: – and pirates are in the Adriatic, we know all that, my lady, most demoralizing for our sailors, but –

PORTIA: Antwerp! Seville! London! Too far!

NERISSA: – but to leave the city?

PORTIA: I love my city, Nerissa, but I hear rumours. Timber is scarce, the number of ships registered by Venice is dropping. Signs, my dear, the signs are there. It's goodbye to Venice, and into the wheatlands of my estates near Treviso and Vicenza and here, Belmont. We'll become growers! Stock-breeders! Cattle and drainage! that's where our fortunes will go.

NERISSA: When you've realized them, that is.

PORTIA: The land! I've decided! [*Pause.*] Good God! [*Looking around.*] What a mess my father's made of my childhood! [*Pause.*] Is this the room?

NERISSA: Facing the sun at eleven o'clock. This is it.

PORTIA: And *here* we are to find the caskets?

NERISSA [*searching*]: Here, somewhere in all this neglect. Your father's puzzle for picking a spouse. One gold, one silver, one lead. [NERISSA *reveals a dusty corner.*] Found! 'By his choice shall you know him.'

PORTIA: What an inheritance! Ten estates in ruin, and a foolish philosophic whim for to find me an idiot husband. Oh father, father, father! What *were* you thinking of? Hear me up there. I will honour the one wish you uttered: whom the casket chooses, I'll marry. But your rules for judging men I will forget, and these ruins will be put back again. The material things of this world count. We *have* no soul without labour, and labour I will, father, hear me.

[*She begins to move about the room pulling down tattered curtains, replacing furniture on its feet, picking up strewn books, perhaps rubbing encrusted dirt from a vase till its frieze can be seen, but moving, moving.*]

NERISSA: How your mother would love to be alive now, with all this possibility of work at last.

PORTIA: Perhaps that's my real inheritance, Nerissa: father's marriage to a peasant. My energy is hers.

NERISSA: And such energy, madame.

PORTIA: All stored and waiting for the poor man's death.

NERISSA: Come, be just. He didn't commit you in marriage at the age of seven as my father did. He gave you tutors.

PORTIA: Ah, thank heaven for them.

NERISSA: A very strange collection, I used to think.

PORTIA: The crippled Ochino from Padua for mathematics, the boring Lamberti from Genoa for history.

NERISSA: The handsome Mansueti from Florence for Greek and philosophy . . .

PORTIA: And for Hebrew, Abraham Cardorso, the sad, old Jewish mystic from the Ghetto Nuovo. I am indebted to them all.

NERISSA: Why in God's name did you want to learn Hebrew, my lady?

PORTIA: To read the words of the prophets in the language they were spoken, why else? Meanings change when men translate them into other tongues. Oh! Those caskets! Those stupid caskets! Take them out of my sight. I loved him dearly, my father, but those caskets will bring me down as his other madnesses brought down my mother, I feel it.

NERISSA: *Such* energy, madame, you tire me to watch you.

PORTIA: And you must have it too, Nerissa. I demand it. You are not only my help but my friend and I'll have you educated and protected from the miseries of an ill-chosen marriage.

NERISSA: If, that is, you can protect yourself from one.

PORTIA: True! My God, and what suitors have announced they're coming. Why, do you wonder, *is* there such interest in me?

NERISSA: Riches, madame, riches, riches, riches.

PORTIA: But my riches are potential, not realized.

NERISSA: The family name?

PORTIA: My family name is illustrious but somewhat moth-eaten.

NERISSA: Your beauty.

PORTIA: No flattery. I won't have it. My beauty is, well – it *is*, but no more than many such women of Venice I could name.

NERISSA: Why, then? *You* say.

PORTIA: I *think* I know, but it's not certain. There are simply – mmm – pulses in my veins. I feel, I feel – I feel I-am-the-new-woman-and-they-know-me-not! For centuries the Church has kept me comfortably comforting and cooking and pleasing and patient. And now – Portia is no longer patient. Yes, she can spin, weave, sew. Give her meat and drink – she can dress them. Show her flax and wool – she can make you clothes. But – Portia reads! Plato and Aristotle, Ovid and Catullus, all in the original! Latin, Greek, Hebrew –

NERISSA: With difficulty!

PORTIA: She has read history and politics, she has studied logic and mathematics, astronomy and geography, she has conversed with liberal minds on the nature of the soul, the efficacy of religious freedom, the very existence of God!

NERISSA: Why! Her brain can hardly catch its breath!

PORTIA: She has observed, judged, organized and – crept out of the kitchen. Knowledge of love and corruption and evil may have lost her sweet innocence but – the fireside chair rocks without her now, and what she will do is a mystery. Portia is a new woman, Nerissa. There is a woman on the English throne. Anything can happen and they are coming to find out.

## SCENE THREE

[SHYLOCK's *study. He and* ANTONIO *have been drinking.*]

SHYLOCK: I gave you wine to cheer you up. It's cheered me down!

ANTONIO: The work's done. You should be happy! I've lost the use of my hand, but what of that? Look, order! Filed, catalogued, all that knowledge. You could save the world.

SHYLOCK: When I can't be certain of saving myself? What a thought! Not even the sages with all their wisdom could save themselves. Here, read this elegy on the Martyrs of Blois by the Rabbi Yom Tov of Joingy. What a lovely old man he must have been. To a question once about whether or not to use a stove on the Sabbath, he replied 'May my lot be with those who are warm, not those who are stringent!' Poor sage. They were all poor sages. Constantly invited to run educational establishments here and there, and never certain whether they were running into a massacre. From the massacre of Rouen they fled into the massacre of London; from the massacre of London into the massacre of York, and from the massacre of York no one fled! [Pause.] Travelling wasn't very safe in those days!

ANTONIO: Are you a religious man, Shylock?

SHYLOCK: What a question. Are you so drunk?

ANTONIO: You are religious, for all your freethinking, you're a devout man. And I love and envy you for it.

SHYLOCK: You are so drunk. Religious! It's the condition of being Jewish, like pimples with adolescence, who can help it? Even those of us who don't believe in God have dark suspicions that he believes in us. Listen, I'll tell you how it all happened. Ha! The scheme of things! I love it! Imagine this tribe of semites in the desert. Pagan, wild, but brilliant. A sceptical race, believing only in themselves. Loving but assertive. Full of quarrels and questions. Who could control them? Leader after leader was thrown up but, in a tribe where every father of his family was a leader, who could hold them in check for long? Until one day a son called Abraham was born, and he grew up knowing his brethren very, very well indeed. 'I know how to control this arrogant, anarchic herd of heathens,' he said to himself. And he taught them about one God. Unseen! Of the spirit! That appealed to them, the Hebrews, they had a weakness for concepts of the abstract. An unseen God! Ha! I love it! What an inspiration. But that wasn't all. Abraham's real statesmanship, his real stroke of genius was to tell this tribe of exploding minds and vain souls: 'Behold! An unseen God! God of the Universe! Of all men! and –' wait, for here it comes, '– and, of all men you are his chosen ones!' Irresistible! In an instant they were quiet. Subdued. 'Oh! Oh! Chosen? Really? Us? To do

what?' 'To bear witness to what is beautiful in creation, and just.
A service, not a privilege!' 'Oh dear! Chosen to bear witness!
What an honour! Ssh! Not so loud. Dignity! Abraham is speaking.
Respect! Listen to him. Order!' It worked! They had God and
Abraham had them. But – they were now cursed. For from that
day moved they into a nationhood that had to be better than any
other and, poor things, all other nations found them unbearable to
live with. What can I do? I'm chosen. I *must* be religious.

ANTONIO: I love you more and more, Shylock. You have a sanity
I could not live without now. I'm spoiled, chosen also.

SHYLOCK: But sad, still. I can see it. I've failed to raise your spirits
one tiny bit.

ANTONIO: *I'm* not a religious man. I had a letter today, from an old
friend, Ansaldo Visconti of Milan, a rich merchant, and well-loved
in my youth. But I'd forgotten him. And in this letter he talked of
his misfortune, his downfall into ruin through strange and cursed
events which I couldn't make any sense of, it was so wordy and
maudlin and full of old times. And in the end he commends to me
his only son, Bassanio, my godson it seems. And I'd forgotten him
also. Poor young Bassanio. Probably a very noble young noble-
man. I even think he must be a young patrician. His father was
born in Venice, if I remember, of patrician stock, if I remember.
No, he's probably a swaggering young braggart! Coming to see
me in the hope I'll put trade his way, or put him in trade's way,
or keep him by me as an assistant, passing on wisdom, or something. [*Pause.*] Here, Bassanio, a little piece of wisdom, here, in
my pocket. [*Pause, mock pomp.*] I am now going to be wise!
[*Pause. Then as if calling a dog*] Here, wisdom, here, boy. Sit. Still.
Quiet now. There, Bassanio, sits wisdom. [*Pause.*] I don't want to
be wise, or to talk about trade, or to see him. Ungodly man!
Doesn't that make me an ungodly man? I should never have had
godsons. Not the type. Bachelor merchant. On the other hand I
suppose that's just the type.

SHYLOCK: When do you expect him?

ANTONIO: Oh, tomorrow, or the next day, or is it next week?
Can't remember which. Bassanio! Humph! [*Shouting out*] I'm not
a religious man, Bassanio.

SHYLOCK: Antonio, my friend, it's late. In ten minutes they lock the gates of the Ghetto and all good Christians should be outside.

ANTONIO [*Still shouting*]: I may be your godfather, Bassanio, but I'm not a religious man.

SHYLOCK: I have a suggestion.

ANTONIO: Bassanio, Bassanio!

SHYLOCK: Stay the night.

ANTONIO: Stay the night?

SHYLOCK: It's not permitted, but with money –

ANTONIO: What about Bassanio, in search of wisdom?

SHYLOCK: We'll send a message in the morning to say where you can be found. Stay. You know my house, lively, full of people in and out all the time. My daughter, Jessica, will look after you – if she deigns to talk that is.

ANTONIO: Very haughty, your Jessica.

SHYLOCK: And free and fractious but – cleverer than her illiterate old father. Gave her all the tutors I couldn't have. But soon I will have one of my own.

ANTONIO [*Trumpeting*]: Abtalion da Modena the illustrious!

SHYLOCK: My very own scholar.

ANTONIO: Arriving any day now, as he keeps assuring us.

SHYLOCK: Any day now.

ANTONIO [*Still trumpeting*]: On his very own pilgrimage from Lisbon to the holy Jerusalem, financed by his very own pupil here, Shylock Kolner, in return for his very own wisdom. [*As if calling a dog*] Here, wisdom, here, boy!

SHYLOCK: Stay! You know how the Ghetto is constantly filled with visitors. In the morning Solomon Usque the writer is coming with the daughter from the Portuguese banking house of Mendes, and in the afternoon we'll go to the synagogue to hear the sermon of a very famous Rabbi from Florence, preaching on the importance of the Talmudic laws on cleanliness, with special reference to Aristotle! Stay. It'll be full of Venetian intelligentsia, they're always coming to attend the festivals, listen to the music. Very exotic we are. We fascinate them all, whether from England where they've expelled us, or Spain where they burn us. Stay. [*Pause.*] He's asleep. He'll have to stay [*Taking an arm of the now half-asleep* ANTONIO, *he struggles with him towards a bedroom.*] And if the gatekeepers remember and come looking don't worry, I'll keep them happy. Happy, happy, happy.


## SCENE FOUR

SHYLOCK's *main room. Next morning. An atmosphere of great activity.* JESSICA, *helped by* SHYLOCK's *old sister,* RIVKA, *and a* MAID, *is supervising the comings and goings, in preparation for the midday meal.* TUBAL, *his partner, is going through accounts.*]

JESSICA: We shall be six to eat at midday. Yesterday it was eight, the day before seven, and tomorrow, no doubt, more again. And is he up? He's not even awake yet. Eleven o'clock and he sleeps.

RIVKA: Yesterday was a very special day for him, Jessica. The books, remember, came out of hiding.

JESSICA: He dusted his dusty books! Heaven help me, Aunt Rivka, I have to look at those books again. From my earliest days I remember nothing but this madness, this illness for books. And at fifteen I thanked God that they had to be hidden away.

RIVKA: That's a sinful thing to say, niece. Your father would be ashamed to hear you talk like this.

JESSICA: My father is an intellectual snob. Every passing scholar or Rabbi or eminent physician has to dine at his table. Some men fawn before crowns, he before degrees. And soon he'll have his very own scholar to come and stay and stay and stay and stay and –

RIVKA: When Abtalion Da Modena comes –

JESSICA: 'When Abtalion Da Modena comes! Wait till Abtalion Da Modena comes!' My father promises him as some men promise the Messiah!

RIVKA: This is not worthy of you, Jessica. Scholarship must be respected.

JESSICA: Oh, I respect scholarship, but there is a world outside the covers of a book, isn't there? Men don't always behave as the philosophers fear, do they? I have the sayings and warnings of sages ringing in my ears so loudly, that music, which I adore above all things, can hardly make sense in my head any more.

TUBAL: Your father is a special man, Jessica. He's animated by ideas. 'Keep me moving,' he cries, 'don't let the dark overtake me, it's my only hope.' A man not afraid to have his mind changed? That's rare. I wish I had such courage.

JESSICA: But he bullies with it all, Uncle Tubal. My father's cruelty is to diminish whoever can't recall a name, a date, an event, or argument. Patterns! The world's fortunes move in patterns. 'The scheme of things.' Well, I do not believe there is a scheme of things, only chaos and misery, and –

RIVKA: That's wanton!

JESSICA: – and in it we must carve out just sufficient order for an ounce of happiness.

RIVKA: Wanton!

JESSICA: Nothing too ambitious. A little modest sweetness, at any price.

RIVKA: At any price?

JESSICA: At almost any price. We have no choice. There are madmen at large in the world. All writing books! Men fired by this ideal, that passion, full of dogma about the way other men should live, assuming moralities for us, deciding the limits of our pleasure, our endeavour, our abilities, our pain. Decreed by whom? By what right? My father is full of them and I am oppressed by them and I think my time is done for them. [*She leaves.*]

RIVKA: She exaggerates. My brother's not a tyrannical father.

TUBAL: Of course not. When their quarrels are over, Shylock makes light of it. But I fear he confuses her frustration for her originality.

RIVKA: He wanted to prove that daughters could achieve the intellectual stature of sons.

TUBAL: A wilful thought I've always thought. But there you are, you can't discuss children with parents, you offend them where they've placed their most cherished endeavour.

[*A young man,* RODERIGUES DA CUNHA, *rushes in. He carries rolls of plans.*]

RODERIGUES: Shylock! Shylock! The plans of the new synagogue! No Shylock?

RIVKA: Asleep still.

RODERIGUES: Asleep still. My appointment was for eleven.

TUBAL: As was mine. 'The accounts,' he cries, 'the accounts are in disorder.'

RODERIGUES: 'The plans,' he cries, 'the plans! You want me to contribute to the building of a new synagogue? Let me see the plans first.' So I stay up all night to draw a new set of plans, and he sleeps!

RIVKA: Go into the kitchen, Roderigues, Jessica is there.

RODERIGUES: All night!

RIVKA: Calm yourself –

RODERIGUES: Well, not *all* night.

RIVKA: – take mid-morning refreshment but don't complain to her, she's a little – heavy. My brother will be with us soon.

[RODERIGUES *nearly succeeds in leaving but is forced back into the room by a storming* JESSICA.]

JESSICA: Did you know they were coming *now*?

RIVKA: Who, my dear, who?

JESSICA: Solomon Usque and Rebecca da Mendes.

TUBAL: But these are honours, Jessica.

JESSICA: Honours for you, work for me, and overcrowding for the Ghetto. Suddenly Venice is alive with Portuguese Anusim.

RIVKA: Fleeing the Inquisition, child, what are you saying?

JESSICA: They will be welcome, but I'm not told, I'm not told.

[*Enter* SOLOMON USQUE *and* REBECCA DA MENDES.]

USQUE: Solomon Usque, playwright of Lisbon, otherwise known as Duarte de Pinel. May I present the Signora Rebecca da Mendes, daughter of the late Francisco Mendes, banker of Lisbon. Peace be unto you, Signor Shylock.

TUBAL: You're both known and welcome, but I'm not Shylock. Tubal di Ponti, his friend and partner, and honoured.

REBECCA: He's always greeting the wrong person –

USQUE: – pushing the wrong door –

REBECCA: – drinking from the wrong shaped glass!

USQUE: When artists aspire to elegance they end by being ridiculous. Please, when will friend Shylock appear?

[SHYLOCK *enters accompanied by* ANTONIO.]

SHYLOCK: He appears, he appears! Friend Shylock appears! Signora Mendes, Signor Usque, I'm ashamed to have had no one waiting for you at the door. May I present my daughter Jessica; my sister Rivka; my good friend Antonio Querini, a merchant of Venice whose head is not his own this morning, and my partner, Tubal di Ponti. Oh yes, and Roderigues – er –

RODERIGUES: – da Cunha.

SHYLOCK: – da Cunha, architect. They're building a new synagogue, to be situated on the south side of the Campiello delle Scuole. Of all people you must know of the plans. Your father, Signora, renowned! Renowned!

REBECCA: There are so many –

SHYLOCK: No, no! We are all indebted. No comparison: benevolence! statesmanship! Whatever I can do for you will be nothing in return. Nothing.

JESSICA: I must attend to the food. Please excuse me.

RODERIGUES: I will join you. Forgive me, everyone, I'm dying of thirst.

SHYLOCK: Thirst! My goodness. Look at me! Jessica, the citronade.

JESSICA [leaving]: It's on the table, father.

SHYLOCK: Soon, dear Roderigues, I'll be with you soon.

RODERIGUES [leaving]: Beautiful! Beautiful plans!

[They go.

SHYLOCK pours drinks which he gives to RIVKA to hand out.]

SHYLOCK: Everything is beautiful to him.

RIVKA: Especially my niece.

SHYLOCK: But not he to her! Stop match-making! He's a sweet boy but not her match. She always match-makes. And always the wrong one. She'll marry the wrong man without your help, push not! [To his guests] Now, what news do you bring?

USQUE: The news is not 'beautiful' either.

SHYLOCK: Tell us.

USQUE: What point in the details, their awfulness is monotonous.

REBECCA: We need help, let's talk about that.

SHYLOCK: Tell us.

USQUE: In the last year the Coimbra Tribunal, which has jurisdiction over the Northern provinces of Portugal, has held thirty-five autos-da-fé drawn from different towns and villages of Traz-os-Montes and Beira alone.

REBECCA: In addition to which the Lisbon and Evora Tribunals have tried Anusim arrested in towns situated in the Eastern department of Braganza.

USQUE: Fifty people burnt at the stake.

REBECCA: Old women, young men, relatives, friends.

USQUE: Marian Fernandes, a cousin from Lisbon.

REBECCA: Maria Diez, my old aunt from Guarda.

USQUE: Sebastian Rodrigo Pinto, a friend from Lamego.

REBECCA: Diego Della Rogna, his wife Isabelle Nones, their four daughters and two sons.

USQUE: An entire family burnt.

REBECCA: Facing each other.

[Silence.]

But there are survivors. It's to those we must attend. Signor Shylock, we are among friends?

SHYLOCK: Everyone, inseparable.

REBECCA: I have been told that you are a courageous man –

SHYLOCK: Please! A fool with my chances, perhaps –

REBECCA: During the next months, a steady stream of the Portuguese community will be making their way to Ancona before leaving for Solonika. Though not easy, Venice is the least dangerous place for them to stop en route and rest. We would like you to arrange places for them to stay, families who would put them up, and a fund started to assist their journey.

RIVKA: And who else but my brother!

SHYLOCK: Who else! I'd have been offended had anyone else been approached. You knew who to come to, didn't you?

REBECCA: We'd been told.

SHYLOCK: They talk, you see, Antonio! I'm a name in my community. From nobody to somebody, a name! Now, you'll stay for food, you must eat with us.

RIVKA: Of course they'll stay and eat with us. You imagine I wouldn't ask them to stay and eat.

SHYLOCK: Say you'll stay, please, please, I insist.

RIVKA: We all insist.

SHYLOCK: We all insist. And you must allow me to show you my collection of manuscripts, come.

USQUE: Signora Mendes is the collector, I only write them.

SHYLOCK: You must persuade him to sign one of his books for me.

USQUE: Ha! they hardly perform me let alone print me.

REBECCA: Fortunately he has other skills.

USQUE: Self-appointed plenipotentiary for refugees.

REBECCA: A constant occupation but one giving him great opportunity for travel – from Constantinople to London.

SHYLOCK: To London?

RIVKA: Are there still Jews in England?

REBECCA: Hardly any. A clandestine existence. But we go back and forth for trade.

SHYLOCK: Then you must look out for a rare manuscript for me – The Fox's Fables.

REBECCA: What's your special interest?

SHYLOCK: There's an edition in the library of Exeter Cathedral written by the author *himself* in which he complains about his life in England and the indifference of its wealthy Jews to intellectual and literary activities.

USQUE: Perhaps *that* accounts for the massacre of London.

[SHYLOCK, REBECCA *and* RIVKA *prepare to leave.*]

REBECCA [*to* SHYLOCK *as they're leaving*]: I shall never understand this habit of using our misery to feed our wit.

USQUE [*parting shot as they go off*]: What else is left to feed it, Signora?

SHYLOCK: And the plans for the synagogue! We simply must look at the plans for the new Spanish synagogue together.

[*Exit with* REBECCA *and* RIVKA.]

USQUE: Is that how it is every day?

TUBAL: Every day! Brother and sister rivalling one another in hospitality, and daughter pushing the other way. A house never still.

ANTONIO: When he's not negotiating loans, he's dispatching men around the world to buy him books, or opening the sights of the Ghetto to visiting dignitaries. Wait till his very own scholar arrives, there'll be time for nothing but tutorials and debate. The very air will be thick with 'wisdom'. So he thinks.

TUBAL: Though in time you'll find he's a very melancholy man, will you agree, Signor Antonio?

ANTONIO: In my warehouse is a young man, Graziano Sanudo, in charge of the import of spices. Now *he's* a happy man, no melancholy in him, and I don't know that I can stand him around. He's of an order of insensitivity I find unbearable. He bends so with the wind, quickly rushing to agree with the next speaker. He has no real opinions, simply a long boring repetitive list of complaints. He's a survivor, not defiantly, which is honourable, but creepily, like a chameleon, blending with everyone to avoid anyone's sting. He's contemplative with fools who contemplate nothing, sad with those who have no reason whatsoever to be sad, laughs when each and every idiot farts his thin wit, fawns on the tyrannical, is reverential before the papal, and manifests the most depressingly boisterous happiness I know. Give me Shylock's melancholy, gentlemen, and take away my man's smiles.

TUBAL: But Jessica is right. Shylock's kind of intelligence *is* an illness.

ANTONIO: Aye! You die from it in the end.

USQUE: I see he has an eternal friend in you, Signor Antonio.

ANTONIO: And I in him. Now, gentlemen, excuse me. I've been expecting a young man to call for me here in search of wisdom, and I fear he's lost.

TUBAL: The message went to your offices, Antonio, first thing this morning. Come at once to the Ghetto Nuovo between the German Synagogue and the Association for the Jewish Poor. Ground floor, ask if lost.

ANTONIO: Thank you, but I've no knowing what kind of soul he is, simple or bright. And in case the former, I'd better go out in search. I think I need the air, besides. [*Leaves.*]

USQUE: Your community lives well, I see. You can build your synagogues and depend upon gentile friends.

TUBAL: Personally I depend upon no gentile but, misery is difficult to wear all weathers. We survive from contract to contract, not knowing if after five years it will be renewed, and if renewed whether it will be for another five, or ten or three but –

USQUE: – Trade is trade –

TUBAL: – Trade is trade and they know it also, and we pay! An annual tribute of twenty thousand ducats; another twenty thousand for renting these squalid walls; fifteen thousand more to the Navy

Board – for God knows what; another hundred for the upkeep of the canals, which stink! And, on top of all that, ten thousand more in time of war which, since our beloved and righteous republic seems constantly fighting with someone or other ensures that sum too as a regular payment. Why, sometimes there's barely pennies in the Ghetto. For days we're all borrowing off each other, till new funds flow in. Only fourteen hundred souls, remember. We're no more than that, trapped in an oppressive circus with three water wells and a proclivity for fires.

[SHYLOCK enters.]

SHYLOCK [calling]: Roderigues! In here! Bring the plans in here, the light's better.

[RODERIGUES struggles in with rolls of plans.]

Signor Usque, you must look at these plans for the Spanish synagogue. [To RODERIGUES] Now, the entrance, why so plain? Why no wrought iron gates? They're Spanish, come from a highly cultured background!

[ANTONIO and BASSANIO enter at this point but hold back to watch and listen.]

TUBAL [continuing to USQUE]: And I make no mention of special demands in times of 'special distress', nor of the unreturned 'loans' to the treasury which bring in no more than a four per cent rate of interest. And did I leave out the cost of upkeeping our own community services and our own streets? I did, I did!

RODERIGUES: And did you leave out the bribes demanded by petty officials?

TUBAL: I did! I did!

RODERIGUES: And payments to the local church? the local police?

SHYLOCK: He did! He did! But never mind about politics. Why is the façade so dull? Is the new mint dull? Or the library and museum of antiquities? Tubal, you should be showing our guest the beauties of Venice not complaining about her.

RODERIGUES: There speaks the eternal guest.

SHYLOCK [returning to RODERIGUES]: And the windows! There's no light!

RODERIGUES: Give me the taxes of Venice and I'll give you light!

SHYLOCK: You don't need money to be bold. You need boldness! Take them away and think again. Bolder! Be bolder!

ANTONIO [*finally making himself known*]: Gentlemen, allow me to introduce my godson, Bassanio Visconti.

SHYLOCK: Ah, Antonio. You found him. Welcome, young man, welcome. You'll stay to eat with us, won't you? Do you know anything about architecture? We're building a new synagogue, look. We don't have a Palladio to build us a San Giorgio Maggiore, but with our modest funds . . .

ANTONIO: I don't think Bassanio plans to stay, but we would like to talk together, and if —

SHYLOCK: But of course. Friend Roderigues is leaving.

RODERIGUES: To be bolder!

TUBAL: And I have sights to show Signor Usque.

SHYLOCK: The first time godfather and son meet is a special and private time. [*To* TUBAL *as he and* SHYLOCK *prepare to leave*] Tubal, you *should* look at these plans for the new synagogue before they're folded away. It's your money too, you know.

TUBAL: I'm plan blind, Shylock. They mean nothing to me. *You* spend my money.

[*They leave.*]

BASSANIO: And that is a Jew?

ANTONIO [*reprimanding*]: He is a Jew.

BASSANIO: I don't think I know what to say.

ANTONIO: Have you never met one before?

BASSANIO: Talked of, described, imagined, but —

ANTONIO: Shylock is my special friend.

BASSANIO: Then, sir, he must be a special man.

ANTONIO [*suspicious and changing the subject*]:Your father speaks highly of you and begs me to help where I can.

BASSANIO: My lord Antonio —

ANTONIO: I'm not a lord, I'm a patrician — lapsed and indifferent to their politicking but, a patrician nonetheless.

BASSANIO: Lord, patrician — you are my godfather.

ANTONIO: I'd forgotten.

BASSANIO: Oh, understandably, understandably! The early years were so full of my father's talk of you and your goodness and your good time together, but — he made no effort to make us known to one another. It was a cause of distress between us.

ANTONIO: There were good times together, were there?

BASSANIO: He spoke of little else. What he shared with you, I shared. What happened between you, I saw happen. If I did wrong he'd say, your godfather would not approve of that. And as I grew I did what I did, thought what I thought, saying to myself – what would the good Antonio do now, how would the wise Antonio decide?

ANTONIO: Ah, wisdom! I feared it.

BASSANIO: You must surely have experienced this yourself, sir, that in your mind there is always one person, a vivid critic, whose tone of voice and special use of words is there in your brain, constantly.

ANTONIO: They call him God, Bassanio.

BASSANIO: I think you're mocking me. Have I come at a wrong time? Perhaps I shouldn't have come at all. To be honest, I hate arriving behind letters of recommendation, it's so undignified and besides, what can the poor host do but be courteous, obliging. Forgive me, sir. You know nothing of me. I'll go. But I'll find ways of making myself known to you, and useful, and in the coming months I'll try to earn your trust. Goodbye, sir.

ANTONIO: No, no, no. Don't go, young man. I've been rude and discourteous, forgive me. Bachelors have special dreads. Old age, loneliness, too much noise, too many requests; we fear opportunists and women. Senile fears. Forgive me. Sit and talk about yourself and what you want of me. Of course I remember your father. We were good for one another in lean years. Talk. I'll help his son. Without question. Trade? Tricks of the trade? Contracts? To represent me? Tell me what you want.

BASSANIO: In Belmont, sir, there is a lady.

ANTONIO: Ah, love!

BASSANIO: Her father's family goes back to the time when Venetians were fishermen, and –

ANTONIO: And would now prefer to forget it!

BASSANIO: – And, like all of those ancient families, became wealthy. These, the Contarinis, added to their wealth with – what shall I call it? – not madness, but – unorthodoxy. The father of my lady, whose name is Portia, was – well – odd! A philosopher.

ANTONIO: Oh, very odd.

BASSANIO: He evolved, it seems, a strange theory that men's

character could be learned by tests, and to this end he devised a huge chart divided into the most important aspects of a man's character. Honour, common sense, loyalty, stamina and so on. And for each virtue and its opposite he devised their tests. His entire estates became manned by men he'd chosen based upon these philosophically evolved examinations. All, with one exception, fell into ruin.

ANTONIO: What an incredibly sad story.

BASSANIO: There is a happy side. The daughter —

ANTONIO: Beautiful?

BASSANIO: Well, not beautiful perhaps, but — striking, vivid. Compelling. Intelligent eyes, mobile features — handsome. In fact, if I must be blunt, determination and strength of will give her face a masculine aspect. She's feminine to the extent that she doesn't deny her sex, yet misleading because she doesn't cultivate, exploit, abuse it.

ANTONIO: Just such a woman I'd like to have met in *my* youth.

BASSANIO: You'll understand, then, the reason for my agitation.

ANTONIO: But not yet how it concerns me.

BASSANIO: Three caskets rest at Belmont. One gold, one silver, one lead. Who chooses the correct casket wins the daughter.

ANTONIO: Aha! The final test. And my role in this?

BASSANIO: I've lived a stupid, wasting life, Signor Antonio. I possess nothing and can lay my hands on nothing. I had hoped to marry wealth but now I've fallen in love with ruins. I mean to choose the right casket, marry that extraordinary woman and work to restore her property to profit. But I'm without means either to dress myself or reach her.

ANTONIO: It will cost?

BASSANIO: To present myself without insult? Three thousand ducats.

ANTONIO: Three thousand ducats!

BASSANIO: I believe no claim was ever made on your godfathership before.

ANTONIO: None.

BASSANIO: And none will be again.

ANTONIO: Bassanio, you come at a bad time. I've ships to sea but no cash to hand. More, I plan retirement, and all my wealth lies in their cargoes. The small change I need for daily living is easily got on credit from friendly traders, but the eyes of the Rialto are on me and I know no one who'll lend me so large a sum except –

BASSANIO: Who?

ANTONIO: Shylock.

BASSANIO: The Jew?

ANTONIO [*defying his contempt*]: Shylock.

BASSANIO: But the interest rate, the conditions.

ANTONIO: Whatever the conditions! It's more than I've ever borrowed in my life, but for the good years of my youth with your father, done!

BASSANIO: With a Jew!

ANTONIO: I've told you, young man, the Jew is my special friend.

BASSANIO: Of course. Forgive me, sir. And now, I'll go. If there's anything I can do for you in the city?

ANTONIO: Yes, take a message to my assistant, Graziano Sanudo. Tell him I won't be in today, but to arrange for dinner on Wednesday. I'm entertaining my friend, Shylock, so no pork. Join us, Bassanio, I keep a good wine cellar.

BASSANIO: With the greatest of pleasure, and honoured. May I bring with me an old friend I've recently met with again? A sort of philosopher.

ANTONIO: 'Sort of'?

BASSANIO: Writes poetry occasionally.

ANTONIO: A 'sort of philosopher' who 'writes poetry occasionally!' Good! Old Shylock might enjoy that. What's his name?

BASSANIO: Lorenzo Pisani.

ANTONIO: Ah! The silk manufacturers.

BASSANIO: You know them?

ANTONIO: The fabric, not the family.

BASSANIO: You won't regret this trust, Signor.

ANTONIO: I hope to God I do not, Bassanio.

[BASSANIO, *leaving, meets* SHYLOCK *on the way out.* SHYLOCK *bows but is ignored.*]

I hope to God.

SHYLOCK: And what was that like?

ANTONIO: I'm not certain. He'd not met a Jew before.

[SHYLOCK *goes into fits of laughter.*]

ANTONIO: What is so funny?

SHYLOCK: That's not a sin. There are a hundred million people in China who've not met a Jew before!

ANTONIO: Still he worries me for other reasons. There was too much calculation in him. You'll be meeting him on Wednesday and can judge for yourself. I've invited him for dinner. With a friend of his, Lorenzo Pisani.

SHYLOCK: Pisani?

ANTONIO: You know him?

SHYLOCK: I know him. He wrote a poem once, too long, 'The Ruin of the Nation's Heart'. A murky thing, full of other people's philosophy. Jessica showed it to me. She seemed very impressed because it called for a return to simplicity . . .

ANTONIO: Of course! My assistant Graziano showed it *me*. Seems it set our youth on fire, full of disgust with the great wretchedness of the world and the sins of men. It had a sense of doom which the poet seemed to enjoy rather more than he was anxious to warn of.

SHYLOCK: That's the one! Ah, children, children! [*which reminds him, so he calls*] Children! Children! Let's eat. [*To* ANTONIO] You must be starving, and the Portuguese must be bored to death with my books by now, and we must be finished eating in time for a sitting. [*Calling again*] Jessica. [*To* ANTONIO] I'm having our portrait painted. It's the day for a sitting. A great painter, an old man now, but exquisite, Moses of Castelazzo. Renowned!

ANTONIO: Shylock?

SHYLOCK: My friend?

ANTONIO: I have a great favour to ask of you.

SHYLOCK: At last! A favour! Antonio of Shylock!

ANTONIO: To borrow three thousand ducats.

SHYLOCK: Not four? Five? Ten?

ANTONIO: I'm not making jokes, Shylock.

SHYLOCK: And why do you think I do?

ANTONIO: For three months?

SHYLOCK: Your city borrows forever, why not three months for you?

ANTONIO: You know my position?

SHYLOCK: I know your position. Your fortune in one voyage, I know. Insane. Still.

ANTONIO: You're a good man, old man.

SHYLOCK: Old man – forever! Good – not always. I'm a friend.

ANTONIO: What shall you want as a surety in the contract?

SHYLOCK: The *what*?

ANTONIO: The contract, Shylock. We must draw up a bond.

SHYLOCK: A bond? Between friends? What nonsense are you talking, Antonio?

ANTONIO: Collateral must be arranged.

SHYLOCK: Between you and me?

ANTONIO: The law demands it.

SHYLOCK: Then we'll ignore the law.

ANTONIO: The law demands: no dealings may be made with Jews unless covered by a legal bond.

SHYLOCK: That law was made for enemies, not friends.

ANTONIO: I don't want it for myself, Shylock, but for you. If word gets out we've made no bond then *you'll* be penalized, not I.

SHYLOCK: And who will tell?

ANTONIO: It's known already. The money is not for me. My godson. No, don't tell me I'm a fool. The boy's father was a good friend. I told him you were the only man I know could raise that sum at once.

SHYLOCK: Good! Then lie to him. Tell him, if you must tell him anything, that a contract exists and it's in my possession.

ANTONIO: Shylock! The law says, in these very words, 'It is forbidden to enter into dealings with a Jew without sign and sealing of a bond, which bond must name the sums borrowed, specify the collateral, name the day, the hour to be paid, and –

TOGETHER: – and be witnessed by three Venetians, two patricians and one citizen, and *then* registered!

ANTONIO: Be sensible! The law of Venice is a jealous one, no man may bend it. The city's reputation *rests* on respect for its laws.

SHYLOCK: Sensible! Sensible! I follow my heart, *my* laws. What could be more sensible? The Deuteronic Code says 'Thou shalt not lend upon usury to thy brother. Unto a foreigner thou mayest lend upon usury, but unto thy brother not.' Your papacy, however, turns your laws against us. But for once, Antonio, let us not quite bend the law but interpret it as men, neither Christian nor Jew.

I love you, therefore you are my brother. And since you are my brother, my laws say I may not lend upon usury to you, but must uphold you. Take the ducats.

ANTONIO: But the laws of Venice are something else, dear Shylock, dear brother. They say we *cannot* be brothers.

SHYLOCK: I will not have soiled a friendship with my fellow man.

ANTONIO [*pressing*]: And if Venice represents anything any longer to anyone in the world it's through its laws, more important even than its constitution.

SHYLOCK: The laws must leave me to conduct my loves as I please.

ANTONIO: Especially now when the economy is so vulnerable.

SHYLOCK: My dealings with you are sacrosanct.

ANTONIO: The French markets are gone, the English are building faster and better ships and there are fools talking about dangerous protectionist policies. We are a nervous Empire.

SHYLOCK: I *will* have trust.

ANTONIO: Shylock listen!

SHYLOCK: My heart needs to know I can trust and be trusted.

ANTONIO: You must not, cannot, bend the law.

SHYLOCK: You can have three thousand ducats but there will be no bond, for no collateral, and for no time limit whatsoever.

ANTONIO: I understand. And it brings me closer to you than ever. But the deeper I feel our friendship the more compelled I feel to press my point, and protect you. You are a Jew, Shylock. Not only is your race a minority, it is despised. Your existence here in Venice, your pleasures, your very freedom to be sardonic or bitter is a privilege, not a right. Your life, the lives of your people depend upon contract and respect for the laws behind contract. What is in your contract with the city councillors they *must* respect. Therefore you, of all peoples, have need of that respect for the law. The law, Shylock, the law! For you and your people, the bond-in-law must be honoured.

SHYLOCK: Oh, you have really brought me down. That's earth I feel now. Solid. [*Pause, not losing his good humour.*] We'll cheat them yet.

ANTONIO: You mean you're still not persuaded?

SHYLOCK: I'm persuaded, oh yes, I'm very, very persuaded. We'll have a bond.

ANTONIO: Good!

SHYLOCK: A nonsense bond.

ANTONIO: A nonsense bond?

SHYLOCK: A lovely, loving nonsense bond. To mock the law.

ANTONIO: To mock?

SHYLOCK: Barbaric laws? Barbaric bonds! Three thousand ducats against a pound of your flesh.

ANTONIO: My flesh?

SHYLOCK: You're like an idiot child suddenly. [*Mocking*] 'A nonsense bond? My flesh?' Yes. If I am not repaid by you, upon the day, the hour, I'll have a pound of your old flesh, Antonio, from near that part of your body which pleases me most – your heart. Your heart, dearheart, and I'd take that, too, if I could, I'm so fond of it.

[*Pause as* SHYLOCK *waits to see if* ANTONIO *accepts.*]

ANTONIO: Barbaric laws, barbaric bonds?

SHYLOCK: Madness for the mad.

ANTONIO: Idiocies for idiots.

SHYLOCK: Contempt for the contemptible.

ANTONIO: They mock our friendship –

SHYLOCK: – We mock their laws.

ANTONIO [*pinching himself*]: Do I have a pound of flesh? I don't even have a pound of flesh.

SHYLOCK [*pinching him*]: Here, and here, and here, one, two, three pounds of flesh!

[*He's tickling him;* ANTONIO *responds. Like children they're goosing each other and giggling, upon which note* JESSICA *and* RIVKA *enter with food,* RODERIGUES *also.*

TUBAL, REBECCA *and* USQUE *enter deep in animated conversation. A meal is to be eaten, the sounds and pleasures of hospitality are in the air.*]

## SCENE FIVE

[ANTONIO's *warehouse. Bales of coloured cloth, some from* PISANI *factories. Sacks of spices.*
GRAZIANO, *throwing cloth over* BASSANIO *to see which suits him. He tends to have conversations with himself, ignoring what others are saying.*
LORENZO, *plunging his hand in a sack drawing spice pebbles which run back through his fingers.*]

BASSANIO: I was amazed. 'And that is a Jew?' I asked. '*He* is a Jew,' my godfather corrected.

LORENZO: I don't like it. A world turned upside down.

BASSANIO: They were all Jews! His friends!

GRAZIANO: But a loan of three thousand ducats? I don't like it!

BASSANIO: You should have heard them, discussing Venice as though the city cared for their voice, existed for their judgement!

LORENZO: Money is a dead thing, with no seed, it's not fit to engender.

GRAZIANO: Well said.

BASSANIO: What could I do, Lorenzo? 'The Jew is my special friend,' he said.

GRAZIANO: Ah, now that *is* understandable.

LORENZO: Is it?

GRAZIANO: Well –

LORENZO: Shylock dares play God with a dead thing, and Venice has only a dead language to answer him with. Of course his usury flourishes. A nation that confuses timidity for tolerance is a nation without principle.

GRAZIANO: A nation turned upside down.

BASSANIO [*to* LORENZO]: Do you know Shylock well?

LORENZO [*moving from sack to sack, the spices trickling through his hands*]: I know him.

GRAZIANO [*Pursuing his own conversation with* BASSANIO *while winding cloth round him*]: Who do you know asserts authority?

LORENZO: A loud, enthusiastic man.

GRAZIANO: Men fear earning hatreds! No leadership! No God!

LORENZO: I've stood by him in the Ghetto when he's showing visitors its sights.

GRAZIANO: Not even the priests have time for God and our painters paint their Virgin Marys like whores.

LORENZO: Thin achievements in stone which he's magnified more from relief they've any stones at all than from their real worth.

GRAZIANO: The aged are in control of Venice, my friends.

LORENZO: There's hysteria in his description of things. His tone is urgent –

GRAZIANO: A burning issue.

LORENZO: – excited –

GRAZIANO: I burn whenever it comes up.

LORENZO: – excited, ornate and proudly erudite.

GRAZIANO: It comes up burning and I burn.

LORENZO: That's his sin: intellectual pride. His daughter can't bear it.

BASSANIO: You know Shylock's daughter?

GRAZIANO: A friend of yours?

LORENZO: You'd not think they're of the same blood. He's proud, she's modest. He imagines knowledge is all, she lives in the world. His voice is metallic with contempt, hers is sweet with reason. And she listens to music.

BASSANIO: And poetry perhaps?

LORENZO: And poetry, perhaps.

BASSANIO: Even praised some?

LORENZO: Even that.

BASSANIO: Good God, Lorenzo, are you in love?

LORENZO: Love? Who knows about love? She admired the poem and those who admire us must have merit we think. We snatch moments together, walk, talk, complain about our separate worlds. Sometimes we don't see one another for weeks, and on the first day there's a sort of longing makes me think the ache is what they call love, but as each day passes she drifts away from my thoughts. I lose her. Can that be love? Respect perhaps.

BASSANIO: What an uncertain young man! Is this the 'he' who wrote 'The Ruin of the Nation's Heart'?

LORENZO: You're right! My nature can't decide itself. I feel passionate appetites within me but for what? The fool depresses me yet I myself believe in God enough to risk being called a simpleton. I despise power yet so much offends me that I want power to wipe out the offence. And where does it lie? In trade or moral principle? The spirit of the trader is in me as in every Venetian but there is such a frenzy of avarice and unbridled ambition that I feel the end of the world must be near, a world which one moment I want to renounce, the next help save from itself.

BASSANIO: Beware, young man, beware. Help the poor world save itself? Would you preach like Savanarola? He also thought Italy lived in horrible times, look how he ended his mission. The trap is that preachers intoxicate themselves so, come to deem themselves lords of life and earth, abuse their powers and weary men by perpetual admonitions. Beware, young man, beware.

GRAZIANO: Beware, nothing! Lorenzo's right. Horrible times. There's little for young men of character here.

BASSANIO: Nonsense! Everywhere I turn I hear of young patricians being schooled for trade, diplomacy, the council's work.

LORENZO: But can those young patricians vote for the Doge if they're under thirty, or become senators before forty? Power doesn't reside in principle but in the hands of a few families.

BASSANIO: Who trade with the world! Come, what are you saying? Venice is a free city. Her doors are open, open!

LORENZO: Her legs are open, open! Venice – brothel of the Mediterranean. And all so that we can boast to everyone of our local codes and a freedom which tolerates corruption.

BASSANIO: Steady there, Lorenzo. Not too far. The tolerance of Jews may be unpalatable to us, but trade, I sometimes think that men in trade have kept our mad world sane, preserved us from destructive politicians, kept very human actions going while the wild men ranted on about their principles. Be honest now, doesn't your father's father own the silk looms of *his* father's father? And don't those looms allow you time for your philosophical speculations and political protests? Venice built its glory on its ancient trading families, after all.

GRAZIANO: And that's where the power lies, in the long ancient families who trade. I should know, coming as I do from one of them.

BASSANIO: *Long* ancient families? You?

GRAZIANO: Don't be surprised, my friends, not all Venetian aristocracy is bright, you see. Least of all I. Me. Least of all me. Or is it 'I'? I'm what they call an academic failure, expect nothing of me. My family are wealthy but not illustrious. They hoped I'd rise to be a statesman and add honour to their fortune, but I've neither tact nor memory, and in shame my family apprenticed me to trade. Personal assistant and happy!

BASSANIO: But what is a 'long family'?

GRAZIANO: A long family it is us, jealously listed in the chronicles and lists of our nobility as one of the twenty-four families. Of old. Who began it all. Or rather, there are twelve, from which I come, who claim the greatest nobility because they go back before 762, or is it 726? When the first Doge was elected, whose name was Orso, a military man, or was that Anafesto? Because some say the first Doge was elected in 679, or was it 697? And that *his* name was Anafesto, or was *his* name Orso? Whoever, my family goes back beyond then. The other twelve families only claim to have elected him. But both are long families. So called. As you see.

BASSANIO: And all were fishermen?

GRAZIANO: No! I mean, yes! I mean, the point is, we don't think of ourselves as descended from fishermen. It's just that we're – old. Go back a long way. The Roman Empire. Venice as a second Rome. Ancient.

BASSANIO: To be ancient is to be noble, you mean?

GRAZIANO: Exactly what I'm trying to say.

BASSANIO: So, a peasant family if it had the memory and evidence of a long past would be noble too?

GRAZIANO: Ah, no.

BASSANIO: So that's *not* exactly what you're trying to say?

GRAZIANO: That's what I'm saying, not exactly.

BASSANIO: Something more is needed to be a noble family?

GRAZIANO: Power!

BASSANIO: Which comes from where?

GRAZIANO: Stop teasing me, Bassanio. The question of Venetian nobility is an anxious one, my family quibble about it constantly.

LORENZO: And pointlessly. The question remains. What's to become of Venice? Does strength lie in trade or moral principle?

BASSANIO: Now you talk of strength. I thought we were talking of power.

LORENZO: You're right. We must distinguish our words or the concepts behind them will become entangled also.

BASSANIO: And strength may lie in moral principle but power resides in trade. See this pebble of pepper – it's this has the power to push men across seas. Three million pounds passed through Venice this year. Do you know what amount of gold that represents? Kings monopolize the spice trade for themselves.

LORENZO: But religious principle is constant, trade is not. A Portuguese sailor circumnavigates the Cape? The spice trade of the Mediterranean dies!

BASSANIO: And who takes over? The Portuguese! Another Catholic nation! And where is religious principle then?

LORENZO: More reason to defend it! For it would then have power to bind the trade of nations who would otherwise fight.

BASSANIO: Precisely! As I said! Trade keeps the world sane while the wild men rant on about their principles. Beware, young man, beware! Gentlemen, it's my time to go. I must cut my suits and sharpen my wits for Belmont. I chase a woman there they say has intellect.

LORENZO: And what is *her* inheritance? Ruins!

BASSANIO: Which she will rebuild.

LORENZO: If the elders will allow her.

BASSANIO: Despite them she will.

LORENZO: If their laws don't cripple her.

BASSANIO: I know her. She will.

LORENZO: If she has cunning and connections and the facility to fawn.

BASSANIO: She will, she will! Rebuild! With my help of course. As youth does, ignoring the evil within, defying the past. We're young! Don't be so solemn, Lorenzo. We'll meet at Antonio's for dinner and talk more. Perhaps we'll get to know you better, Graziano.

GRAZIANO: You'll love me, I promise you.

BASSANIO: And old Shylock too. What more will he be made of, I wonder?

LORENZO: Nothing much for loving there.

GRAZIANO: I know what he means, I know what he means.


# SCENE SIX


[SHYLOCK's *main room.*
*Chairs and easel are being set up for a portrait sitting.*
SHYLOCK *enters with* USQUE, *followed by a bustling* RIVKA, *and*
RODERIGUES *who is planning to do his own sketch of* JESSICA.
*The old Jewish portrait painter* MOSES OF CASTELAZZO *arrives.*]

SHYLOCK: Ah! Moses, you're here!

MOSES: No! I'm not here!

SHYLOCK: Signor Usque, playwright, allow me to introduce you to the painter, the renowned Moses of Castelazzo.

MOSES [*ignoring the niceties of introduction and going straight to the easel*]: Renowned! Renowned! Who cares about renown at eighty!

[SHYLOCK *and* RIVKA *take up positions.*]

RODERIGUES: And where's Jessica? How can I draw a subject who's not there?

MOSES [*mocking*]: And where's Jessica? How can I draw a subject who's not there! Look at him! If you must be in love don't show it. If you must show it don't draw it! Let me see. [*Snatches sketch book.*] You can't draw! Why are you trying to draw when you can't draw? Suddenly everybody imagines he's an artist!

RODERIGUES: The very old like him should be kept apart from the very young like me. I can see it now.

SHYLOCK: Stop squabbling. Moses can begin without Jessica, and Signor Usque has promised to tell us about his new play.

MOSES: Another one! Suddenly! Everyone! An artist!

USQUE: It will be a debate.

SHYLOCK: Between whom?

USQUE: Between rabbis who were interpreting –

SHYLOCK: – the interpretations of the interpretations of the great scholars who interpreted the meaning of the meaning –

USQUE: Precisely! You will remember that Catherine of Aragon had been the widow of Henry the Eighth's dead brother, Arthur, and now Henry wanted his marriage with her annulled. The Pope would probably have said yes, but was worried about Catherine's nephew, Charles V. Both – Henry and the Pope, that is – found support for their views in the Bible.

SHYLOCK: Naturally!

USQUE: Henry's wishes were supported by the book of Leviticus which said marriage to the widow of a dead brother was forbidden. While Rome's refusal supported itself with Deuteronomy which allows such a marriage in the case of a previously childless match.

SHYLOCK: Sons! Sons must be born to perpetuate the man's name! Power, lineage, lust – and all rushing for succour to the Bible.

USQUE: But the problem of interpretation was perplexing.

SHYLOCK: Naturally!

USQUE: And so to whom did they turn for guidance?

SHYLOCK: We can't wait to hear.

MOSES: To the bickering old Jews of Venice.

SHYLOCK: *You* know?

MOSES: Around 1530. Big quarrels.

RIVKA: Old fools of Venice, more like.

MOSES: And all a lot of nonsense. There was a man I remember came all the way from England to get the opinions of the Italian Rabbis –

RIVKA: Who immediately formed different camps!

MOSES: Now what was his name – er – er –

USQUE: Richard Cooke.

MOSES: Cooke. Yes. Names! Why can't I remember names?

RIVKA: They didn't know the King of England or the Pope but they fought for them!

MOSES: I used to remember everybody's names. Age!

RIVKA: Old fools!

MOSES: Damn age!

USQUE: But, who do *you* think was right, Shylock? Remember my play will not be seeking interpretations of history, but of the scriptures.

[JESSICA *enters and takes up her pose the other side of* SHYLOCK.]

SHYLOCK: You're late.

JESSICA: This is the last time I sit, father.

SHYLOCK: Don't you understand how insulting it is to be late for an appointment?

JESSICA: Signor Castelazzo was not held up by me.

SHYLOCK: This is my house, and while under my roof –

JESSICA [*challengingly*]: While under your roof, *what*?

SHYLOCK: An appointment is sacred.

JESSICA: You exaggerate.

SHYLOCK: To keep another waiting is to say to him you don't care for him.

JESSICA: Or that you care more for what you've left. Or that what you've left presented problems unanticipated. Or that what you've left was a dying man, you were needed, or you were compelled, or forced – really! Father! You're so full of tight, restricting little codes.

SHYLOCK: An appointment is a bond. Between two people. They depend upon each other honouring it, and if it's broken – lives can be affected, deals fall through, hearts broken, disappointment –

JESSICA: The scheme of things! The scheme of things! Stop lecturing me with your scheme of things.

MOSES: I have a painting to paint. Please.

USQUE: You've not answered my questions, Signor Shylock.

SHYLOCK: Ask my daughter. She's the clever one.

USQUE: My new play, about a quarrel between rabbis, some interpreting Deuteronomy on behalf of the Papacy, others Leviticus on behalf of Henry the Eighth. The positions were this –

JESSICA: With respect, Signor Usque, I don't need to have their relative positions described. The idea is offensive. To scurry backwards and forwards in and out of the Bible's pages for such an obscene quarrel – the rabbis should have been ashamed of themselves. The cause doesn't interest me.

USQUE: The cause doesn't interest me, either, but the nature of interpretation does.

SHYLOCK [*but proud*]: Forgive her. She's had good tutors to exercise her mind but no mother to shape her manners.

RODERIGUES [*sketching furiously*]: But keep her angry, she looks beautiful when she's angry. Beautiful!

MOSES: Idiot!

RIVKA: I thought women only looked beautiful when they were in love, Roderigues.

JESSICA [*topping her*]: This is the last time I pose, father.

SHYLOCK: You've told me already.

JESSICA: As you've told me a thousand times that this is your house and your roof.

SHYLOCK: Under which you are deprived of nothing.

JESSICA: Except the sweetness of feeling that it is *my* house and *my* roof also. You want a debate for your play, Signor Usque? Then debate this question: to whom does a house belong? Only the father? Not even the mother? And if not the children and the mother, then how must their relationship be described? As temporary occupants? As long standing visitors? At what point is the child's right of movement and taste taken into consideration? Does she only become whole when taken from the possession of her father to the possession of her husband? What do Leviticus and Deuteronomy have to say on those things? Look how my father swells with pride at his daughter's intellect. He's given me teachers to nourish and exercise my mind, while he continues to exercise control.

SHYLOCK: If she is talking about control and the child's rights it can only mean she wants to go out again one day soon. I feel her tremors long before she erupts.

JESSICA: He talks as though the world elected him.

SHYLOCK: *She* talks as though the tutors' fees were well spent!

JESSICA: Tell him his daughter must be taken seriously.

SHYLOCK: Tell her she should not be neglecting her music studies.

JESSICA: Tell him you can be oppressed by study.

SHYLOCK: Dancing, singing, the instruments I bought for her – tell her.

JESSICA: Tell him not everyone wants to perform, some are content to listen.

SHYLOCK: Tell her –

JESSICA: Tell her, tell her! Tell her nothing more –

[*She storms out.* SHYLOCK *is shocked.*]

RIVKA: Mean! Mean! To withhold praise from your daughter, mean. From your own daughter.

SHYLOCK: The Talmud says: praise not a man more than ten per cent of his worth.

USQUE: Forgive me, Signor Shylock, I do not think you've judged well. You'll drive her into a hasty marriage.

RIVKA: He doesn't *want* her to marry.

[USQUE *turns to* SHYLOCK *for a response.*]

SHYLOCK: The *Pope* calls for the vows of chastity, but *God* only ever ordained matrimony. To whom should I listen? [*But he is thinking of other things.*]


# SCENE SEVEN

[ANTONIO's *house.*

*Present are* BASSANIO, LORENZO *and* GRAZIANO. *They have just eaten.*

SHYLOCK *has been with them but is out of the room, unwell, accompanied by* ANTONIO.

*Contented pause of men who've eaten, drunk and conversed well.*]


GRAZIANO: Well, the poor Jew is very sick, for sure. He's been gone a quarter of an hour.

BASSANIO: I think you gave him too much wine.

LORENZO: Or the food was too rich for him.

BASSANIO: The man looked anxious. Worried. Sad.

GRAZIANO: I must say, he did drink fast. Very nervously. He came in and at once downed two glasses of wine.

LORENZO: It was not that. He eats and drinks and talks at the same time. There's no grace in the man.

BASSANIO: I find him most interesting. *You* see many Jews in Venice – at least ten thousand, I'd say –

GRAZIANO: Fourteen hundred.

BASSANIO: Really? As few as that? Well, they seem more. But where I lived, just outside Milan, we saw none. Everyone talked about them, but I'd never actually met one. So for me – interesting.

[SHYLOCK *and* ANTONIO *enter.*]

SHYLOCK: Oh, I love Venice.

GRAZIANO: A noble city, Signor Shylock, you're right.

LORENZO: You were born here, of course.

SHYLOCK: Yes, I was born here, of course.

LORENZO: I ask because so many of you come from here and there and everywhere.

SHYLOCK: I know why you ask.

LORENZO: It must be very difficult for your tribe to produce much of art or thought, as civilized nations do who have roots in territory.

SHYLOCK: Very.

LORENZO: Would you not agree that –

[SHYLOCK, *bored and despising* LORENZO, *turns aside to talk with his friend,* ANTONIO. *He's still a little drunk.*]

SHYLOCK: I love Venice, Antonio, because it's a city full of men busy living, and passing through, and free to do both as their right, not as a favour.

ANTONIO: Venice is distorted through your gratitude, Shylock, you've forgotten your yellow hat.

SHYLOCK: If I'd been a damned physician, I'd not have to wear this damned yellow hat every time I took a walk. Physician! Now *there* was a profession to belong to instead of my own seedy lineage. Failures! [*Pause.*] I descended from German Jews, you know. My grandparents. Grubby little things from Cologne. Came to Venice as small-time money lenders for the poor. But my parents – they tried a new profession. Very brave. Second-hand clothing! My mother went blind patching up smelly old clothes and my father became famous for beating out, cleaning and reconditioning old mattresses. Bringers of sleep – not a dishonourable trade don't you think, gentlemen? Mattresses; bringers of sweet sleep.

LORENZO: And sweet plagues.

SHYLOCK [*hisses*]: Yes! I know! Better than you, I know! [*Relaxing again.*] But he was not an ambitious man, my father. Had no confidence in himself. Not like the really big pawnbrokers, men who built up huge stores of carvings, furniture, paintings. Tintorettos would pass through *their* hands while stained pantaloons passed through my father's. Those pawnbrokers were so stocked up in their warehouses that even the dukes had to come to them in order to hire furnishings for their banquets. You could always be certain of buying dazzling tapestry in the Ghetto. Except from my father. Verminous vests you could get from him.

LORENZO: It's true. The Ghetto *is* notorious for its smells.

ANTONIO: I will not have discourtesies in my house.

LORENZO: You must forgive me, Signor Antonio. But I too am a guest, and we can't pretend that animosity doesn't exist between your guests. You ask me to respect your Jewish friend but what respect has he shown for me? Respect has no merit if it's unilateral. And disputation is a sacred right in our city. On several occasions this evening I've attempted to engage Signor Shylock in a theological discussion. He's turned away. If courtesy is esteemed then such a manner is not an efficacious way to achieve it.

SHYLOCK: Efficacious! Unilateral! Disputation! What a rich vocabulary! Perhaps I'm too frightened to dispute with you, friend Lorenzo. Yours is a university trained mind. Mine is the Ghetto's.

BASSANIO: You must not be surprised if with such scorn you attract hostility.

LORENZO [*with evangelist fervour*]: 'They are not humbled even unto this day, neither have they feared, nor walked in my law, nor in my statues, that I have set before you and before your fathers.' Thus sayeth Ezekial.

SHYLOCK: It was Jeremiah. Oh dear. You want theological disputation? Listen. You have us for life, gentlemen, for life. Learn to live with us. The Jew is the Christian's parent. Difficult, I know. Parent-children relationships, always difficult, and even worse when murder is involved within the family. But what can we do? It *is* the family! Not only *would* I be your friend but I *have* to be your friend. Don't scowl, Signor sweet Christian. For life. Old Shylock, Jew of Venice. For ever! The prophets, perseverance, protest, account books and all!

[*Long pause.*]

GRAZIANO: Yes. Well. A very noble city. You are absolutely right, Shylock. We were discussing nobility the other night.

SHYLOCK: Now what is he talking about?

GRAZIANO: Nobility and power. What *is* the nature of nobility and in what does power reside?

SHYLOCK: Power? Were we talking about power?

GRAZIANO: Bassanio here believes that power resides in our ability to trade.

SHYLOCK: Good God! There was no one in the room when I was talking!

BASSANIO: While Graziano here believes power resides in the family who trades, which power in turn gives the family nobility.

GRAZIANO: Exactly! The *accumulated* knowledge of superiority *gives* one superiority: Venice is as a second Rome.

BASSANIO: Lorenzo-the-silent on the other hand believes power resides in the strength of moral superiority. Only Christian principle should activate our republic.

SHYLOCK: Perhaps they will understand *you*. They obviously thought I was speaking Hebrew.

ANTONIO: I have no stomach for it really. Venice as a second Rome is such nonsense. We're a commercial enterprise and no more.

BASSANIO: Come, Antonio, that's cynicism. I agree in part but that's not the whole truth. What about Venetian rule of law? Her Christian pride and fervour? All vital organs of the Empire.

ANTONIO: The most vital organs of our Empire are warehouses, ships' holds, barges and pack-horses. St Mark may be our architectural pride but it's a spiritual offering to hide our real gods Mercury and Neptune, the Gods of commerce and the sea! We're not even honest industrialists, we're simply importers and exporters, rich because the commerce of other people flows through us, not because we produce it ourselves. And as for Venice's sense of justice, it's to retain for her patricians the best opportunities for long-distance trade. Our motives are opportunist and our power rests on a geographical accident, so let's have no nonsense about Venice being a second Rome.

SHYLOCK: No, no, friend Antonio. Forgive me, I must quarrel with you as well. Oh, this is terrible. You defend me and I cross you. But I must. You both miss the point of Venice, of all Italy. Venice as Rome or not, as a commercial enterprise or not is irrelevant. What you say may be true but there is a scheme of things much grander. Let me remind you of three distinct developments affecting the history of this extraordinary land of yours and let's see where real power resides.

LORENZO: Are we now to be given a history lesson about our own lands by a German Jew?

SHYLOCK: Don't be offended, Lorenzo-the-silent. Remember, the synagogue existed in Rome before the Papacy.

GRAZIANO [incredulous]: The rabbi before the Pope?

SHYLOCK: The Roman wars. Jewish slaves. The Princes of Israel. Now ssssh! And listen. It's a very thrilling story. Three developments! But first, who said: 'Religionem imperare non possumus –

ANTONIO: – quia nemo cogitur –

SHYLOCK: – ut credat invitus'? Mmm? How do you like my pronunciation of Latin, eh?

GRAZIANO: 'We cannot enforce acceptance of a creed, since no one can be compelled to believe against his will.'

SHYLOCK: Excellent, Graziano, bravo!

GRAZIANO: Had to learn it by heart at school.

SHYLOCK: But who said it?

[Pause.]

ANTONIO: Cassiodorus!

SHYLOCK: The last and lovely link between Imperial Rome and Gothic Italy.

ANTONIO: Born 479, died 575.

[Then SHYLOCK tells his story with mounting excitement and theatricality, using whatever is around him for props, moving furniture, food, perhaps even people, like men on his chessboard of history. ANTONIO is singled out to be 'Cassiodorus'.]

SHYLOCK: A sweet and intellectual man. Dubious elasticity of conscience, perhaps – always able to make himself necessary to the different rulers of the country, but still. A statesman! A scholar! And for what is this man remembered most? His administrations on behalf of monarchs? Never! And here is development one. At sixty he retired from politics and then, only then began his real life's work.

And what was this work, gentlemen, for another thirty-six years until he died aged ninety-six? [Pause.] During his life he'd succeeded in preserving through all the devastations of civil wars and foreign invasions, a great collection of Greek and Roman classic manuscripts, which, during his retirement to Bruttii, he made certain were scrupulously copied by the monks. *What* a work! What a faith! But why? Why should he have bothered? What makes one man so cherish the work of others that he lovingly guards it, copies, preserves it? And a Christian, too, preserving the works of pagans! I love it! From monastery to monastery, especially among the Benedictines, busy, busy, scribbling, for centuries, right up until the twelfth century, at which point the book trade creeps from the monasteries into the universities. The scholars take over from the monks. The pattern takes shape. Development number two: the destruction of the Roman Empire! Italy breaks into three pieces. The north goes to the German Holy Roman Empire, the centre becomes dominated by the Papacy, and the French house of Anjou takes over the South. Look how fortunes change, rearrange themselves.

LORENZO: Your pleasure in history is superficial, signor – playful. Its patterns please you but not its meanings. How can you expect us to listen seriously to your analysis? Such delight in chance is spiteful. You'd have us believe there was no cause and effect. I have no sympathy with such approaches.

SHYLOCK: Aha! Spirit! I might even come to respect you, young man, but –

LORENZO: And don't play with me, either, signor.

SHYLOCK: But – you read me wrong if you believe I read history so carelessly. I'm perfectly aware how causes work their effects – but *within their time*. The line *I* stretch joins together men and moments who could never possibly have forecast one another's acts. Did old Cassiodorus working away in the year 539 see how Italy's development would shape? Hear me out. It's thrilling, thrilling – believe me.

The land in three pieces, then. But, does everything stand still? Impossible? Watch in the north how the German Holy Roman Empire cracks, disintegrates. Watch the centre shake as the powerful families of Rome brawl among themselves and drive a weary papacy to Avignon for seventy years. Listen in the south, the noise of war! The French house of Anjou is fighting the Spanish house of Aragon. Nothing stands still! And as the dust of war and madness settles all is revealed! The northern half of the peninsular fragmented! And into what? Into what, gentlemen? City States! The magnificent City States of Milan, Genoa, Florence, Venice! The Empires have broken up, the Papacy has slunk off, and suddenly – every city is left to its own government. What can it do? How *does* one govern? Industry and trade grows. Can't help itself. What! The centre of the Mediterranean basin and *not* trade? So – it begins! The Italians invent partnership agreements, holding companies, marine insurance, credit transfers, double-entry book-keeping! Progress! But listen! Listen what else happened in the fourteenth century, and don't forget old Cassiodorus lurking away patiently down there in the sixth century. More business meant more complex agreements, which meant more law, which complicated the business of government, which meant men of greater education were needed, which meant a *new* kind of education, more practical, more – ah! worldly! And where, where I ask you, could that worldly, new education come from to produce that new law, that new government? Tell me. [*Pause.*] Why, from books! Where else? And where *were* the books? Old Cassiodorus! In the monasteries! He'd preserved the ancient manuscripts of Rome and Greece, hallelujah! Praise be to wise old men!

Aren't you enjoying it? Admit it, doesn't it thrill you to watch it take shape? Be generous. Let yourselves go, for here comes development three. The year 1450. Two beautiful births: a wily old German from Mayence named Gutenberg gives birth to an extraordinary invention called – the printing press: and a great classical scholar named Aldus Manutius is born. Manutius? Manutius? Who's he? Where did he come from, suddenly? What's he got to do with anything? [*Pause.*] Here! In our very own city of Venice, at the age of forty-five, less than a hundred years ago, the great Manutius sets up his divine press and produces the incredible Aldine Editions. Suddenly – everybody can possess a book! And what books! The works of – Plato, Homer, Pindar and Aristophanes, Xenophon, Seneca, Plutarch and Sophocles, Aristotle, Lysias, Euripides, Demosthenes, Thucydides, Herodotus, and all printed from manuscripts kept and preserved in monasteries as far apart as Sweden and Constantinople which Italians were now bringing back home. Amazing! Knowledge, like underground springs, fresh and constantly there, till one day – up! Bubbling! For dying men to drink, for survivors from dark and terrible times. I love it! When generals imagine their vain glory is all, and demagogues smile with sweet benevolence as they tighten the screws of power – up! Up bubbles the little spring. Bubble, bubble, bubble! A little, little lost spring, full of blinding questions and succulent doubts. The word! Unsuspected! Written! Printed! Indestructible! Boom! I love it!

[*Bells ring. Time to return to the Ghetto.* ANTONIO *rises to give* SHYLOCK *his yellow hat. He looks at* ANTONIO *and shrugs sadly, as though the hat is evidence to refute all he's said.*]

ANTONIO: What little lost spring can help you now?

[*And yet . . . he defiantly places it on his head, embraces* ANTONIO, *bows to the other three and goes off chuckling and mumbling . . .*]

SHYLOCK: Bubble, bubble, bubble! Bubble, bubble, bubble! Bubble bubble . . .

# ACT TWO

## SCENE ONE

*[A room in Belmont.*
PORTIA *and* BASSANIO *in conversation.* NERISSA *reading.]*

BASSANIO: Wrong, madame, wrong! It may be true that trade in
spices and the old wares is less profitable and safe these days, but
land and agriculture are not where the fortunes lie. Precious metals!
Trade in those. Gold! A bank! The bank of Contarini! – doesn't
that thought dazzle you? Besides, where will you obtain your
capital for implements?

PORTIA: I've sold estates, and will perhaps sell even more with your
help, but now dear friend, you must choose. Choose wisely. None
of the others did. Some chose swiftly, some with pride. Others
stood thinking for so long they terrified themselves out of the
simple ability to choose at all. So take your place and take your
time. I'll talk with Nerissa. She's reading the letters of Seneca and
I've asked her to select a favourite one. I think I know which one it
will be.

*[*BASSANIO *takes up his place by the caskets.* NERISSA *approaches*
PORTIA.]*

NERISSA: This one, my lady, letter forty-seven. *[She begins to read.]*
'I'm glad to hear, from these people who've been visiting you,
that you live on friendly terms with your slaves. It is just what one
expects of an enlightened, cultivated person like yourself . . .'

*[Her voice lowers as the main melody takes over. Attention must be
focused upon* BASSANIO.]*

BASSANIO: What an eccentric test of love. Whose mind constructed
this? 'By his choice shall you know him.' *[Contemptuously, and
gradually drawn into a conversation with* PORTIA'S FATHER *'up there'.]*
What shall you know of him? That if he choose gold he will be

a man without a soul, with a purse where his heart should be? But a man without a soul may have cunning, surely? Greed does not preclude perception, and a greedy man may well detect misfortune where his instinct leads. Suppose an even more human condition: the man who loves gold has plagues of guilt and so is ripe for self-disgust? Now there's a man who'd shy away from the shiny stuff. No, I don't see the point of such a simple trick. And silver? What's one supposed to think of that, stuck between gold and lead? Oh, here's the mediocre man! Here's the man plays safe with life and neither dares much nor achieves! Or is silver the test of the temperate man, the sober man? Perhaps the diplomat is being looked for here? The statesman? The judge? Not unworthy men! Yet I'm hardly any of those. A little bit of each in me I'd like to think, but – I hardly riot in those qualities. Still, if such a man is wanted for that extraordinary lady, and that extraordinary lady is what I want, then perhaps the statesman, diplomat and judge in me had *better* blossom. Hm! Not such a simple test after all. Come on now, Bassanio, use your wits. You've not survived this far without an arsenal of guile. Think! Think! What father, wanting his daughter to marry a statesman, diplomat or judge would devise such a scheme? A very wise father I'd say, if I didn't know that he was very stupid. Perhaps, then, a better question would be: does Portia look the kind of a daughter who'd have the kind of father would *want* her to marry a statesman, diplomat or judge? [*Pause.*] I will go mad.

The wrong approach! These caskets can't be a test for a profession but – a sort, a kind, a spirit. The question then is: what kind of, sort of spirit would such a woman's father want for her? The father! Look to the father. He's the key. Good! That's something. So. The father descends from a long illustrious line. An aristocracy. But by the time the blood of rulers reached her father it had been watered down to the blood of a philosopher. And now, abundant though the estates' possibilities are, yet they're in ruin. Very decorous ruin, but – ruin. What metal would a ruined ruinous philosopher choose? [*Long pause, smile, he's seen through the strategy, but at first cunningly misleads.*] There can only be one answer. Simple! The end of philosophy is despair. He looked around him, saw the constant battles being fought, the waste, disintegration and decay, and he concluded: for my daughter, none of that! Gold! The hard, determined, merciless pursuit of gain, security and comfort. Gold! With gold is bought beauty, art, obedience, the power for good. Gold! For my daughter shall be trapped a man of gold. The sun is golden, the harvest too – energy and sustenance. These things I will, for my only child, these things which I with my engagement in philosophy neglected to provide. Gold! [*Pause.*] And then he changed his mind! For who can change the habits of a foolish lifetime? [*To* PORTIA] Lead, my lady. Lead I choose. My brain has battled. There's its choice.

PORTIA: Your brain, Bassanio? Not your heart? Still, heart or brain, you've chosen as my father wished.

BASSANIO: Not you?

PORTIA: I? You must forgive me. It *is* possible for eyes to meet and feel their love at once, I know. But I'm not made that way. Love grows with me. My mother taught love ripens on the mind, is made of passions, laughter, all the minutiae of living *shared* rather than surmised. Is that pedantic, you think? Would you rather I embrace you now and say, with routine ardour, that *your* choice decides? Don't think from my response that I'm a calculating woman, though sometimes I wish I were. The truth is I'm impulsive. My responses shape at once. I know a man, a situation at a glance, but my mother said 'humility, your impulse may be wrong.' You'd rather have my love relaxed and confident, Bassanio? Be patient. We will live together. All I have is yours, you know that. Settle here. Rehearse the role of husband. We'll work together, find each other carefully. We *may* be born for one another, part of me believes we are. I want my *all* to know it though. See, I'm trembling as I talk. I think you must embrace me after all.

[THEY *embrace.*]

Now leave. I must arrange and scheme for you.

BASSANIO [*facilely*]: I have no words.

PORTIA [*catching the tone, cools*]: I'm touched.

[BASSANIO *leaves.*]

Perhaps I should be his mistress only. That gives him no holds over

236

me then. As his wife the State chains me. *There's* something to exercise your logic on, Nerissa.

NERISSA: You're uncertain?

PORTIA: Oh, I am that.

NERISSA: You should not love someone you don't like.

PORTIA: What a ridiculous carrier of passion – a casket. I'm uncertain all right. What if I should tire of him? God forbid a woman should tire of a man. Of his vanities and little faults which always, always magnify with time. He has such a blindness for his image, such an incredible satisfaction with his long-considered thimbleful of thoughts, his firm decisive manner over that which should be racked with doubt, his – his – his silly coloured feathers which he feels to be his masculinity. Oh! his masculinity!

NERISSA: Have you watched the way a man walks? As though balancing a cannon-ball on each shoulder, careful that the width of him is seen, felt?

PORTIA: There is such presumption in him, such an air of arrogance, as though what else could woman be but his rib, a mere bone of his body. After all, my dear, men have won battles with a bone missing!

NERISSA [*ribaldly*]: And lost many even with one there.
    [*Great laughter between them.*]

PORTIA: Heaven help us, but there are so few poets among them!

NERISSA: They are such clumsy things. So weighed down with dull earthiness.

PORTIA: Except at wooing-time, and then, ah! Then – have you noticed that collapse of features which they feel is tenderness? That slow softening of the eyes into a milky melancholy they think is love-sick helplessness?

NERISSA: That sudden clenching of the jaw and fist which struggles to be passion?

PORTIA: What feeble and pathetic arts they have. And we must pretend! Poor gimcrack men! Oh! There are such stirrings in me. Such untried intellect. Such marvellous loves and wisdom. I could found cities with my strengths, Nerissa, cities undreamed of by any man.
    [*Bells peal out as we change to –*]

## SCENE TWO

[*The 'logetta' beneath the campanile of St Mark's. Normally a meeting-place for patricians.*
TUBAL *and* RODERIGUES *approach from different parts. It is night.*]


TUBAL: Nothing?

RODERIGUES: Nothing!

TUBAL: You've asked discreetly?

RODERIGUES: Discreetly and indiscreetly. What do I care now!

TUBAL: The entire Ghetto is out looking for her, taking risks. Foolish girl.

RODERIGUES: 'I know your daughter,' I told him, I warned him.

TUBAL: You warned? I warned! Who didn't warn?

RODERIGUES: 'She's too intelligent to be constrained, too old to be teased and too hot to be predictable,' I told him.

TUBAL: Foolish girl!

RODERIGUES: But he understands nothing. 'If I'd beaten her, been a drunkard, gambled my money away like those other old men, playing cards and dice all day between synagogue services . . . But we loved one another!' As if loving helps!

TUBAL: Nor is that to be his only tribulation. There are other calamities in the wind. The sea's wind. Your clever patron signed a bond with his best friend, Antonio. It was to be a joke, to mock the laws of Venice: a loan of three thousand ducats with a pound of flesh as bond if, within three months, the loan was not repaid. And now –

RODERIGUES: A pound of flesh?

TUBAL: And now his ships are threatened.

RODERIGUES: A pound of flesh?

TUBAL: A pound of flesh, his ships in threat, the Ghetto penniless, and the time is up at six the evening after tomorrow.

RODERIGUES: A pound of *human* flesh?

TUBAL: Yes, yes, yes, YES!

RODERIGUES: But, of course, the ships are not sunk.

TUBAL: No! Captured only! By pirates. The market is buzzing with the news.

RODERIGUES: And the bond is a joke.

TUBAL: There are no more jokes left in this world, Roderigues. The next, perhaps – ach! I am so loath to lend and deal in this trade any more.

[*Enter* GRAZIANO.]

GRAZIANO: Ah, signor Tubal, if anyone knows where Antonio is, it will be you.

RODERIGUES: Here comes everyman's everything and I'm in no mood for him.

TUBAL: What's the news of Antonio's ships?

GRAZIANO: Bad, bad, bad, oh bad.

TUBAL: Bad, we know. Facts we want.

GRAZIANO [*cheekily*]: The facts are that the news is bad.

TUBAL [*with powerful anger*]: No courtesies and games. Tell us the news.

GRAZIANO [*portentously*]: Grave. The news is grave. In view of how huge the cargo is the maritime office have ordered armed ships to the rescue.

TUBAL: Good, that's news worth taking back. Come, Roderigues.

GRAZIANO: But the damn winds are not helping, they fear a storm. The armed ships are paralysed.

TUBAL: Oh, Abraham! Abraham! Someone's God is angry. I'm too old for all this, too old, too old . . .

[TUBAL *and* RODERIGUES *leave.*]

GRAZIANO [*mocking as he, too, leaves*]: Oh Abraham, Abraham! I'm too old for all this, too old, too old . . .

[LORENZO *and* JESSICA *who have been looking for each other now meet, clutch one another in relief. She is agitated.*]

LORENZO: You're trembling.

JESSICA: I'm frightened and I'm ashamed, so I'm trembling.

LORENZO: Oh, those eyes. Those sad, sad eyes.

JESSICA: Forget my eyes, Lorenzo, and tell me what is to happen next.

LORENZO: First be calm, if for no other reason than not to command the staring of others.

JESSICA: I've spent so much, you see. It's cost so much.

LORENZO: I know, I know.

JESSICA: The decision to break away. You can't imagine. To be cut off.

LORENZO: I know.

JESSICA: So I'm drained. I'll be all right soon but for the next hours my reason is numb and you must do it all.

LORENZO: Trust me.

JESSICA: I'm a woman suspended.

LORENZO: Trust me.

JESSICA: Kiss me.

> [*He hesitates.*]

All these months of meetings and you've not kissed me.

> [*He hesitates again.*]

Haven't you kissed a woman before?

LORENZO: A hand, a cheek.

JESSICA: Not lips?

LORENZO: Not lips.

JESSICA: Then mine will be the first for you.

LORENZO: And mine?

JESSICA: Will be the first for me.

> [*They kiss.*]

Oh, I have known that kiss all my life.

LORENZO [*lifting her and whirling her round*]: Now, I would like to nail your name, proclaim you, claim you!

JESSICA: And say this is mine, and this, and here I've been before, and that skin, that smell, that touch so belongs, belongs, belongs that surely I was born the twin to it.

LORENZO: Nail your name and claim your strength!

> [*They kiss as* SHYLOCK's *voice is heard.*]

## SCENE THREE

[SHYLOCK's *study. He's trying to read a letter from his daughter.*]

SHYLOCK: 'Dear Father. I am not what you would like me to be, and what I am, brings me to this. To write more will urge upon me the necessity to think more. I have thought and reassured enough, not conclusively, but sufficient to drive me out. Reflect on our quarrels. They have said all. Your daughter, Jessica.'

[RIVKA enters.]

RIVKA: And where has your joking got you?

SHYLOCK: I have a letter from my daughter, now be silent, Rivka.

RIVKA: Have you asked yourself why she's gone?

SHYLOCK: I'm trying to find out, don't nag at me.

RIVKA: Are you certain there was no wrong in *you*?

SHYLOCK: You're the only person I know who asks accusations.

RIVKA: And he still makes jokes.

SHYLOCK: He? He? Who? Where? Me?

RIVKA: Please, Shylock, I beg you. Be a kind man, be a considerate brother. I've no health for laughter. Be finished with joking.

SHYLOCK: I have a letter from my daughter.

RIVKA: You've read it seven times, already. Talk with me. I'm not a fool.

SHYLOCK: What would you have me talk about, sister?

RIVKA: The meaning of your bond.

SHYLOCK: It has meanings? Clauses, perhaps, but meanings?

RIVKA: Clauses, meanings, meanings, clauses! If *you* won't read the meanings like a man, then this old woman will. What you wanted to mock now mocks you! That's what your bond means.

SHYLOCK: I don't see what meaning that meaning means.

RIVKA: Oh yes you do.

SHYLOCK: I see problems. I see possibilities. I see maybes and perhapses. The problem of Antonio's ships captured, the possibility of rescue, though maybe the wind will delay it and perhaps the ships will return late. But on the other hand maybe we will hear soon of the rescue, and perhaps Antonio's creditors will advance him more money and he'll have the possibility to repay me in time, and then there'll be no problem.

RIVKA: In time? What time? The clocks will soon strike six and that will only leave one day.

SHYLOCK: I have a letter from my daughter. Please.

RIVKA: I know you know the meanings that I mean. You're wriggling so.

241

SHYLOCK: I must hear this nonsense through I suppose.

RIVKA: Don't be rude to me, Shylock! You have a friend. Good. A gentile and gentle man. Good. You made some peace for yourself. I was happy for you. Good. But could you leave it like that, my wise man, always throwing his voice, his ideas about, on this, on that, here, there, to anyone, could you leave it well alone like that? Oh Shylock, my young brother. I've watched you, wandering away from Jewish circles, putting your nose out in alien places. I've watched you be restless and pretend you can walk in anybody's streets. Don't think I've not understood you; suffocating in this little yard, waiting for your very own scholar to arrive. It made me ache to watch you, looking for moral problems to sharpen your mind, for disputations – as if there weren't enough troubles inside these peeling walls. But you *can't* pretend you're educated, just as you can't pretend you're not an alien or that this Ghetto has no walls. Pretend, pretend, pretend! All your life! Wanting to be what you're not. Imagining the world as you want. And now, again, as always, against all reason, this mad pretence that Antonio's ships will come in safe. [*Pause.*] You've mocked their law.

SHYLOCK: Which mocked at us.

RIVKA: A hero! Shylock to the defence of his people. Can't you see what you've done?

SHYLOCK: Asserted dignity, that's what I've done.

RIVKA: That? That's what you've done? Nothing else? [*Pause.*] To assert the dignity of your mocked people you have chained your friend's life to a mocking bond, *that's* what you've done.

SHYLOCK: Go to your room, Rivka, you're becoming excited.

RIVKA: Shylock! Go and find the money! Knock on every Ghetto door, beg, plead, bully – but get it. Now. Before it's too late.

SHYLOCK: Foolish woman. Do you think I haven't tried? The Ghetto is drained. The last tax emptied every purse.

RIVKA: Oh God! Well, there's your moral problem, then. [*Pause, carefully spelling it out for him.*] Antonio could have been saved one of three ways: You could have found him the money, but the Ghetto is drained. Or he could have borrowed from his friends, but they don't trust his future now. Or, to save a citizen's life the court *will* relieve you of your bond. You do *know* that don't you?

SHYLOCK: Tomorrow. Tomorrow we'll talk about it.

RIVKA: They will even let you bend the law and lend him further ducats for repayment when the hour is passed. You do *know* that, don't you?

SHYLOCK: Rivka, please.

RIVKA: More! They'll wait days, weeks, even months. But – and here your moral problem begins – not everyone in the Ghetto will agree to the bending of the law.

SHYLOCK: Please, Rivka.

RIVKA: *Some* may. Some may even beg you to do that rather than have the blood of a Christian on their hands. But others will say, no! Having bent the law for us, how often will they bend it for themselves and then we'll live in even greater uncertainties than before. They'll be divided, as you are, my clever brother. Who to save – your poor people or your poor friend? You can't see that?

SHYLOCK: We'll talk about it tomorrow.

RIVKA: It's not only your problem now, it's the community's. You can't see that?

SHYLOCK: Tomorrow, tomorrow.

RIVKA: And who *will* you choose? The one foreign friend you love or the families of your blood you barely know? [*Pause.*] Well, am I a fool or not? Are there to be jokes or not? Have you a problem or not?

SHYLOCK: Tomorrow, tomorrow. We'll talk about it tomorrow.

RIVKA: Tomorrow! Tomorrow! *What* tomorrow? The clocks will soon strike six and it will be tomorrow. [*Long pause. She rises to leave.*] Me you can get out of the way, your problem – not! [*She leaves.*]

[SHYLOCK *turns to his letter.*]

SHYLOCK [*aloud*]: 'Reflect on our quarrels. They have said all. Your daughter, Jessica.' [*It is as though he has not understood.*] 'Our quarrels.' What quarrels? How could she have called them quarrels? *Enemies* quarrel. 'I am not what you would like me to be.' *What* did I want you to be, Jessica? My prop, my friend, my love, my pride? Not painful things, those. Are they?

Oh, Jessica. And where are you now? What wretched, alien philosophy has taken up your mind, muddied it with strange fervours? Which of the world's fervourists has lighted your sweet nature with its ephemeralities? Oh, vulnerable youth. You must be so lonely. So lost and lonely. So amazed and lost and lonely. Oh daughter, daughter, daughter.

[ANTONIO *enters. He too appears burdened with worries.*
*They confront each other in silent and all-knowing commiseration,*
*then embrace.*

SHYLOCK *at once begins to fuss over his friend, sitting him down,*
*pouring wine.*]

SHYLOCK: It'll be all right. Your ships will find their harbour and my daughter will find her home.

ANTONIO: But whose harbour and whose home and when?

SHYLOCK: Ah! I see you're gloomy.

ANTONIO: And I see you pretend you're not.

SHYLOCK: And supposing you lose your ships, what? You've no credit, no friends? What?

ANTONIO: I'm in debt to all Venice.

SHYLOCK: No skills to start again?

ANTONIO: Shylock, your own loss has stupefied you. Can you see me starting again? Wanting to? I've lived too long cushioned by huge sums, I'm not only naked without them, but my judgement's been flabbied by them.

SHYLOCK: Oh, now –

ANTONIO: Don't protest. You're evading the implications.

SHYLOCK: What, of a ship sinking or a daughter fleeing?

ANTONIO: Jessica's disappearance is a sad and awful thing, but other threats press.

SHYLOCK: Drink! I think we both need a little, little helpful drink.

ANTONIO: The implications must be faced and talked about.

SHYLOCK: Nothing presses, nothing threatens, drink.

ANTONIO: We've signed a foolish bond.

SHYLOCK: The bond will not be called upon – drink.

ANTONIO: It's known the ships were attacked, and my entire fortune staked in a single convoy. We've signed a foolish bond.

SHYLOCK: The storm will drop.

ANTONIO: We've signed a foolish bond, whose forfeiture is due.

SHYLOCK: The maritime office's fleet will sail – drink.

ANTONIO: At six o'clock there will be only twenty-four more hours to go.

SHYLOCK: Perhaps the days have been miscounted.

ANTONIO: SHYLOCK! [*Pause.*] What will you do with a knife in your hand and my flesh to weigh?

> [*Long pause.*
>
> SOLOMON USQUE *and* REBECCA *arrive.*]

REBECCA: Signor Shylock, is it true? We heard that your daughter is missing.

SHYLOCK: No commiserations, please. You're welcome. I love my friends around me, but there's been no death in my family, simply – a holiday. Every young person must have a holiday from home. Sit. I'll pour drink for you. Are you hungry? Tell me news.

REBECCA: Little change, families wanting passage to Constantinople, old men waiting for our funds for their voyage to Jerusalem, but your daughter, signor.

SHYLOCK: Who can write plays in such misery, eh, Signor Usque?

USQUE: No, who is there *great* enough to write plays in such misery!

SHYLOCK: Ah ha! Who is there great enough to write plays in such misery!

> [TUBAL *and a crestfallen* RODERIGUES *arrive.* SHYLOCK *looks to them expectantly*].

RODERIGUES: I told you! I warned! [TUBAL *stays him.*]

TUBAL: She has joined the man called Pisani.

SHYLOCK: Pisani?

TUBAL: They left tonight for an estate named Belmont.

SHYLOCK: Lorenzo Pisani? A nothing!

ANTONIO: To join Bassanio, my godson.

SHYLOCK: A man of whom it can only be said, 'He's there!' A sour, silly young man with little talent but that of envy, who confuses complaint for protestation, and even that betrays with a lazy mind. Jessica! you have been grabbed by air!

> [GRAZIANO *enters. Everyone knows what he has come to announce. They wait. He's terrified both of such an audience and the news he brings. He wants to hand the list to* ANTONIO.]

ANTONIO: Read me the list. [*Pause.*] Yes, here.

GRAZIANO: A ship carrying raisins from the Island of Zante, olive oil from Corfu and the cotton from Syria. Another with wine, corn and cheese from Crete. The Danish ship you chartered for the English cloth and the Spanish wool. The assignment of timber and, the last, from –

ANTONIO: – from the sugar estates of Cyprus. All. They have taken or sunk the consignment I swore would be my last. I do not possess one ducat, Shylock.

[*A clock strikes six.*

TUBAL *motions to the others that they should leave the two friends alone.*]

ANTONIO: I cannot raise the money now.

SHYLOCK: I know.

ANTONIO: Nor can you lend it me again.

SHYLOCK: The Ghetto's drained, I know.

[*Long pause.*]

SHYLOCK: They'll let us drop the bond.

ANTONIO: We cannot, must not.

SHYLOCK: You understand?

ANTONIO: I understand.

SHYLOCK: I'm frightened that you don't.

ANTONIO: I do.

SHYLOCK: I will not bend the law.

ANTONIO: I understand.

SHYLOCK: I must not set a precedent.

ANTONIO: I know.

SHYLOCK: *You* said. *You* taught.

ANTONIO: Shylock, Shylock. I'm not afraid.

SHYLOCK: Oh friend! What have I done to you?

[*Pause.*]

ANTONIO: Your yellow hat belongs to both of us. I'm party to the mockery as well.

SHYLOCK: I know.

ANTONIO: To strike a mad bond with you in such times!

SHYLOCK: I know.

ANTONIO: An act of schoolboy defiance when such times should be taken seriously. We shall both be put to death.

SHYLOCK: I know.

ANTONIO: I by you. You by them.

SHYLOCK: I know, I know.

ANTONIO: We know, we know! We keep saying we know so much.

SHYLOCK: Gently, gently, dear friend. I'm not afraid either.
[*Pause.*]

SHYLOCK: Just promise me silence in the trial.

ANTONIO: Will we make no explanations? The court must understand.

SHYLOCK: Understanding is beyond them! I protect my people and my people's contract. Besides, honour would be accorded me if I pleaded such explanations. 'He saved his people!' It would be grotesque. Just promise me silence at the trial.

ANTONIO: Silence, that's contempt, Shylock. Unworthy of you.

SHYLOCK: You must let my pride have its silence.

ANTONIO: They won't think it's pride, they will mistake your silence for contempt.

SHYLOCK: Perhaps they will be right. I am sometimes horrified by the passion of my contempt for men. Can I be so without pity for their stupidities, compassion for their frailties, excuses for their cruelties? It is as though these books of mine have spoken too much, too long; the massacres by kings, the deathly little spites of serfs, the oppressive jealousies and hurts of scholars, who had more learning than wisdom. Too much, Antonio, too much. Seeing what men have done, I know with great weariness the pattern of what they will do, and I have such contempt, such contempt it bewilders me. Surely, I say to myself, there is much to be loved and cherished. I tell myself, force myself to remember. Surely? Sometimes I succeed and then, ha! I'm a good man to know, such a good man. Children warm to me in the streets. They don't cry out 'Shylock old Jew' then. It's as though the light of men's noble endeavours has cracked through my dried-up bitterness and shines out of my eyes, and they can see it, those children. And they skip at my side and hold my hand, and on those days I walk so upright, like a young man, and I feel myself respected and loved. And love I myself also. Why, you rush to ask, if such joy comes to us through praising men, why do not we praise them all the time, look all the time for explanations, reasons, whys and whats, to account for their nastiness? You ask! The balance, dear friend, the balance! We can't always cheat the scales of history. Take those books, one by one, place on one side those which record men's terrible deeds, and on the other their magnificence. Do it! Deed for deed! Healing beside slaughter, building beside destruction, truth beside lie. Do it! Do it! [*Pause.*] My contempt, sometimes, knows no bounds. And it has destroyed us.

ANTONIO: Ah, Shylock, Shylock, why didn't we know one another when young?

SHYLOCK [*smiling*]: I'd have been wiser you mean?

ANTONIO: No, fool! It was myself I was thinking of.

SHYLOCK: I love thee, Antonio.

ANTONIO: And I thee, old man.

## SCENE FOUR

[*Belmont. The garden.*
PORTIA. BASSANIO *enters with* LORENZO *and* JESSICA.]

BASSANIO: My dear friends. What a pleasure to meet people you love in new places. Lorenzo, here she is. You've heard her described, now you see her in the flesh. Here, Portia, is the man I spoke to you about – philosopher, prophet, a man who may one day lead Venice – Lorenzo Pisani.

PORTIA: I hope, signor Lorenzo, you are not as intimidated by what is expected of you as I feel stripped by the words describing me! Nevertheless, says flesh to prophet: welcome!

BASSANIO: And Jessica welcome too. We've not met before and so both Portia and I have this pleasure together.

PORTIA: Oh those sad eyes.

LORENZO: We're honoured and grateful for your hospitality but those sad eyes carry sad news.

BASSANIO: Whose sad news?

LORENZO: Antonio's sad news. The ships are gone. The wreck of one was found and it's assumed the others either shared the same fate or have been taken off for use by the pirates.

PORTIA: But I don't understand the problem. Antonio owes Shylock three thousand ducats. What's that? I'm able to raise that sum and more besides to set him up in trade again.

LORENZO: No good! The hour is up and the Jew has turned mad. He accepts no deviation from his contract and Antonio insists upon sharing responsibility for it. The dilemma for the Doge is unprecedented. 'My people! My bond! My people! My bond!' as though the Jewish population were in threat instead of a poor, beguiled friend of the Jew who must now have the skin of his breast scraped from his bones.

JESSICA: Forgive me, Lorenzo . . . but . . .

LORENZO: You're right. My anger's made me indelicate.

JESSICA: It's not simply that —

BASSANIO: I warned him! A Jew to be trusted?

JESSICA: Please! Gentlemen! Remember me! I'm raw. My rhythms still belong to the Ghetto. I can't slip so quickly from God to God like a whore.

LORENZO: Jessica!

JESSICA: Yes, I'm also angry. You misrepresent the bond. Whatever else my father's flaws you know the bond had mockery not malice in it.

PORTIA: And that I understand. There's not enough of mockery in Venice. We're a city boasting very little of intelligent self-scrutiny or ridicule. But to mock the law is one thing, to squeeze it of its last punitive drop is another.

JESSICA: He must have his reasons.

PORTIA [*warmly*]: You must be hungry. Nerissa and I have prepared a light meal. Nothing too heavy.

BASSANIO: And I must go to prepare my luggage. Antonio will expect me to be near him while the court conducts its inquiries.

LORENZO: I'll join you, there's a principle affecting the future of Venice tied up in this case. Someone must air it.

BASSANIO [*leaving*]: Forgive me?

PORTIA: The decision is yours. [*To* LORENZO] I'll be very happy to look after your Jessica for you. It's a tragic affair but there's nothing we can do in it.

[PORTIA *follows* BASSANIO *off.*]

LORENZO: You look so sad. 'Those eyes'. They tell me I'm unworthy of you, that I don't appreciate your sacrifice. I do. Have courage. You've joined the world now.

JESSICA [*sardonically*]: Is that what I've joined?

LORENZO: Come, lie in my arms these last minutes. You're shocked still. Let me tell you about yourself.

JESSICA [*trying to relax*]: Oh do, Lorenzo, do tell me about myself, what I've done. Make sense of my actions for me. It seemed such a natural, inevitable thing to do. And now this bond, this wretched stupid bond threatens, threatens.

LORENZO: Hush, then.

JESSICA: I feel so full of discontent.

LORENZO: Quiet, then.

JESSICA: As though it's not in me ever to be happy.

LORENZO: Sssssh!

JESSICA: I'm frightened and . . .

LORENZO: Ssssssh!

JESSICA: All right. I'm quiet. Look. Start.

LORENZO [*after a pause, portentously*]: Some families are doomed.

JESSICA: That's not a very joyful start.

LORENZO: You should find all truths joyful.

JESSICA: Oh dear.

LORENZO: Even unhappy ones.

JESSICA: Oh dear, dear.

[*He wants to be solemn. She tries to be gay.*]

JESSICA: So, some families are doomed.

LORENZO: Parents have ill-chosen one another.

JESSICA: Parents have ill-chosen one another, so?

LORENZO: So, as parents can ill-choose one another, similarly can men ill-choose one another, similarly can men ill-choose their gods.

[JESSICA, *slowly realizing with disgust his meaning, rises angrily, and backs away.*]

JESSICA: I see.

LORENZO: Not with those reproachful eyes, Jessica. You *know* that is the truth about yourself. The sadness Portia saw was also of a forsaken race, married to a God they'd thought had chosen them. Doomed!

JESSICA [*icily*]: You think so?

LORENZO: But there are always survivors. I will make you a wife, a woman and a Christian.

JESSICA [*with controlled fury*]: Sometimes I think the sadness in my eyes comes from the knowledge that we draw from men their desperate hates. Poisons rise in our presence, idiocies blossom, and angers, and incredible lapses of humanity. That is my doom! to know that secret: that at any time, for any reason, men are capable of such demented acts. So I regard a stranger, with dread, reproach, fear. Forever vigilant. That's difficult for him to bear, to be looked at like that, for no reason, to be thought guilty before the act, to be known for the beast in one, the devil in the making. Who can forgive eyes that have such knowledge in them?

LORENZO: I see there's a great deal of unthreading to do.

JESSICA: Yes, I see there is.

[NERISSA *enters.*]

NERISSA: Signor Lorenzo, you must leave at once. The wind is right. I've prepared food for your journey.

LORENZO: There's no better place to be left, Jessica.

[*He embraces her. She cannot respond.*]

Trust me, please.

[LORENZO *leaves.*

JESSICA *looks very much alone.*

PORTIA *enters. At once, women together, they relax.*]

PORTIA: Good, the three of us alone. Talk to me, Jessica. Tell me about the Ghetto. My tutor in Hebrew studies was a strange man called Abraham Cardorso. *He* came from the Ghetto.

JESSICA: We knew him.

PORTIA: You did? What a coincidence.

JESSICA: Hardly a coincidence, madame, the quarter is so small.

PORTIA: And the buildings. So tightly packed together.

JESSICA: Yes. Always a danger of fire. Last week one young man, a friend in fact, threw himself into the flames attempting to save his mother. [*It's all too much for her. She is weeping. After a moment –*]

PORTIA: Tell me what you love in him.

JESSICA: I loved his questioning the wisdom of age, his clamouring to give youth its voice, his contempt for what men wrote in books.

His strength, his seriousness, his devotion. I loved, I suppose, escape from oppressive expectations.

PORTIA: And now?

JESSICA: Now, I'm feeling his strength is arrogance, his seriousness is pedantry, his devotion is frenzy, and I am confused and drained and without ground beneath my feet.

PORTIA: And the truth about the bond?

JESSICA: Antonio asked my father for the loan which he would have given ten times over without a contract.

PORTIA: Shylock didn't want a contract?

JESSICA: Not with his dear friend, no. They almost quarrelled, till Antonio finally persuaded him – the law must be respected! The Jews have need of the laws of Venice and so – the bond, in defiance.

PORTIA: Then I understand nothing.

NERISSA: Why don't *you* attend the court in Venice, madame?

PORTIA: Attend the court in Venice?

NERISSA: Perhaps you'll understand more there.

PORTIA: And having understood, what then?

NERISSA: A word, a thought, have faith in that 'untried intellect'.

PORTIA: Faith in that 'untried intellect' I have, but knowledge of the law I have none.

NERISSA: Perhaps it isn't law that's needed.

PORTIA: But there's so much work to do here.

NERISSA: Two men's lives are at stake.

PORTIA: But not men I know.

NERISSA: One, her father.

PORTIA: What can I do? I pity men their mad moments but a bond is a bond. The law demands its forfeitures. A pound of flesh is a satanic price to conceive, even as a joke but – [*She becomes a woman struck, as if by revelation. She can't believe the thought that has come to her. She rejects it but it persists.*] Holy Mary mother of Christ! I have it! But no. No! No, no, no, no, it's too simple. The law is complex, devious. This is common sense. Justice. The law is not to do with justice. No. It *can't* be applicable. And yet – who could possibly deny ... the law may not be just when it demands strict adherence to an agreement which may cause misery, but it does demand strict adherence. Then surely ... dare I? I'm no advocate. My temper's not for public places . . . and yet . . . a wrong is a wrong . . .

JESSICA: To whom is she speaking?

PORTIA [*triumphantly*]: Why don't we all three go to Venice and attend the court? There is a contract I must scrutinize and a father with whom you should be.

JESSICA: Are women granted entry to the courts?

PORTIA: They'll grant these women entry to the courts!

[*The scene immediately becomes the Courtroom of the Doge's Palace.*]


# SCENE FIVE

[*The women turn and sweep into the Courtroom of the Doge's Palace, Venice.*

PORTIA *and* NERISSA *walk straight up to ask the Doge permission to enter. He grants it.* JESSICA *is embraced by* RIVKA *and* TUBAL, NERISSA *moves to the Christian side. Present are* USQUE, REBECCA, RODERIGUES *and* SENATORS.

(NOTE: *If the set can hide* PORTIA *from the proceedings, good. If not, she must leave the court and reappear on her line.*)

*The* YOUNG MEN *are surprised.*]


BASSANIO: Portia!

LORENZO: Jessica!

BASSANIO: Did the women say they were coming?

LORENZO: On the contrary, Portia felt there was nothing to be done.

BASSANIO: Nor is there. Silence! For two hours this court of inquiry has had nothing but silence from him. Shylock! Will you speak!
[*No response.*]
He says nothing, offers no explanations, simply claims the bond.

JESSICA: Explain it to them, father, explain!
[SHYLOCK *growls and turns away. He hates scorning her, but can't help himself. She retires in distress to the Christian side.*]

BASSANIO: Look at that scowl. Have you ever seen such meanness in a face before? [*To* SHYLOCK] He was your friend! You boasted a gentile for a friend!

GRAZIANO: When a man says nothing you can be sure he hides evil and guilt, you can be sure.

BASSANIO: But why hasn't Antonio said something?

GRAZIANO: Well, of course, he wouldn't. Bewitched wasn't he? Forced into the bond. [*Calling out*] What did you say, old Jew? Not only would I be your friend, but I have to be your friend. Friendship? Ha!

BASSANIO: Shylock, will you speak!

LORENZO: Perhaps it's not Shylock who should speak but some of our own city councillors. Why were they silent? What Jewish money do they owe? It must be huge if they're prepared to let a fellow citizen be skinned alive. [*Calling out*] Fellow Venetians, is this city so far gone in its quest for profit and trade that there's no morality left? Usury is a sin against charity. When God had finished his creation he said unto man and unto beasts, and unto fishes: increase and multiply, but did he ever say increase and multiply unto money?

ANTONIO: Profit is the fruit of skill, young man!

JESSICA: And this bond was the fruit of friendship, Lorenzo, not usury, you know it!

TUBAL: Besides, most people at some moments in their life become short of money – illness . . .

USQUE: . . . A bad harvest . . .

RODERIGUES: . . . Domestic misfortune . . .

TUBAL: What shall they? I mean it's a problem!

LORENZO: I promise you that when the young patricians take their seats there'll be more God than Mammon on our statute books. Usury is a sin against charity. The –

TUBAL: And to deprive the people of an opportunity to obtain help is a sin against humanity!

LORENZO [*ignoring him*]: Usury is a sin against charity. The –

TUBAL: Listen to me!

LORENZO: The people suffer from it!

ANTONIO: The people suffer from ignorance, Lorenzo, believe me. To deprive them of knowledge is the sin.

LORENZO: Knowledge! Knowledge! How Shylock's books have muddied your mind. A man can be strong and happy with no knowledge, no art. Turn to the shepherd and the tiller and the sailor who know of the evils of usury, without books, without art.

Real knowledge, simple knowledge is in the wind and seasons and the labouring men do.

ANTONIO: You say a man is happy with no knowledge or art? There is wisdom in the wind, you say? The seasons tell all there is to know of living and dying? I wonder? Is it really understanding we see in the shepherd's eye? Is the tiller told more than the thinker? I used to think so, sitting with sailors roughened by salt, listening to their intelligence. They perceive much, I'd say to myself. But as I sat a day here, a day there, through the years, their intelligence wearied me. It repeated itself, spent itself upon the same complaints, but with no real curiosity. Only one thing was observed again and again: that there is much to know. But to know that there is much to know and yet not ask – I can't respect that man. How alive can he be with muscles but no curiosity? You wonder why I bind my fate to Shylock, what I see in him? Curiosity! *There* is a driven man. Exhilarating! I thank the shepherd for my clothes and the tiller for my food, good men. Blessed. Let them be paid well and honoured. But they know, I, we know: there is a variousness to be had in life richer than laying seeds in the narrow troughs of a turned and turned hungry earth. Why else does the labourer send his sons to schools he can? He knows what self-respect knowledge commands. All men do, wanting for their children what fate denied them, living without meat and keeping warm with mere sticks to do it. I'd have died before now if no man had kindled my soul with his music or wasn't there with his bright thoughts keeping me turning and taught about myself. Yes. Even at such an hour, I remember these things. Don't talk to me about the simple wisdom of the people, Lorenzo. Their simple wisdom is no more than the ignorance we choose to keep them in.

[*Silence.*]

GRAZIANO: As I thought. Bewitched. A knife hangs over him and he defends the man who holds it.

LORENZO: Be quiet, Graziano.

GRAZIANO: Lorenzo!

LORENZO: Stop meddling. You're a fool! The situation is too complex for you and I've not time for your tavern-tattle.

BASSANIO: Quiet now. The Doge is ready.

[*The* DOGE *returns to the official proceeding leaving* PORTIA *to continue perusing papers.*]

DOGE: Antonio Querini?

ANTONIO [*stepping forward*]: Most serene Prince.

DOGE: Shylock Kolner?

SHYLOCK: Most serene Prince.

DOGE: This court has never had before it such a case. The issue's clear, the resolution not. We must retrace and nag at it again. Signor Shylock, are you fully aware that the court is prepared to release both parties from the need to see this contract through?

SHYLOCK: I am, excellency.

DOGE: Yet you refuse, and state no reason?

SHYLOCK: I refuse and state no reason. Yes.

DOGE: And do you know this man may bleed to death?

SHYLOCK: I have our greatest doctors standing by.

DOGE: To do what? What can even Jewish doctors do to stem such awful draining of a man's life-blood? A strange perverted charity is that. You, Querini, dear fellow patrician, we beg you break your silence, or does this man have some hold over you? We've noticed your absence from the council's meetings. You once enjoyed the affairs of running our city, tell the court. Don't be afraid. What has happened?

ANTONIO [*impatiently*]: Nothing has happened, excellency, more than I've lost my appetite for the intrigues and boredom of administration. I can't pretend this is a city of holiness and light. These are empty boasts, wind fit for the lungs of impatient youth but they have nothing to do with our humiliation in this court. Please, may we proceed.

DOGE: Then *you* say why we're here humiliated in this court. Say why you shared the madness of a bond which twice endangers you: from a man insisting that you pay a forfeiture of flesh, and from the law which must punish you for mocking it.

[*No response.*]

Your silence does not help.

GRAZIANO: I knew it! I told it! I warned it!

ANTONIO: Graziano, be quiet!

GRAZIANO: A plot! A plot! A Jewish plot!

ANTONIO: Be quiet, I say.

GRAZIANO: I can't be quiet, I love you.

ANTONIO: You love no one and nothing but a safe place with the multitude. Now be quiet.

DOGE: Why do you attack your friends, Antonio? These men who've come to speak for you? And why are you not speaking for yourself?

[Pause.]

LORENZO: Incredible! The man has even chained his victim to silence. Most serene Prince, I beg you –

DOGE: Be careful!

LORENZO: – the reason for humiliation in this court is linked with principles which go beyond this case.

DOGE: Do not attempt to make capital!

LORENZO: We should not be inquiring into silence but questioning if Jews and usury, no matter what the bond, should be permitted to pollute the fabric of our city's life. The real question is –

TUBAL: Do you think we enjoy the indignity of lending to your poor at twelve per cent . . .?

LORENZO: . . . the real question is . . .

RODERIGUES: Collect for your poor among yourselves!

LORENZO: . . . the real question is . . .

USQUE: You have pious fraternities, collect from them for your poor!

TUBAL: Or use taxes!

LORENZO: . . . THE REAL QUESTION IS . . .

DOGE: The question of the city's contracts with the Jews is a matter for the Council. The laws of Venice are very clear and precise and cannot be twisted this way and that for political significance or gain, nor denied to foreigners, otherwise justice will not obtain. And the principal foundation of our city, is justice. The people of Venice must have justice.

ANTONIO [finally angry]: Justice? For the people of Venice? The people? You pride yourselves you mirror Rome! But one benefit that great empire had and we lack is: equal political citizenship. Here, in Venice, political power rests quite firmly in the hands of two hundred families and those only. That, though he talks of principle, is what Lorenzo cannot wait for, to share that power, take it over, perhaps, but not eradicate its sure corrosiveness. You use the people's name, for through their grievances, you'll come to power. One of their grievances is what you call usury. The usurer's a Jew, and the Jew the people's favourite villain. Convenient! Easy! But the Jew pursues what he hates to pursue in order to relieve *us* of the sin. Usury *must* exist in our city, for we have many poor and our economy can't turn without it. Do we condemn the Jew for doing what our system has required him to do? Then if we do, let's swear, upon the cross, that among us we know of no Christian, no patrician, no duke, bishop or merchant who, in his secret chambers, does not lend at interest, for that is what usury is. Swear it! On the cross! No one, we know no one! [*Pause.*] Who's silent now? [*Pause.*] You will inflame the people's grievances in order to achieve power, Lorenzo, but will you ever question its necessity? I doubt it, for once there you'll sing such different songs I think.

DOGE: You do not make inquiry easy for this court, Signor.

BASSANIO: How can you make inquiries into silence, most serene Prince, the inhuman silence of an arrogant chosen people. Heretical! They still refuse to acknowledge that they are no *longer* the chosen people.

SHYLOCK: Oh horror of horrors! Oh heresy of heresies! Oh sweat! Oh flutter! Oh butterflies, gooseflesh, hair-on-end! Oh windbag of windbags! And *you* I suppose, have been chosen instead?

LORENZO [*flooding the proceedings with conciliatory warmth and charm*]: Most serene Prince. If my friend misapplies the word inhuman, we can perhaps understand. But I must pursue my original plea and ask the court to remember this: the Signor Shylock is not here because he is a Jew. The patricians of Venice are good men and justly fear being accused of such prejudice. No! What is on trial in this court is, I insist, the principle of usury whose evil this bond so tragically exemplifies, and from whose consideration we should not be detracted. The *bond* is inhuman, not the man. *No* one doubts the Jew is human. After all, has not a Jew eyes?

SHYLOCK: What is *that* fool attempting now?

LORENZO: Has not a Jew hands?

SHYLOCK: Is he presuming explanations on *my* behalf?

LORENZO: Has not a Jew organs, dimensions, senses, affections, passions?

SHYLOCK [*enraged*]: Oh no!

LORENZO: Is not the Jew fed with the same food, hurt with the same weapons, subject to the same diseases, healed by the same means, warmed and cooled by the same winter and summer as a Christian is?

SHYLOCK: No, no!

LORENZO: If you prick him, does he not bleed?

SHYLOCK: No, no, NO! I will not have it. [*Outraged but controlled*] I do not want apologies for my humanity. Plead for me no special pleas. I will not have my humanity mocked and apologized for. If I am unexceptionally like any man then I need no exceptional portraiture. I merit no special pleas, no special cautions, no special gratitudes. My humanity is my right, not your bestowed and gracious privilege.

GRAZIANO: See how ungrateful the Jew is? I knew it! I told it! I warned it! The Jew was silent because he knew that the moment he opened his mouth he'd hang himself with his arrogance. The Jew . . .

SHYLOCK [*furious but low and dangerous, building*]: Jew! Jew, Jew, Jew! I hear the name around and everywhere. Your wars go wrong, the Jew must be the cause of it; your economic systems crumble there the Jew must be; your wives get sick of you – a Jew will be an easy target for your sour frustrations. Failed university, professional blunderings, self-loathing – the Jew, the Jew, the cause the Jew. And when will you cease? When, when, when will your hatreds dry up? Dear God of Abraham, will your mindless hungerings for *our* flesh ever be satisfied? There's nothing we can do is right. Admit it! You will have us all ways won't you? For our prophecies, our belief in universal morality, our scholarship, our command of trade, even our ability to survive. If we are silent we must be scheming, if we talk we are insolent. When we come we are strangers, when we go we are traitors. In tolerating persecution we are despised, but were we to take up arms we'd be the world's marauders, for sure. Nothing will please you. Well, damn you then! [*Drawing knife.*] I'll have my pound of flesh and not feel obliged to explain my whys and wherefores. Think what you will, you will think that in any case. I'll say it is my bond. The law is the law. You need no other reason, nor shall you get it – from me.

[*He turns to the* DOGE, *justice must be done.* ANTONIO *joins him on the other side of the* DOGE. *They turn to face one another – doomed friends. Though no Jew must take another's life yet* SHYLOCK *has made the decision to damn his soul for the community which he feels is threatened.*]

PORTIA: Most serene Prince, I have read the documents. [*Pause.*] Your Excellency, forgive my presumption, I know nothing of the law, but I cannot see that there is sufficient detail in this contract to make it legally valid.

[*Murmurs in court.*]

And if not valid, then not binding.

[*Excitement grows.*]

But I'm anxious in case my intelligence is merely foolish faith in little more than a hair of the law.

DOGE: The courts of Venice are open to justice no matter how tenuous a hair binds it to the law.

PORTIA: Then it seems to me this contract contains nothing but contradictions.

[*Tense silence.*]

There is in this bond a call for flesh but none for blood.

[*Noise in court.*]

There is in this bond a call for a precise pound weight but none for more or less.

[*Growing noise.*]

It cannot be executed because torn flesh draws blood.

[*Still growing noise.*]

It cannot be executed because precise weight cannot be achieved.

[*Yet more noise.*]

This contract is not binding because – impossible.

[*A swift silence in court.*]

SHYLOCK [*stunned, moves first to embrace* ANTONIO]: Thank God!

Thank God! Of course! Idiots! Cut flesh draw blood. No blood no flesh. Oh, Antonio, how could such a simple fact escape us? Pedants of the law! Shame on you, a disgrace to your tribe. Go down Shylock, to the bottom of the class. Oh, Tubal, what a fool you've had for a partner. No wonder we never owned the really big warehouses. [*Offering knife to the three men*] There! For you! *You* need it. You've no wit to draw blood with your brains or tongue, take this. Cruder, but guaranteed. Ha ha! No blood, no flesh. I love the lady. Young lady I love you. You have a future, I see it, a great future.

PORTIA [*with sadness*]: But not you, old Shylock.

SHYLOCK: Not I? Are you mad? I've been delivered of murder – I've got a clean and honest life to continue. Oh, not for a hundred years, I know, and it's a pity because today, TODAY I feel I want to go on living for ever and ever. There's such wisdom in the world, such beauty in this life. Ha! Not I, young lady? Oh yes, I! I, I, I! A great future, also. Back to my books.

DOGE: No Shylock, no books.

SHYLOCK: No books? Will you take my books?

ANTONIO: You take his life when you take his books.

SHYLOCK: What nonsense now?

DOGE: No nonsense, I'm afraid, Shylock. An old Venetian law condemns to death and confiscation of his goods the alien who plots against the life of a citizen of Venice.

SHYLOCK: I? Plot? Against a citizen of Venice? Who? Antonio?

DOGE: You pursued that which would end a man's life.

SHYLOCK: But was 'that' which I pursued 'plot'? Plot? Malice aforethought.

DOGE: Malice aforethought or not, the end was a citizen's death.

ANTONIO: However –

SHYLOCK: But there's no perception, no wisdom there.

ANTONIO: However –

SHYLOCK: As I warned, as I knew, no pity there.

GRAZIANO: Pity's called for now!

ANTONIO: HOWEVER! The law also says the offender's life is at the mercy of the Doge –

DOGE: Which mercy I make no delay in offering you. But the State must take your goods. The people of Venice would not understand it if –

SHYLOCK: Oh! The people of Venice, of course.

LORENZO: See what contempt he has.

SHYLOCK: The people again. What strange things happen behind the poor people's name.

DOGE: – The people of Venice would not understand it if the law exacted no punishment at all for such a bond.

SHYLOCK: Of course.

ANTONIO: And I? What punishment do the people of Venice exact of me?

DOGE: Your foolishness, Signor, was punished by the pain of threatened death. Enough!

ANTONIO: The wisdom of patrician privilege, of course.

DOGE: But do not strain it, friend. Do not.

ANTONIO [*bowing*]: I thank you.

[*The* DOGE *and all leave, except* SHYLOCK, ANTONIO, PORTIA JESSICA.]

SHYLOCK [*turning to* PORTIA]: And the lady, where is the lovely lady, what does she say to all this?

PORTIA [*with sad apology*]: The lovely lady can say nothing more to merit the name.

SHYLOCK [*tenderly, as to a daughter*]: All that intelligence? Gone?

PORTIA: Not gone, but limited in power. Your lovely lady used her common sense to read a bond. That is the best not only she could do, but can be done. The law takes over now.

SHYLOCK [*sardonically*]: Oh! I forgot! The law. Yes. Impartial justice. Is that to be applied now?

PORTIA [*poignantly*]: Oh, Signor Shylock, please don't look to me for help.

SHYLOCK: There, there! I'm sorry. Shuh, shuh.

PORTIA [*raging at the departed* DOGE]: I would not carry a sword in one hand and scales in the other. That image always seemed to me ambiguous. Is my sword held high to defend the justice my left hand weighs? Or is it poised threateningly to enforce my left hand's obduracy?

SHYLOCK: Impartial justice, lovely lady, impartial justice.

PORTIA: Impartial! How? *I* am not a thing of the wind, but an intelligence informed by other men informed by other men informed! *I* grow. Why can't they? What *I* thought yesterday might be wrong today. What should I do? Stand by my yesterdays because *I* have made them? I made today as well! And tomorrow, that I'll make too, and all my days, as my intelligence demands. I was born in a city built upon the Wisdom of Solon, Numa Pompilius, Moses!

SHYLOCK: You waste your breath, young lady, there was never any such city in the world.

PORTIA [*returning tenderly to* SHYLOCK]: I can't console you, Signor Shylock, forgive me. Rage against the slowness of the law is all I can do for you. Not much help, though, is it?

[*They exchange sad smiles.*]

SHYLOCK: In all law part is diseased. A diseased law inspired the mad bond, another now demands a price to be paid. [*Shrugs.*] What can one do?

PORTIA: Wisdom, inconsiderately, does not translate in a moment. [*They exchange another smile.*]

SHYLOCK [*with sad pleasure, taking her hand, still as to a daughter*]: You have a future, young lady, I tell you, a great future.

[JESSICA *finds this tender moment between her father and another young woman unbearable and flees.*]

ANTONIO: Shylock! Don't be a stubborn old man. Explain to the court you did not want to set a precedent in law. You'll save your books.

SHYLOCK [*sardonically and with finality*]: No. Take my books. The law must be observed. We have need of the law, what need do we have of books? Distressing, disturbing things, besides. Why, dear friend, they'd even make us question laws. Ha! And who in his right mind would want to do that? Certainly not old Shylock. Take my books. Take everything. I do not want the law departed from, not one letter departed from.

[*Sound of song.*]

Perhaps now is the time to make that journey to Jerusalem. Join those other old men on the quayside, waiting to make a pilgrimage, to be buried there – ach! What do I care! My heart will not follow me, wherever it is. My appetites are dying, dear friend, for anything in this world. I am so tired of men.

[SHYLOCK *moves away, a bitter man. Everyone has left except* PORTIA. *The scene has changed to Belmont. We hear the distant sad singing of a woman. The song is 'Adio querida', a Sephardic song.*★]

## SCENE SIX

[*Belmont. The garden. A warm, heavy, melancholy evening.* PORTIA *strolling,* JESSICA *stands aside.*

*The woman singing in the distance.*

*The air is broken by the sound of raucous laughter.* BASSANIO, LORENZO *and* GRAZIANO *enter carrying food.* NERISSA *follows them. A picnic is prepared.*

*They talk, spread a rug, light candles while* NERISSA *prepares platters of food.*]

BASSANIO: A farewell supper! Our friends are leaving, Portia. Tonight must be made memorable. Lorenzo! Jessica! Food!

[*But they seem reluctant to join the three young men.* LORENZO *alone notes the indifference, especially of* JESSICA.]

GRAZIANO: It's a splendid house. The most beautiful I've seen. Really, Signorina Contarini, splendid. About two hundred and twenty-three years old, I'd say. And what a library! It made me pick up a book for the first time in years.

LORENZO [*acidly*]: Which book?

GRAZIANO: No, no, Lorenzo. You can't keep getting at me. We've been through a lot together now and you know me to be your faithful admirer. I know my limitations and I'm happy to be factotum to your cause. Or causes. Name them, I'll follow. Plot them, I'll execute them. Don't be ungracious. There's a lot to be said for a sycophant.

[ANTONIO *appears.*]

PORTIA: I'm so grateful you stayed, Signor Querini. These two weeks have been made bearable, and I've found a new friend.

★ See EMI label ASD 2649, sung by Victoria de los Angeles.

ANTONIO: While I've found a woman who's made me mourn my
youth. What mixed blessings in these last years of my life, to meet
an acerbic old Jew who disturbed my dull complacency; and you,
blossoming with purpose, reminding me of a barren life. An unfair
restlessness at this depleted age. [*Pause.*] He will haunt me, that
man.

[*Silence but for the singing.*]

What will you do?

PORTIA: Honour my father's wishes, marry the man who chose
lead, dutifully take my role of wife, look to what must be grown.
And you?

ANTONIO: Sort out what has been salvaged from my ships. See my
friend off to the holy land. Visit him, once, perhaps, before I die,
and you often, if I may, before I die.

PORTIA: Oh please! I would be so indebted.

ANTONIO: But what will happen to her?

LORENZO [*Calling her to eat*]: Jessica!

[*She ignores him. He waits throughout the next exchange for her to
turn to him. She does turn, contemptuously, then turns away.*]

PORTIA: I'll look after Jessica. My marriage is a parent's will, not
hers, though. Mine can't be held back, hers, I will see, never takes
place.

ANTONIO: But *which* place will she take? There's no father's house
to return to.

PORTIA: But there is a Jerusalem, where he can be followed.

ANTONIO: I don't think I really fear for Jessica, but you ...

PORTIA: I! I'll fill my house with poets and philosophers, and
politicians who are poets and philosophers. Bassanio will come to
know his place, accept it, or leave it. I am to be reckoned with,
you know, not merely dutiful. Although, something in me has
died struggling to grow up.

[LORENZO *turns angrily away from looking at* JESSICA, *finally
understanding that he's lost her.*]

LORENZO: I don't think I shall ever lose the image of that man's
scowl from my mind. Remember? And how silent he was, to
begin with.

GRAZIANO: To begin with he would be very silent.

LORENZO: Fortunately the law is a terrifying thing and the courts are an awesome place.

GRAZIANO: Ha! But he was awed.

BASSANIO: 'And you I suppose have been chosen instead!' How he spat the words out. A man full of despite and contempt.

[PORTIA *and* ANTONIO *move away to different corners of the garden. They, with* JESSICA, *are three lonely points of a triangle which now encircle the grating sounds of an inane conversation.*]

LORENZO: Perhaps now they will learn, the elders. Virtue consists in simplicity, suffering, renunciation!

GRAZIANO: But we forget Portia, his wife ...

BASSANIO: Not yet, not yet!

GRAZIANO: His wife to *be*. Now there's a mind to be careful of. Should we envy him or fear for him.

BASSANIO: It was in my stars to make such a match for my bed.

GRAZIANO: You're mad to think only of bed with an intellect like that at your side.

BASSANIO: It shall be cherished but not spoilt. I shall turn to it but not let it rule! Ah! Here comes Nerissa with drink for the heroes.

NERISSA: And heroes you are, sirs, true. No denying it. True, true, heroes indeed. True. True, true, true. Heroes!

[*Only the singing now and a fading, warm and sad evening.*]

## MORE ABOUT PENGUINS
## AND PELICANS

*Penguinews*, which appears every month, contains details of all the new books issued by Penguins as they are published. It is supplemented by our stocklist, which includes almost 5,000 titles.

A specimen copy of *Penguinews* will be sent to you free on request. Please write to Dept EP, Penguin Books Ltd, Harmondsworth, Middlesex, for your copy.

*In the U.S.A.*: For a complete list of books available from Penguins in the United States write to Dept CS, Penguin Books, 625 Madison Avenue, New York, New York 10022.

*In Canada*: For a complete list of books available from Penguins in Canada write to Penguin Books Canada Ltd, 2801 John Street, Markham, Ontario L3R 1B4

*In Australia*: For a complete list of books published by Penguins in Australia write to the Marketing Department, Penguin Books Australia Ltd, P.O. Box 257, Ringwood, Victoria 3134.

## ARNOLD WESKER

(... 'the outstanding playwright of his generation'– Clive James)

## THE WESKER TRILOGY

In *Chicken Soup with Barley*, *Roots* and *I'm Talking About Jerusalem* Wesker dramatizes the struggles of two Jewish families in their efforts to preserve, re-define and put into practice their socialist ideals.

'The passion of Mr Wesker's themes is matched by the living fire in his writing ... Its quality is undiminished by the passing years' – Bernard Levin in the *Sunday Times*

'A trilogy which will act as a monument to its era' – *Daily Mail*

## THE KITCHEN, THE FOUR SEASONS and THEIR VERY OWN AND GOLDEN CITY

In *The Kitchen* Wesker presents, as a microcosm of the world, the stifling hell of an overcrowded kitchen, using a mixture of realistic and symbolic techniques. In contrast, *The Four Seasons* is an almost classical portrayal of the seasons of love that hovers somewhere between poetry and ballet; while Andrew Cobham's dream of building co-operative Golden Cities in *Their Very Own and Golden City* is a vision of the future.

# ARNOLD WESKER

(... 'a moral thermometer for the rest of us' – *Queen*)

## CHIPS WITH EVERYTHING,
## THE FRIENDS, THE OLD ONES,
## and LOVE LETTERS ON BLUE PAPER

*Chips With Everything*: 'A gauntlet of a play has been flung down on the stage ... furious, compassionate and unforgiving' – *Observer*

*The Friends*: 'Bold and finally beautiful in its dramatic sweep, as his characters crumble before our eyes' – *Evening Standard*

*The Old Ones*: 'It works a singular magic through its author's stubborn belief that his bruised people, undefeated in defeat, are worthy of respect' – the *Observer*

*Love Letters on Blue Paper*: 'The quality of a masterpice is unmistakable ... a bold, uncompromising exploration of death' – *Yorkshire Post*

*and*

## LOVE LETTERS ON BLUE PAPER and other stories

In this new selection of short stories, taken from *Love Letters on Blue Paper*, *Six Sundays in January* and *Said the Old Man to the Young Man*, courage and humour animate an unforgettable collection of stories that linger powerfully in the memory.

'Integrity and a deep sense of pity are the qualities that emerge from these thoughtful stories' – *Sunday Times*

'Wesker's writing is finely sensitive, sharply humane and quite convincing' – *New Statesman*

*All the world's a stage ...*

## THE NORMAN CONQUESTS

### Alan Ayckbourn

'A superb comic trilogy ... Mr Ayckbourn is the most remarkable British dramatist to have emerged since Harold Pinter' – J. W. Lambert in the *Sunday Times*

'One of the most remarkable enterprises in the British theatre since the war. Mr Ayckbourn uses farce to illuminate small nooks of human desolation; and he demands a devastating psychological accuracy which Chekhov would have been impressed by' – *The Times Literary Supplement*

## THE RETURN OF A.J. RAFFLES

### Graham Greene

On his return from South Africa after mistaken reports of his death on Spion Kop, Raffles was momentarily disconcerted to find Bunny about to go to Covent Garden with Lord Alfred Douglas. But Lord Alfred was quick to take advantage of the cricketing cracksman's return. Why not burgle the home of his moronic father, the Marquess of Queensbury?

'Glorious Comedy' – B.A. Young in the *Financial Times*

## DEATH OF A SALESMAN

### Arthur Miller

*Death of a Salesman* was written in six weeks in the spring of 1948, but it had been brewing in Miller's mind for ten years. Its 742 performances put it among the 50 longest recorded Broadway runs; it received the Pulitzer Prize for Theatre and was later filmed. Miller himself defined his aim in the play as being 'to set forth what happens when a man does not have a grip on the forces of life'.

*And all the men and women, merely players . . .*

## THREE AWARD-WINNING
## TELEVISION PLAYS

### Jack Rosenthal

*Bar Mitzvah Boy* – Numbed by the torrent of circumstantial social arrangements for his bar mitzvah, the central and least noticed character walks out in the middle of his initiation ceremony.

'Rosenthal's ear for the ragged desperation of Jewish humour is impeccable' – *Sunday Times*

*The Evacuees* – Two young Jewish brothers are evacuated from Manchester to Blackpool in the early war years

'A masterly blend of history, comedy and social comment, and Rosenthal's ear (and memory) for pre-war schoolboy conversation is astonishing' – *Financial Times*

*Spend, Spend, Spend* – The dramatization of a true story of a pair of pools winners to whom the cheque brought only boredom, isolation and tragedy.

'A remarkable . . . and revealing piece of work' – *Daily Mail*

## FIVE PLAYS

### Ben Travers

Here, collected in paperback for the first time, are four of Ben Travers's most famous Aldwych Farces: *A Cuckoo in the Nest*, *Rookery Nook*, *Plunder* and *Thark* together with *The Bed Before Yesterday* with which the author found new fame at the age of ninety.

'The single-track dirty mind, the *double entendre*, the treble think, the quadruple bluff: funny names, funny local yokels, domineering women, pretty girls and the ever-swinging bedroom door . . . Explosively funny' – Richard Usborne in *The Times Literary Supplement*

1854